QUEST FOR JUSTICE

Towards Homosexual Emancipation

ANTONY GREY

SINCLAIR-STEVENSON

First published in Great Britain by
Sinclair-Stevenson
7/8 Kendrick Mews
London SW7 3HG, England

British Library Cataloguing in Publication Data
A CIP catalogue record for this book is available
from the British Library.

ISBN (hardback): 1 85619 136 2
ISBN (paperback): 1 85619 155 9

Typeset by Rowland Phototypesetting Limited
Bury St Edmunds, Suffolk

Printed and bound in Great Britain by
CPI Antony Rowe, Chippenham and Eastbourne

FSC

Mixed Sources

Product group from well-managed
forests and other controlled sources

Cert no. SGS-COC-2953
www.fsc.org
© 1996 Forest Stewardship Council

QUEST FOR JUSTICE

*It is better to light one candle
than curse the darkness*

Motto of the Christopher Society

I dedicate this book to

A. E. Dyson (UK)
Dr Franklin Kameny (USA)
The late Bob Angelo (Netherlands)
Lamplighters for homosexual liberation

CONTENTS

ILLUSTRATIONS

ACKNOWLEDGMENTS

I am most indebted to Rodney Bennett-England, the former Chairman of the Albany Trust, for allowing me to quote whatever I wished from the Trust's archives. The Rev. Andrew Hallidie Smith kindly gave me his permission to do the same from his unpublished book, *The Right to Exist*.

I owe grateful thanks to those who read my draft text and gave me the benefit of their comments: Professor Peter Campbell, Maureen Colquhoun, Lord Jenkins of Hillhead, C. H. Rolph, and Eric Thompson.

The enthusiasm and encouragement of my publisher, Christopher Sinclair-Stevenson, and his editorial director, Penelope Hoare, sustained me from the outset and all through the lengthy process of writing and producing the book.

I am also grateful to the following copyright holders for their permission to reproduce quotations and illustrations acknowledged at the appropriate place in my text: Messrs. Allison & Busby, American Psychiatric Association, *British Journal of Psychiatry*, Gerald Duckworth & Co. Ltd, Wally Fawkes, Sigmund Freud Copyrights, The Institute of Psycho-Analysis and Hogarth Press, GMP Publishers Ltd, Hamish Hamilton Ltd, William Heinemann Ltd, Her Majesty's Stationery Office, King's College, Cambridge, and the Society of Authors as literary representatives of the late E. M. Forster's estate, Longman Group UK, Macdonald & Co (Publishers) Ltd, John Murray (Publishers) Ltd and executors of Sir Osbert Lancaster, Peter Owen Ltd, Oxford University Press, Penguin Books Ltd, Pilgrim Press (USA), Random Century Group, Routledge, *Social Work Today*, Unwin Hyman, Weidenfeld & Nicolson Ltd.

NOTE ON TERMINOLOGY

While I have endeavoured to be as consistent as possible in my use of terms, I realise that it is impossible to satisfy everyone's preferences about language. Though I prefer to avoid words which have a pejorative flavour, I am resigned to the fact that the essentially political nature of language makes this virtually impossible; whatever I choose will offend someone. I can only apologise in advance.

'Gay' has become an essentially political statement as the chosen self-description of men who are open and unapologetic about their homosexuality. Openly homosexual women prefer to call themselves Lesbians, so I shall use 'Gay' as referring only to men who are 'Glad to be Gay', and not as an umbrella term for all homosexual men and women. 'Homosexual' was originally coined by the Hungarian K. M. Benkert in 1869 as a scientifically neutral medical description for the state of being exclusively or predominantly sexually attracted to persons of one's own sex. It has since inevitably acquired scapegoating overtones, and is disliked as a description of themselves by many homosexual people. I myself consider it an adequate working tool, when properly used as an adjective followed by the appropriate noun – for example, 'homosexual man', 'homosexual people'. I have endeavoured to use it consistently in this way myself, although it is not possible to do so when quoting others.

FOREWORD

I believe profoundly that my own and everyone else's sexual preferences and mutually consenting personal relationships are the peculiarly private business of each one of us, and that we should not be required to explain or to justify them to others. So, paradoxically, I have spent much of my life engaged in public debate about sex, while heartily endorsing D. H. Lawrence's view that we British are a bad case of 'sex in the head': healthy sex is about doing and enjoying, rather than about thinking, talking, looking or reading.

So what point is there in my adding yet another pebble to the mountain of books about sex? First, to record accurately my own work for homosexual law reform in the 1950s and 1960s, and to comment on the disappointing aftermath. Secondly, to urge social and educational changes in the hope that – even in the age of AIDS – girls and boys entering their teens in AD 2000 will experience a happier and healthier sexual climate than today's.

Despite all the ceaseless and largely mindless chatter about sex which permeates the atmosphere we breathe, the basic sexual issue of today is that far too many people are still experiencing a lack of emotional and physical fulfilment. There is still far too much sexual loneliness, shame and personal misery. Widespread sexual deprivation, and the unhappiness it brings, matter far more than the sexual 'depravity' which generates so much vociferous indignation among the puritans and the prurient – although sexual cruelty (like all cruelty) is utterly abhorrent.

Most of the pervasive guilt and loneliness which so many people have to endure stems from the ignorance and censoriousness of misguided moralisers and the media's tongue-in-cheek tut-tutting and tittle-tattling. In essence, the 'sexual problem' is one of improving personal and social education so as to bring a more honest, tolerant and mutually understanding society into being. Well informed and balanced attitudes towards homosexuality must be an integral part of such a society.

I

Personal Prologue

'I, a stranger and afraid
In a world I never made.'

A. E. Housman

I did not become Secretary of the Homosexual Law Reform Society merely by accident. I had in fact known since I was a teenager that I intended to do something significant about my own plight as a homosexual person, and that of my fellows.

My own personal experience has been as a male who is exclusively homosexual by conscious preference and behaviour. I do not say 'as a gay man' – because my awareness and experience of my sexuality began when I was still a young boy, and 'gayness' was not then the visible option that it is today: if it had been, my own story would have been very different.

Though being homosexual has affected the course of my life profoundly, and I would not recognise myself if my sexuality were other than it is, I do not regard this aspect as the most important or interesting thing about me (or anyone else). I certainly do not consider the possession of a homosexual orientation as being a handicap or a misfortune – except socially, because homosexual people still encounter widespread ignorance, prejudice, discrimination, and pervasive verbal abuse which can sometimes spill over into physical violence.

Today there is still a general insensitivity towards the feelings and needs of homosexual and bisexual people which would not be so thoughtlessly displayed towards members of any other social minority. Homosexual men and women are nowadays the only such minority liable to be mocked or persecuted even by people claiming to represent 'respectable' opinion and religious orthodoxy.

Those of us who are homosexual or bisexual are entitled, as much

1

as any other members of society, to our basic rights and equalities as citizens; to our human dignity; to the freedom to be what we are; to equal opportunities with everyone else to live our lives fully and openly, forming and sustaining whatever intimate personal, domestic and social relationships we choose, without official or unofficial pressures to desist, dissemble or conform.

I gradually came to realise these facts as I was growing up. But for me, as for so many other boys and girls who are homosexual, adolescence was a deeply puzzling time. Ever since I became aware of my feelings (when I was about nine), I knew that those who preoccupied and attracted me were boys, not girls. This did not seem to be a problem until I realised that others – including everyone in authority – *did* regard it as a problem, and a very unwholesome one. Like many who are homosexual, my first awareness of my attraction was emotional, not physical; explicitly erotic interest followed a good deal later. But from kindergarten school until university, I fell in love with a succession of my fellow-students. And I do not say 'fell in love' lightly; these loves were as tender, as longingly passionate and as agonisingly frustrated as any that I have experienced in my adult life.

I never ventured to declare myself to a single one of these objects of my affection. I do not think any of them ever had an inkling of how I hero-worshipped them. They all appeared to be single-mindedly heterosexual anyway, and would (I told myself) have been uncomprehendingly aghast at my feelings if I had dared to reveal them. A good deal of physical sex went on between boys at school, of course; there were plenty of dormitory and locker room sex games at all the schools I went to, of the 'healthy horseplay' variety to which the teachers turned a blind eye unless the situation threatened to get out of hand (so to speak), but emotion hardly entered in. I found these boyishly randy pastimes enlightening and enjoyable, but they did not satisfy my yearnings for an ideal companion.

By the time I reached my teens and went to boarding school, I knew that I was 'a homosexual'. Painstaking circular tours through the dictionary had taught me that there were such beings – people who had 'a sexual propensity for persons of one's own sex' (*Concise Oxford*). I also became aware that there was a hideous aura of criminality, degeneracy and abnormality surrounding the matter. I found this incomprehensible; for how could something which seemed to me

2

so desirable, natural and indeed inevitable be looked upon in this way? Like Harry Daley a quarter of a century earlier, I couldn't believe that love and affection, with their potential for so much happiness, were things to be ashamed of.[1] But, growing up during the war, I increasingly felt where sex was concerned like a member of the Resistance in enemy-occupied territory.

As an undergraduate I certainly was not aware of the widespread 'cult' of homosexuality amongst intellectuals and the upper middle classes which Lord Annan so interestingly delineates in *Our Age*.[2] The first helpfully enlightening information I came across was when a fellow undergraduate at Cambridge lent me an abbreviated paperback version of Havelock Ellis' *Psychology of Sex*. Its humane and surprisingly modern broadmindedness reassured me. Later, soon after I had started living in London, I nervously bought a copy of Donald Webster Cory's *The Homosexual Outlook*[3] – a pioneering work for its time (the early 1950s), which, with its forthright call for self-acceptance by homosexuals and an end to society's anti-democratic discrimination against them, gave me a constructive new perspective on my own situation. I did not know then that I would not only meet Cory[4] in New York years later, but that I should also have a memorable meeting in her extreme old age with Havelock Ellis' life-partner of many years, Françoise Delisle.

Although I had clearly identified myself as 'a homosexual' by the time I was sixteen, I remained mostly celibate after leaving school until well into my twenties. While I was reading history at Cambridge, I fell romantically in love with a contemporary who was not himself gay, but who, luckily, was a classical scholar with a sympathy for the culture of ancient Greece which enabled him to put up with my unavailing hero-worship of him with exemplary kindness and good humour. I am glad to say that we are still friends.

By the time I left Cambridge, in 1948 aged twenty, I was determined to do whatever I could to fight the iniquitous laws which had destroyed the genius of Oscar Wilde and brought untold misery to many thousands of otherwise blameless men. If I achieved nothing

---

[1] Harry Daley, *This Small Cloud* (Weidenfeld & Nicolson, 1986), p. 48.
[2] Weidenfeld & Nicolson, 1990. Chs 7 and 8.
[3] Peter Nevill, 1953.
[4] Pseudonym of the American sociologist, Dr Edward Sagarin.

else, I would do my best to remove this unjust stigma from the way I wished to be affectionate. Journalism seemed one way of contributing, and it attracted me for many other reasons. My first job was with a provincial daily newspaper. When they did not keep me on permanently I decided in 1949 to go to London and read for the Bar, which I did while I was working in the Secretary's Department of the British Iron and Steel Federation. I remained there for the next twelve years, getting my first experience of parliamentary lobbying and doing the bulk of the research and much of the drafting for a large-scale history of the steel industry.[5]

Even when I arrived in London, aged twenty-two, I did not seek out sexual adventures. Although I knew where most of the West End gay pubs and clubs were, and visited them sometimes, I made few gay acquaintances and always returned alone to my digs. The knowledge that the kind of love which my emotions and my body craved was criminal cast a stain of shamefulness and worry over all my early desires and thoughts about love. I was too shy to chat up anyone I fancied in the bars and clubs; convinced of my own unattractiveness I retreated from these alluring persons into the furthest corner of the room, and spurned most of the people who spoke to me: I did not fancy *them*.

So at the age of thirty I was still sexually inexperienced. After some years of sharing a home with my unmarried aunt, who was more like a sister to me, I was living on my own again and going out much more frequently to gay meeting places. In the 1950s London's gay life was more discreet than it had been during the war when the presence of Allied servicemen made the capital a much more cosmopolitan and openly pleasure-seeking city than it had been previously or would be in the immediate post-war 'austerity' years.[6]

There was one internationally famous gay pub, the Fitzroy Tavern in Charlotte Street, which retained the boisterously bohemian atmosphere of wartime London. Although the best-known pickup place in town, and only just round the corner from Tottenham Court Road police station, it enjoyed for many years an immunity from police raids (because, so it was said, of its generous contributions to the

---

[5] J. C. Carr and Walter Taplin, assisted by A. E. G. Wright, *A History of the British Steel Industry* (Blackwell, 1962).

[6] For an account of homosexuality in wartime London, see John Costello, *Love Sex & War: Changing Values 1939–45* (Collins, 1985).

police benevolent funds). One of the old-established clubs, the A & B (standing for 'Arts and Battledress', denoting its wartime origins) was just off Wardour Street. There was also the Rockingham Club, behind Shaftesbury Avenue: its striped regency wallpaper, elegant (some said piss-elegant) furnishings and white grand piano giving it an air of equivocal respectability. I went to all of these quite often, but almost always left as I arrived, alone.

This will doubtless seem extremely naïve, and even bizarre, to a young gay man of the 1990s, whose experience of 'coming out', even if initially worrisome, will, I am glad to think, have been totally different from mine. To be lonely, scared and sexually inhibited at thirty is thankfully no longer necessary, even in today's still ignorant and hostile social climate. But forty years ago homosexual activity was a serious crime, and virtually unmentionable except in those baffling Sunday paper reports of erring vicars and scoutmasters accused of what was obscurely termed 'a serious offence' who were, if found guilty, often jailed for long periods.

Respectable middle-class families thought of homosexuality – if they thought about it at all – as something sick and depraved; it was utterly incomprehensible to my own parents, when I finally broached the subject. Gay men with thicker skins than mine lived their lives as they chose, viewing the threat of the law as a hazard akin to a traffic accident. But I was not of their number. I remained solitary, frustrated and apprehensive until, at the age of thirty-two, I met, by a happy accident, the companion with whom I have now spent half my life.

II

The Roots of Oppression

'There is probably more nonsense written about homosexuality, more unwarranted fear of it, and less understanding of it, than of any other area of human sexuality.'

Dr Wardell B. Pomeroy, 1969

The 'problem' of homosexuality

Almost a quarter-century after the limited legal reform of 1967, homosexual people are still being morally, socially and legally scapegoated. Homosexuality continues to be misunderstood and misrepresented, even by professionals such as teachers, sex educators and doctors (all of whom should surely, by now, have received adequately informed and balanced training). Being attracted to one's own sex is frequently a source of personal unhappiness and social disadvantage, rather than productive of joy and contentment, as it should be, to those who happen to experience it.

Open persecution of, and discrimination against, racial and religious minorities is nowadays widely deprecated, and in some respects curbed by law. But active hostility towards those who are homosexual is still commonly thought to be respectable and even justifiable by many otherwise humane and intelligent people, and is commonplace in some sections of the media. When vulgar prejudice against homosexual people is articulated, it is frequently in abusively offensive terms which would not be tolerated if applied to religious or ethnic minorities. While there is nowadays a general public awareness of the social unhealthiness and moral nastiness of anti-Semitism, and of racial prejudice, this is not the case where homosexuality is concerned. Incessant sneers in some popular tabloids[1] at 'poofters' and

---

[1] And, every now and then, hostile articles in the 'quality' broadsheets.

other silly names for homosexual people are designed to provoke contemptuous attitudes in the same way that terms like 'nigger' and 'wog' used to be applied unthinkingly to black people. The deliberate use of these anti-gay expressions to stir up hostility is complacently condoned, if not actively encouraged, by many who consider themselves to be socially responsible. It is still too meekly endured by many of its targets.

While more people today – especially younger people – now know that homosexual and bisexual people exist,[2] as yet too few realise that these are essentially ordinary folk, and that their different sexual preferences do not make them into 'alien beings from outer space', compulsive child-molesters or sex-fiends who must be loathed, feared, laughed at, or attacked in 'self-defence'. The hoary myth that uncurbed homosexual seduction and corruption will 'spread like a prairie fire' is still powerful.

Such attitudes constitute a grave moral flaw in contemporary society. And they are reinforced by the homosexual person's option of 'passing' (choosing not to reveal his or her homosexuality) which, in contrast to the obvious nature of racial and religious difference, contributes in a paradoxical way to homosexual vulnerability because what is invisible is not perceived as significant. Yet no race or age has been without its homosexually orientated people. It is not, I think, the case that our society gets the homosexual men and women it deserves; they are, by and large, considerably better people than the usually shabby treatment meted out to them would lead one to expect. Because society has far more power to inflict harm upon homosexual people than the latter have to damage society, society has only itself to blame if many of its homosexual citizens are angry, embittered and sometimes cynically irresponsible. Social loyalty has to be earned through social justice.

If homosexuality *does* constitute a 'problem', this is essentially because of social attitudes which are themselves symptomatic of a wider malaise in public perceptions of sexuality as a whole.[3] And the sexual debate is itself just one aspect of the still larger issue, crucial for democracy, of how to reconcile the aspirations of individuals and

---

[2] Those who are bisexual are almost certainly more numerous (though less thought about and talked of) than the exclusively homosexual. I myself first knowingly encountered bisexuality with considerable, and I now realise naïve, surprise when I was in my late twenties.

[3] For a provocative discussion of these wider issues, see Francis Bennion, *The Sex Code: Morals for Moderns* (Weidenfeld & Nicolson, 1991).

groups within society at large. In the last resort the 'problem' of homosexuality is the problem of all humanity.

In the present climate it is hardly to be expected that homosexuality – about which, as Kinsey's senior colleague Wardell Pomeroy has rightly said,[4] much nonsense is talked – will be widely understood. Yet homosexuality and bisexuality permeate all of sexual life. Sexual variety in taste, expression and behaviour exists throughout the entire natural world, and is most pronounced in the human species.

The Variety Show of Sex

The concept of sexual 'deviations' as 'pathology' was a mid-nineteenth-century innovation, partly spurred by a humane desire within the emerging profession of psychiatry to decriminalise behaviour which doctors saw as a medical rather than a criminal matter. At the end of the nineteenth century, Freud considered bisexuality (by which he meant a capacity to experience sexual attraction to persons of either sex) to be an innate potential of every human being. His concept was reinforced in the mid-twentieth century from a behavioural standpoint by Kinsey, who postulated a 'spectrum' of sexual emotion and behaviour ranging from a hundred percent heterosexual through varying degrees of bisexuality to a hundred percent homosexual. Not surprisingly, a majority of Kinsey's large samples fell somewhere in between these two extremes. Charlotte Wolff, in her sensitively perceptive study of *Bisexuality*,[5] maintains that it is 'the root of human sexuality'. The concept is at least as old as Plato, and the fascinating richness of its ramifications throughout history is explored by June Singer in her book *Androgyny*.[6]

Sexual Politics

The implication of these researches is that in real life there are no such people as Mr Norman and Mrs Norma Normal and their wholly heterosexual 2.4 children, who are supposed to comprise the archetypical 'nuclear family unit' so beloved of today's conventional social

---

[4] In Weltge (ed.), *The Same Sex* (Pilgrim Press, Philadelphia, 1969), p. 3.
[5] Charlotte Wolff, *Bisexuality: A Study* (Quartet, 1977, 1979).
[6] June Singer, *Androgyny: Towards a New Theory of Sexuality* (Routledge & Kegan Paul, 1977).

moralists and politicians. Convention itself is a myth, and we are all of us in the same boat of sexual desires and needs which are to some extent unorthodox. A more widespread grasp of this essential truth would enlarge the mutual comprehension and compassion which are vital ingredients of good social health.

It would also expose the artificial nature of 'heterosexism', the unthinking assumption that heterosexuality is 'natural' and 'normal' while all other forms of sexual desire and expression are deviant, degenerate and anti-social. It is the bogus superiority of heterosexism, and of its stable-mate sexism – the assertion of male superiority over women – which provides the primary challenge and battleground of sexual politics today and for the foreseeable future. Sexual politics are here to stay as a valid strand of social debate; and those who find the rhetoric of sexism and heterosexism unfamiliar or distasteful must recognise that the discussion is about forms of discrimination which are as real and as cruel as racism, and even more pervasive.

Variation and Choice

Much has been discovered and written in recent years about the development of sexual preferences. Apart from a minority of biologists who are committed to their belief in the predominating role of hormonal and genetic programming, most sexologists now believe that people's sexual preferences and desires are acquired primarily through social conditioning as a learned process in the very early years.[7]

If the concepts of variation and of bisexuality as characterising human sexuality are valid, it follows that exclusively heterosexual and homosexual preferences (and antipathies) result from *inhibition* rather than from morbid or perverse stimulation: the significant factor is the *absence* of desire for heterosexual intercourse in the exclusively homosexual, and for homosexual experience in the exclusively heterosexual, rather than the *presence* of such desire. The path of individual change, where this is freely sought, lies through stimulating a person's potential option towards an active bisexuality rather than in vainly endeavouring to inhibit or even eliminate the exclusively heterosexual or homosexual desires already present.

[7] See, e.g., John H. Gagnon and William Simon, *Sexual Conduct: The Social Sources of Human Sexuality* (Aldine, Chicago, 1973).

Although they obviously do frequently overlap, homosexual preference and homosexual behaviour are two separate and distinct issues. Not everyone who experiences homosexual desires practises homosexual behaviour or lives a homosexual lifestyle, and not all those who behave homosexually are primarily homosexual; but they may find homosexual activity preferable to abstinence if they lack heterosexual opportunities or for commercial reasons.

Those men and women who publicly 'come out' as gay men and lesbians are themselves a minority of those who are in fact homosexual or bisexual: and they are not by any means typical or representative, of the homosexual population.

Awareness of these matters is crucial for competent parenthood. There is no cause for parents to blame themselves or to ask, as they often do, 'where did we go wrong?' when they discover that they have a homosexual child. Nor does the accumulating evidence about the complex ways in which people's sexual preferences develop deny their scope for choice about behaviour, or the existence of ethical responsibility, which is not affected by the 'nature versus nurture' debate. If society requires people to be individually responsible in sexual matters, it needs itself to practise collective social responsibility – which it is not doing at present.

Myths and Scapegoats

Homosexuality is still widely perceived as both a social and a personal 'problem'. For some of those who are not homosexual or bisexual and who are disturbed by the fact that other people are, the mere existence of homosexuality constitutes an offensive state of affairs. These homophobic[8] people, in their turn, generate grievous social and personal problems for homosexual and bisexual men and women, who are made the targets of prejudice, stigma and discrimination.

Though no longer 'the love that dare not speak its name', homosexuality is still the subject of widely believed myths. And it is the

---

[8] 'Homophobia' is commonly used (in ironically pseudo-medical fashion) by homosexuals to denote the state of mind of those who vociferously condemn them. It was defined by American psychiatrist Dr George Weinberg, in *Society and the Healthy Homosexual* (Colin Smythe, 1972), as an *irrational* fear, revulsion and *hatred* of homosexuals resulting in prejudiced antagonism towards and *mistreatment* of them (my italics). Despite its etymological confusion, it is eloquently descriptive.

non-homosexuals' myths about the depraved nature and sinister potentialities of homosexuality which shape the contours of public debate.
Ignorance breeds prejudice, which generates fear and loathing, which
incite persecution. The ugly and absurd stereotypes of effeminate, evil
perverts preying upon innocent little children are still alive and potent.
Early in 1990, for example, when there was a minor furore about the
rumoured homosexuality of some Scottish judges, I happened to tune in
to a radio phone-in programme where an indignant woman was saying:
'Well! We don't want people like *that* judging us, do we? I mean, they
are all mentally unbalanced, aren't they?'

Failure to recognise that homosexuality is simply one facet – and an
unremarkable one – of human loving allows our sexually guilt-ridden
society to project on to the homosexual, as the most obvious and con-
venient scapegoat,[9] a huge load of morally and legally sanctioned fear,
hatred and aggression, which largely springs from the self-loathing
which is itself the real contemporary sexual sickness. The deplorable
result is greatly to inflate the misery that homosexuality brings, not only
to homosexual people themselves, but also to their non-homosexual
parents, wives, husbands, children and friends. All of this human anxiety
and disruption is needless.

Aspects of Oppression

1 THE PILLORYING OF SAME-SEX LOVE

Homosexual and bisexual people can (and commonly do) experience
deep, passionate love for someone else of their own sex, and not
merely lust or sexual indulgence. That two men, or two women,
can form profoundly loving attachments that are as authentic and
meaningful to them as those of happily married heterosexual couples
is an essentially straightforward concept but it is not comprehended
by many 'straight' people who persist in imagining that homosexuality
is merely a depraved and degenerate way of getting cheap thrills.

Homosexual people throughout their lives experience an invalida-
tion of their deepest feelings and most significant relationships, not only
when, like nearly all adolescents, they have 'crushes' on people which

---

[9] Until recently. The nowadays ubiquitous child molester (usually misdescribed as a
'paedophile') currently holds this dubious distinction.

their parents and other grown-ups find rather laughable if these are het-erosexual and shocking if they are not; but, often much more painfully, as adults, when their elders and heterosexual contemporaries are either simply unaware of the direction of their sexual emotions or, if they have 'come out', discount their attachments as being less 'real' than those of heterosexual people. Gay couples who have lived together for years are frequently treated as if they were single by their own families, and are expected to behave as such, especially at the Great Family Festival of Christmas. When one of them dies after years of committed devotion, the other is commonly not perceived or treated as a bereaved spouse, and is sometimes even insulted and denied access to their lover's death-bed or funeral.[10] The reality of homosexual experience is thus often denied and discounted in our society.

2   HOMOSEXUALITY SEEN AS SICKNESS

The assertions that sexual 'deviations' are a medical problem, and that homosexuality is 'pathological', arose in the mid-nineteenth century, partly as a humane reaction to brutal legal punishments. But the switch from a rhetoric of sin and crime to one of disease has benefited neither homosexuals nor society as a whole, because it is based upon a mis-taken model of sexuality. This 'medical model' was developed by Krafft-Ebing, Ulrichs, Benkert (who coined the term 'homosexual-ity'), and others. At the turn of the century, Freud gave a big impetus to this process, with his ambitious theory of sexuality as the root driving force of all human energy, activity, thought and culture. In his well-known 1935 letter to an American mother,[11] he wrote:

> Homosexuality is assuredly no advantage, but it is nothing to be ashamed of, no vice, no degradation, it cannot be classified as an illness; we consider it to be a variation of the sexual function produced by a certain arrest of sexual development.

Many post-Freudian analysts have been less tolerant, and in the 1940s and 1950s American psychoanalysts such as Bieber, Bergler and Socarides mobilised an almost McCarthyite zeal in labelling homo-

---

[10] The admirable work of the Gay Bereavement Project testifies to this sad state of affairs.

[11] Reproduced in *American Journal of Psychiatry*, CVII, April 1951, p. 787. Copyright, the American Psychiatric Association. Reprinted by permission.

sexuals as sick, inadequate personalities, and 'grievance collectors'.

From a homosexual standpoint, 'sickness theories' are just as oppressive as those of sinfulness and criminality – indeed, more so: for it is less objectionable to be treated as a (responsible) criminal than as an (irresponsible) sick person. The 'anti-psychiatry' stance of Gay Liberation[12] is an extreme, though fundamentally healthy, reaction against the pseudo-scientific and patronising 'medical model'.

3 HOMOSEXUALITY SEEN AS SIN

Historically, religion has been in the vanguard of homosexual oppression. Recent re-evaluations by some Churches, and their wish to soften past condemnation, still encounter the so-far immovable obstacle of traditional theology. There has always been a love/hate rivalry between sex and religion. Both are pathways to ecstasy; and priests have sought down the ages either to harness or else to subdue the sexual impulse in the service of their various gods. Sexuality has been integrated into religion as ceremonial orgy or temple prostitution, or proscribed and controlled within strict and narrow limits as intrinsically undesirable and potentially sinful.

Christ is not portrayed in the Gospels as being nearly as preoccupied with sex as so many later Christians have been. He told the woman taken in adultery that he did not condemn her; and when he added: 'Go, and sin no more,' it could well have been the breach of her marriage vows, rather than her sexual enjoyment, that he regarded as 'sin'. Yet when a bishop of the Church of England said a few years ago that sexual faithlessness was not necessarily the worst marital offence, a minor furore inevitably broke out, followed by a major one when the same bishop naïvely speculated that Christ himself might have been homosexual.

Ever since St Paul fulminated against sexual indulgence, and grudgingly pronounced that it was 'better to marry than to burn' (with lust, presumably), the seeds of the Manichaean heresy, which saw the flesh and everything to do with it as evil, have permeated the Church. The more worldly-wise (though also homophobic) St Augustine of Hippo, with his disarming cry of: 'Lord, make me chaste, but not yet,' represents a minority viewpoint, still generally

---

[12] See chapter XIV.

thought of by most Christians as too lax. The heresy of Dualism has played such havoc with traditional Christian attitudes to sex that contemporary Christians are still wrestling with the manifold problems it has spawned in an anguished attempt to produce a Christian sexual ethic that will seem relevant to today's generation. Their continuing overemphasis upon the sins of the flesh, as against those of the mind and the spirit, makes their search a forlornly uphill task.

Sexual guilt has always been one of the Church's most powerful weapons for controlling people. Obsession with how, when, where, and with whom, semen is spilled and orgasms are obtained is a prurient human characteristic which is unlikely to be eradicated in the foreseeable future; though one may hope that its more morbid manifestations will be progressively curbed as they come to be perceived as antisocial and individually harmful.

Christ is not recorded in the Gospels as having said anything about homosexuality. This has not deterred his followers from stigmatising it for almost two millennia as one of the worst of human abominations. It is only within the past forty years that some 'liberal' Christians have endeavoured to re-evaluate this traditional attitude.[13] Despite careful scholarship, their doubly apologetic attitude – to the Churches, for the existence of homosexual people and the need to tolerate them; and to homosexual people, for the traditionally hostile Christian attitude towards them – has not as yet proved widely acceptable. Most Christians continue to reject those who are homosexual; and most homosexual and bisexual men and women still reject Christianity.[14]

Though belief in God, or in the clergy as His divinely inspired loudspeakers, is no longer as widespread in our society as it was even half a century ago, it is undeniable that the social ignorance and prejudice concerning homosexual people, and the negative concepts of homosexuality which still prevail, are *historically* rooted in Christianity: not-

---

[13] E.g. Derrick Sherwin Bailey, *Homosexuality and the Western Christian Tradition* (Longmans, Green, 1955); Norman Pittenger, *Time for Consent* (SCM Press, 1967, 1970); Leonard Barnett, *Homosexuality: Time to Tell the Truth* (Gollancz, 1975); Peter Coleman, *Christian Attitudes to Homosexuality* (SPCK, 1980). A pioneering book in the United States was Robert W. Wood, *Christ and The Homosexual* (Vantage Press, 1960).

[14] 'He was obliged . . . to throw over Christianity. Those who base their conduct upon what they are rather than upon what they ought to be always must throw it over in the end, and besides, between Clive's temperament and that religion there is a secular feud. No clear-headed man can combine them'. (E. M. Forster, *Maurice.*)

withstanding the Churches' notable support in the 1960s for more humane laws and attitudes, religion bears a heavy responsibility for the continuing denigration of homosexual people's right to be themselves. Even today, those who are both homosexual and religiously inclined face the unpalatable demand to deny and suppress their sexuality in accordance with the requirements of the Church. If they are unable to do this, they must either conceal their true nature or openly flout Church doctrine.

The open existence of 'Gay Christians' has not, as yet, substantially altered this state of affairs; they are not within sight of obtaining full acceptance as equal, healthy and wholesome members of the body of Christ, rather than (as Lord Runcie condescendingly labelled them) 'handicapped' human beings. They vainly seek to square the circle of theological orthodoxy.

Burdened with this history, it is not surprising that more enlightened churchpeople have a sense of shame over the Churches' treatment of the issue; spurred on by this, some of them played a prominent part in bringing about the limited law reform of 1967. But the Churches' record since then has not been an encouraging one. Various working parties have deliberated but none has advocated a clean and courageous repudiation of the traditional scriptural condemnation. And the emergence of vociferous, bitterly homophobic 'evangelical' groups has made the re-evaluation processes much more contentious in recent years.

4   HOMOSEXUALITY SEEN AS VICE AND CRIME

The notion of homosexuality as depraved and vicious stems from religion, as does the concept of the law as a 'moral guardian'. After centuries of comparative leniency,[15] punishment of sexual 'sinners' was, at the instance of Henry VIII – not exactly a paragon of sexual virtue himself! – transferred from ecclesiastical to secular courts at the Reformation. For the next 300 years, homosexuals were commonly perceived as 'wicked heterosexuals' – degenerate people who were jaded with 'normal' pleasures, and who sought fresh stimulation in 'unnatural' lusts.

The death penalty for buggery (anal intercourse – the 'abominable

[15] See, e.g., John Boswell, *Christianity, Social Tolerance, and Homosexuality* (University of Chicago Press, 1980).

crime, not fit to be mentioned before Christians'), whether homosexual or heterosexual, persisted throughout the seventeenth, eighteenth and early nineteenth centuries, and sporadic examples were made, the unhappy victims frequently suffering cruel treatment in the pillory from a jeering mob as a prelude to their barbarous execution. The criminal code was slightly eased in the early nineteenth century, and the 1861 Offences Against the Person Act substituted penal servitude for life for the death penalty; but Labouchere's amendment, inserted with Government support into the 1885 Criminal Law Amendment Act as Section 11, for the first time made all other forms of male homosexual behaviour ('gross indecency') criminal, whether committed with or without consent, and even in private. This swiftly and justifiably became known as the 'Blackmailer's Charter'.[16]

Within a few years of the Labouchere Amendment, several homosexual scandals, such as the Cleveland Street male brothel affair of 1889–1890,[17] and notably the Oscar Wilde case of 1895, completed the demoralisation of those homosexuals and their sympathisers who might otherwise have fought publicly to get the law repealed.

The evil stench of Oscar Wilde's downfall tainted the atmosphere in which English homosexual men lived. In May 1895, Wilde was sentenced to two years' hard labour for gross indecency with male persons – the maximum sentence which could be imposed for this offence, but 'totally inadequate for such a case as this', in the opinion of Mr Justice Wills, who considered that 'people who can do these things must be dead to all sense of shame', and that Wilde had been 'the centre of a circle of extensive corruption of the most hideous kind among young men'.[18]

Wilde eloquently defended from the dock the 'love that dare not speak its name' as 'beautiful, fine, the noblest form of affection'. But a sordid procession of pimps and blackmailers had been paraded

[16] See Sir Travers Humphreys' Foreword to *Trials of Oscar Wilde*, ed. H. Montgomery Hyde (Hodge, 1948).

[17] Fully described by H. Montgomery Hyde in *The Cleveland Street Scandal* (W. H. Allen, 1976) and by Simpson, Chester and Leitch in *The Cleveland Street Affair* (Little, Brown, 1976). The case was remarkable for allegations that Lord Salisbury's Conservative government stifled full investigations and prosecutions because of pressure from the Prince of Wales (later King Edward VII), whose eldest son Prince 'Eddy', Duke of Clarence, was rumoured to have been one of the patrons of the Cleveland Street establishment.

[18] Montgomery Hyde, *Trials*, p. 339.

through the witness box, ensuring that he would occupy a prison cell for the next two years and an infamous place in social history for half a century. Wilde's highly coloured and self-pitying self-justification in his letter *De Profundis*, written in prison to Lord Alfred Douglas who had been the chief although unwitting agent of the calamity, struck another literary homosexual, Denton Welch, as 'very tawdry and mawkish' when he first read it as a student nearly half a century later. Welch was 'frightened of the prison reek all about it. I had only just heard the gruesome Wilde story, and was filled by its disgusting quality'.[19] His reaction is fairly typical of his and my generation.

This renowned case – which, in the opinion of the historian-politician H. Montgomery Hyde, represented the high water mark of popular prejudice against homosexuality in Victorian England[20] – reverberated briefly around London's social overworld, of which the witty author and playwright had been a fashionable ornament, and lastingly throughout the sexual underworld of which he was an habitué. Its impact clamped a lid of silence down upon discussion of homosexuality, and the rights and wrongs of the laws affecting it, for almost sixty years.

Isolated voices – notably those of the (heterosexual) pioneer sexol-ogist, Havelock Ellis, the (bisexual) distinguished literary critic John Addington Symonds, and the (homosexual) idealistic socialist Edward Carpenter – were raised against the total legal outlawry and social ostracism of sexual 'inverts', but they gained no public, and little private, support. Though Carpenter escaped legal persecution not-withstanding his domestic partnership with another man, Ellis' book *Sexual Inversion* – the first volume of his monumental *Studies in the Psychology of Sex* – was successfully prosecuted in England and banned as obscene, with the result that the subsequent major work of one of Britain's greatest thinkers and writers about human sexual behaviour first went into print in the United States.

---

[19] *The Journals of Denton Welch*, edited by Michael De-la-Noy (Allison & Busby, 1984), p. 251.
[20] H. Montgomery Hyde, *The Other Love* (Heinemann, 1970), p. 2.

5   HOMOSEXUALITY SEEN AS ANTISOCIAL

Many people see homosexuality as disruptive of family life and a threat to conventional values and ways of living. They overlook the fact that almost all homosexual people were born into conventional families and have family ties (often very close and affectionate ones) with their parents, siblings, nieces and nephews. Yet these same homosexual men and women are bitterly criticised for being open about their relationships, which frequently involve sharing a home together for many years, and even more for wishing to parent or to adopt children – one of the triggers for the notorious Section 28 of the Local Government Act 1988, with its illiterate and asinine ban upon the teaching in any local authority maintained school of 'the acceptability of homosexuality as a pretended family relationship'.[21]

A further common criticism of homosexual people, although not consistent with the previous ones, is that they are antisocial because they do not contribute to the birth rate. Faced as we are with today's potentially disastrous global population explosion, homosexuality should surely be congratulated for being non-procreative. But logic is not a strong point with homophobes.

[21] See chapter XIX.

III

Wolfenden – A Gleam of Light

'Research into "causes" and "cures" of homosexuality is a complete waste of time and money. Why does this particular form of sexual activity make such an assault upon other people's sensitivities?'
Kevin O'Dowd
Psychotherapist

During the first half of this century, homosexuality in Britain was shrouded in a conspiracy of silence. Harsh laws compounded social ignorance and homosexuals' fearfulness. Nevertheless, as biographies and memoirs of the period indicate, the 'silent years' between the 1890s and the 1950s saw a great deal of homosexual behaviour, most of it discreet and undetected.[1]

The law imposed a heavy burden of unnecessary misery upon those – especially the sensitive young – who discovered homosexual feelings within themselves. And it was undoubtedly a 'Blackmailer's Charter': it is ironic that an attempt to extend the law against private homosexual behaviour to lesbianism in 1921 was defeated in the House of Lords on precisely this ground.[2]

In the years immediately following the Second World War, which had brought greater frankness into heterosexual relations, homosexuality was still rarely mentioned, and then only in shocked tones. This

[1] As the Wolfenden Report pointed out, the effect of the law upon people's sexual behaviour is often exaggerated. The existence of prohibitive criminal laws does not deter most people from engaging in mutually desired conduct of an essentially private and personal nature.

[2] Hyde, *The Other Love*, pp. 176–182. I have never found any credible evidence for the persistent legend that lesbianism had been overlooked by the Victorian law because the Queen herself refused to believe in its existence. This story, while *ben trovato*, is almost certainly a slander on a monarch who was better informed and more broadminded on sexual topics than many of her subjects.

was the social atmosphere into which I grew up and grappled with the thorny issue of my own sexual identity.

As Lord Wolfenden recalled in his autobiography,[3]

> [When the Wolfenden committee was appointed in 1954] the topics with which we were to be concerned [homosexuality and prostitution] were not mentioned in polite society. Most ordinary people had never heard of homosexuality; and of those who had the great majority regarded it with something nearer to disgust than to understanding. . . . The way in which these subjects are treated nowadays [i.e. in 1976], in plays, films, television programmes, the Press, and general conversation would have been unthinkable then.[4]

Homosexual men were smothered by this blanket of silence and lived in an atmosphere of secrecy, of insecurity and frequently of considerable ignorance. Knowing about the existence, location and extent of the underworld of 'friendly' pubs and other meeting places was a matter initially of chance, fuelled by individual enterprise and often affected by social class. But whether in a small provincial town or in a large city (even London), and whether or not a member of a local clique known to one another, there could hardly have been, as Allan Horsfall has said,[5] a less satisfactory basis for a social or sexual existence:

> Had it been conceivable to produce a gay man's survival guide at that time it would have urged him never to reveal his name or address, never to discuss how he earned his living or where he worked, never to take anybody to his home or give anybody his telephone number and never to write letters, whether affectionate or not, to anybody with whom he was sexually involved or even to anybody he knew to be gay.

It is hard for anyone now aged under fifty to imagine what living in this oppressive atmosphere was like. While some of the more robust took it (like the wartime blitz) fatalistically in their stride, believing that you simply had to carry on regardless until the blow fell, which

---

[3] *Turning Points* (Bodley Head, 1976), p. 131.

[4] He was amused to have lived long enough to have made himself obsolete: 'We, who were thought by many to be so outrageous in 1957, (are) now regarded as Victorian fuddy-duddies' (op. cit., p. 146).

[5] Allan Horsfall, 'Battling for Wolfenden', in *Radical Records: Thirty Years of Lesbian and Gay History*, ed. Cant & Hemmings (Routledge, 1988), p. 18.

it would do anyway 'if your number was on it', more timid souls (of whom I was one) were overcast by a constant cloud of apprehensive fear. Between 1945 and 1955 the number of annual prosecutions for homosexual behaviour rose from under 800 to just over 2,500, of whom over 1,000 were given custodial sentences. When cases came to court, men were frequently sent to prison for private consenting behaviour with other adults committed years before.[6]

During the 1950s homosexuality began to be mentioned in the press and discussed as a serious social problem. The publicity given to court cases involving Lord Montagu of Beaulieu,[7] John Gielgud, Rupert Croft-Cooke[8] and other well known men led to demands in Parliament and the newspapers for Government action to curb the spread of this 'detestable vice'. A number of books about it by reputable authors began to appear. A particularly dire one, I remember, was *They Stand Apart*,[9] which, while claiming an 'objective' stance, editorially asserted that 'there can be no question of the potential evil . . . resulting from [these] corroding practices', referred to the homosexual's 'filthy errand', and contained a contribution by Lord Hailsham stating that 'the problem of male homosexuality is in essence the problem of the corruption of youth by itself and by its elders'. Other professional researchers referred to homosexuality as 'a severe mental sickness', and supported the claims of psychoanalysts that it was a personality deficiency.[10] In this atmosphere, it was not easy for even sensible and socially concerned homosexual people who read these works to sustain a high morale.

But there were also calls in the Commons by Labour's Desmond Donnelly and Tory Sir Robert Boothby for the existing law and practice to be reviewed; and they were backed up by the *Sunday Times*, in

---

[6] Allan Horsfall, op. cit., knew a case of a man who was convicted for a single private act which had occurred *ten* years previously.

[7] The circumstances surrounding this case are graphically and movingly described by one of Lord Montagu's co-defendants, Peter Wildeblood, in his book *Against the Law* (Weidenfeld & Nicolson, 1955).

[8] See R. Croft-Cooke, *The Verdict of You All* (Secker & Warburg, 1955).

[9] *They Stand Apart. A Critical Survey of the Problem of Homosexuality*, edited by His Honour Judge Tudor Rees and Harley V. Usill (Heinemann, 1955).

[10] Gordon Westwood (pseudonym of Michael Schofield), *Society and the Homosexual* (Gollancz, 1952); D. J. West, *Homosexuality* (1st edn, Duckworth, 1955). In their later works, both these authors progressively modified these early opinions.

a solemn and carefully argued leader.[11] The Home Secretary Sir David Maxwell-Fyfe (later Lord Kilmuir, and a notorious homophobe) reluctantly responded to these promptings in August 1954 by appointing a Home Office departmental committee, under the chairmanship of John Wolfenden,[12] Vice-Chancellor of Reading University, to examine and report on the state of the law relating to homosexual offences and prostitution.[13]

Some of those affected by these unjust laws saw this as an opportunity which must be grasped to press for reform. I was one who ventured to approach both the legislators and the press, and wrote a long, anonymous letter to the *Sunday Times*.[14] This marked the start of what was to become my major personal preoccupation, and also my professional occupation, for most of the next two decades.

The appointment of the Wolfenden Committee had no perceptible impact upon the police or the courts. In Birmingham, in July 1954, twenty-eight men were given prison sentences amounting to thirty-six years on charges covering isolated incidents which had occurred over a long period. There was no question of public corruption or mass orgies – the case had originated from the police's possession of one man's diary; nevertheless, in passing sentence, the judge referred to 'these disgusting practices which corrupt the life of the community'. After being interviewed by the police at Evesham in March 1956, a forty-two-year-old barman gassed himself and a forty-six-year-old

---

[11] 'Law and Hypocrisy', 28 March 1954.

[12] J. F. Wolfenden (1906–1985; CBE 1942; knighted 1956; life peer 1974) had been headmaster of Uppingham and of Shrewsbury schools before becoming Vice-Chancellor of Reading University in 1950. He was subsequently Director of the British Museum. He was widely regarded as 'the best committee chairman in England' (see his obituary, *The Times*, 19 January 1985). In his memoirs, *Turning Points* (Bodley Head, 1976) he recounts his experiences as chairman of the famous departmental committee which bore his name. After its publication, 'I enjoyed the high privilege of being officially cursed, out of the blue, by Jehovah through the typewriter of His Prophet George. My only regret was that I was sent not the original but a carbon copy.' (Ibid., p. 141.)

[13] The lumping together of these two quite dissimilar topics in a single enquiry confused them in the public mind and gave the headline writers of the popular press the gift-tag 'VICE REPORT' to describe the Wolfenden Committee's work. Home Office officials were so coy about their own committee's subject-matter upsetting the department's female typists that in their internal memoranda they referred to homosexuals and prostitutes as 'huntleys' and 'palmers'! See Richard Davenport-Hines, *Sex, Death and Punishment* (Collins, 1990), p. 314.

[14] Reproduced as Appendix 1.

22

carpenter threw himself under a train, leaving a widow and three children; in April, an eighty-one-year-old man died of a stroke before sentence could be passed upon him. In court, it was considered a fit thing to say of these three that they were 'facing a higher tribunal'. A few months later a man was sent to prison for a homosexual offence committed three years previously, though in the meantime he had ceased homosexual practices, married, and become a father. It is hard to see what was achieved by the prosecution of such men other than the wanton wrecking of homes and destruction of lives.

On 5 September 1957 the Wolfenden Report was published.[15] It achieved shock headlines with its main recommendation that 'homosexual behaviour between consenting adults in private be no longer a criminal offence' – an enlightened proposal which predictably outraged most of the 'popular' press and, one suspected, the Government which had appointed the Committee.[16] It gave a tremendous fillip to those of us who scented an anticipatory whiff of victory in our overdue quest for justice.

The Wolfenden Committee underpinned its stance with the refreshingly robust argument that

> unless a deliberate attempt is to be made by society, acting through the agency of the law, to equate the sphere of crime with that of sin, there must remain a realm of private morality and immorality which is, in brief and crude terms, not the law's business.[17]

This subsequently much debated piece of homely philosophy formed the bedrock of the case for reform, as it was developed over the succeeding decade. There was no attempt to contend that homosexual behaviour was not sinful or immoral – although the Wolfenden Com-

---

[15] *Report of the Committee on Sexual Offences and Prostitution* (CMND. 247, HMSO, 1957).

[16] 'I have not the faintest idea at this moment what we shall ultimately recommend,' Wolfenden told the Committee at its first meeting, 'but whatever it turns out to be my guess is that it will be unwelcome to approximately fifty per cent of Her Majesty's subjects. In short, we can't win.' He hoped they would be able to establish one or two general principles, so that their ultimate recommendations would hang together logically, and not just be an accidental collection of isolated and unconnected items (*Turning Points*, pp. 134–5).

[17] 'Every sentence in the final document has a history, of discussion, rewording, expansion, deletion, fresh approach, and eventual acceptance.' (Wolfenden, op. cit., p. 138.)

mittee firmly rejected the view of those witnesses who had told them it was a sickness. The argument for reform was essentially practical and pragmatic, and very English in its hearty dislike of the notion of policemen prying into what went on in consenting people's bedrooms.

The Wolfenden Report contained eighteen recommendations relating to homosexuality. Besides decriminalisation of the private behaviour of consenting adults aged over twenty-one, the Committee proposed a bar on proceedings in respect of homosexual acts (other than indecent assaults) committed more than twelve months previously, and added that such acts committed in private by those aged under twenty-one should be prosecuted by the Director of Public Prosecutions or with the consent of the Attorney General. They also urged that, except for some grave reason, homosexual offences revealed in the course of blackmail investigations should not be prosecuted. Revised maximum penalties for buggery, gross indecency and indecent assaults were proposed – notably an increase to five years' imprisonment for consenting buggery or gross indecency committed by a man aged over twenty-one with a youth aged over sixteen but under twenty-one. Gross indecency should be triable summarily with the consent of the accused, and men accused of importuning for immoral purposes should be entitled to claim trial by jury. Other recommendations concerned male prostitution, approved schools, the prison medical service and treatment of offenders in prison, psychiatric reports and the institution of research. There was one note of dissent to the main recommendation – from a Scottish legal member, James Adair, who detected 'a marked degree of sentimentalism' in much of the evidence presented to the Committee and maintained that 'the presence in a district of . . . adult male lovers living openly and notoriously under the approval of the law is bound to have a regrettable and pernicious effect on the young people of the community.' But several other members of the Committee added their own reservations because they did not think all the recommendations went far enough, and considered that some of the proposed penalties were too severe.

The first parliamentary debate on the Wolfenden Report took place in the House of Lords on 4 December 1957. It was initiated by Viscount Pakenham, better known nowadays as the Earl of Longford. Frank Pakenham was an Oxford University don, a leading Roman Catholic layman who had held Cabinet office in Mr Attlee's Labour

Government. In those days – long before he became so linked in the public mind with his later anti-pornography crusades – he had already made a name for himself as a passionate social reformer and prison visitor; one of the results of the Montagu trials had been Lord Paken-ham's association with Peter Wildeblood and the future chairman of the Homosexual Law Reform Society, C. H. Rolph, in setting up the New Bridge, a charity to assist ex-prisoners. It was therefore character-istic of him to test the parliamentary waters for Wolfenden.

It was, he asserted, a social document of the first importance. He approached it from a Christian standpoint, and endorsed the Commit-tee's emphasis on the distinction between crime and sin. If he thought that a change in the law would appreciably expand homosexual con-duct, he would oppose it; but even if there were to be an initial increase, he thought it would be swamped and a great reduction effected on balance through a rational national approach to the whole question of homosexuality (something we are still waiting for!). He concluded:

> One day this change will be wrung from us without, if it were
> long delayed, much credit to anybody. Let us take advantage of
> a point in time, while it is still in our power to do the civilised
> thing.

Of the seventeen other peers who spoke, eight supported Lord Paken-ham in calling for reform broadly along the lines proposed by Wolfenden – although the Archbishop of Canterbury (Dr Geoffrey Fisher) made a tentative case for retaining consenting buggery as an offence while repealing the Labouchere Amendment. He also made the eminently sensible observation that

> the threat to general public moral standards from homosexual
> offences done in private is far less, and far less widespread, than
> the damage openly done to public morality and domestic health
> by fornication and adultery.

Speaking for the Government, Lord Chancellor Kilmuir said they did not think the general sense of the community was with the Wolfenden Committee's main recommendation, and that the subject required further study and consideration. Certainly, there was no prospect of early legislation. A member of the Wolfenden Committee, the Mar-quess of Lothian, commented that when they had embarked upon their study three years earlier many of them held very ill-informed views on 'these unpleasant subjects'.

> But one thing has become plain to me, and that is that in a free country the control of sexual appetites is, for the average adult, a personal and not a public challenge.

An opposing view came from the eminent judge Lord Denning, who saw the difficulty as being that 'the law must either condemn or condone; and in cases such as this it must condemn even though convictions are rare'. This 'evil' should be left to the discretion of the judges.

It was clear that the Wolfenden proposals would not have a swift or easy passage into law. Nevertheless, as Barbara Wootton[18] commented, 'what had once been said between the covers of a Blue Book would never seem quite so shocking again'. But the Report's publication and the Lords' debate had no immediate impact upon the activities of the police and the courts. In a letter to the *Spectator* in January 1958, Dr R. D. Reid of Wells described the provincial 'pogroms' which were continuing unabated following publication of the Wolfenden Report:

> The pattern is much the same in all these cases. The police go round from house to house, bringing ruin in their train, always attacking the younger men first, extracting information with lengthy questioning and specious promises of light sentences as they proceed from clue to clue i.e., from home to home, often up to twenty. This time the age range is seventeen to forty, which is about average. Last time a man of thirty-seven dropped dead in the dock at Assize.

Dr Reid called for the formation of a society to help the victims and their families. In subsequent correspondence, A. E. Dyson, of the University College of North Wales, suggested that it would be even more to the point to establish a society to work for a reform of the law. On 7 March 1958 the following letter (drafted by Dyson) appeared in *The Times*:-

HOMOSEXUAL ACTS

Sir, We, the undersigned, would like to express our general agreement with the recommendation of the Wolfenden Report that

---

[18] Later Baroness Wootton of Abinger.

homosexual acts committed in private between consenting adults should no longer be a criminal offence.

The present law is clearly no longer representative of either Christian or liberal opinion in this country, and now that there are widespread doubts about both its justice and its efficacy, we believe that its continued enforcement will do more harm than good to the health of the community as a whole.

The case for reform has already been accepted by most of the responsible newspapers and journals, by the two Archbishops, the Church Assembly, a Roman Catholic committee, a number of Non-Conformist spokesmen, and many other organs of informed public opinion.

In view of this, and of the conclusions which the Wolfenden Committee itself agreed upon after a prolonged study of the evidence, we should like to see the Government introduce legislation to give effect to the proposed reform at an early date; and are confident that if it does so it will deserve the widest support from humane men of all parties.

Yours, etc.,

N. G. ANNAN; ATTLEE; A. J. AYER; ISAIAH BERLIN; +LEONARD BIRMINGHAM; ROBERT BOOTHBY; C. M. BOWRA; C. D. BROAD; DAVID CECIL; L. JOHN COLLINS; ALEX COMFORT; A. E. DYSON; +ROBERT EXON; GEOFFREY FABER; JACQUETTA HAWKES; TREVOR HUDDLESTON CR; JULIAN HUXLEY; C. DAY LEWIS; W. R. NIBLETT; J. B. PRIESTLEY; RUSSELL; DONALD O. SOPER; STEPHEN SPENDER; MARY STOCKS; A. J. P. TAYLOR; E. M. W. TILLYARD; ALEC R. VIDLER; KENNETH WALKER; LESLIE D. WEATHERHEAD; C. V. WEDGWOOD; ANGUS WILSON; JOHN WILSON; BARBARA WOOTTON.

A reply to this letter appeared at the beginning of April, signed by the Bishops of Carlisle and Rochester, Lord Lawson and Earl Winterton, arguing that very few men were convicted for private behaviour, and that the introduction of legislation would 'divide the nation' and bring 'a most unsavoury subject into undesirable prominence'. Soon afterwards a further letter supporting reform was published, signed by fifteen prominent married women. This and other published correspondence drew together those who supported the Wolfenden proposals, and the Homosexual Law Reform Society formally came into being on 12 May 1958. The first chairman of its executive committee was the distinguished surgeon, psychiatrist and sexologist, Kenneth

Walker, and the other original members were A. E. Dyson (Vice-Chairman), Ambrose Appelbe, Canon John Collins, Victor Gollancz, Jacquetta Hawkes, Dr W. Lindesay Neustatter, C. H. Rolph, Stephen Spender, Dr E. B. Strauss and the Rt. Hon. Kenneth Younger, MP.

Soon unobtrusive advertisements began appearing in the classified columns, inviting people who supported the Wolfenden Report's main recommendation on homosexuality to get in touch with the Homosexual Law Reform Society at an address in Liverpool Road, Islington. I did so, and soon had my first meeting with Dyson, the Society's founder.

Tony Dyson, a man of about my own age, was then a lecturer in English Literature at the University College of North Wales, Bangor. An intelligent and idealistic person who had been shocked and concerned by some human tragedies caused by the law, he was determined to seize the opportunity presented by the Wolfenden Report to press for reform. Single-handed, he had undertaken the practical and financial burden of all the negotiation and correspondence involved in getting the Society going, and was now looking for energetic helpers. I and a small group of half a dozen or so similarly motivated men became the active inner core around him. As committed as myself were a City businessman, Nigel Bryant; an architect, Duncan Wright; and the couple who owned the Liverpool Road house, Len Smith and Reiss Howard.

Len and Reiss were both people of strong individuality and the greatest integrity. Before they met and started their homosexual relationship, they had each been (heterosexually) married. Both were pacifists, and Len, who was also a long-standing member of the Independent Labour Party, had been imprisoned as a conscientious objector during the war. Reiss, a Canadian, was an artist, and together they ran an antiques business from their combined home, studio and shop in Liverpool Road. Len, for the year or so that he was solely responsible for the HLRS records and bookkeeping, never went to bed until all was meticulously written up and entered, however late. Their action in offering their private address to enable the Society to begin operating was one of signal bravery; police surveillance of anyone known or suspected as a practising homosexual was very much a reality in those days, and Len and Reiss knew very well that if they were to be arrested and convicted they would get heavy prison sentences. Yet the atmosphere at 219 Liverpool Road was invariably one of tranquil serenity and efficient cheerfulness; I and the others who used to go there regularly on a working rota for at least one evening a week looked forward to our visits because of the kindly welcome and friendliness we knew we would find there and the fulfilling sense of a task well done.

In addition to his sagacious skill in picking a reliable team of helpers (no easy task, I am sure anyone who has been involved in running a voluntary organisation will agree), Tony Dyson proved even more adept in securing the adherence of distinguished supporters to adorn the Society's masthead. Within a few months of its foundation the HLRS boasted an Honorary Committee who were sourly dubbed 'the pick of the lilac establishment' by a hostile newspaper. Both the Anglican archbishops and several bishops of the Church of England, distinguished representatives of other churches (including the Roman Catholic), the academic world, the arts, the law, other professions and all the political parties became and remained Honorary Committee members throughout the arduous arguments of the law reform years.

The executive committee was by no means a cypher, and played an active policy-making role throughout the campaign. They did not, however, have any direct contact in the early days with the Liverpool Road working party, except through Tony Dyson, and this inevitably led to some stresses and strains. The working party did most of the dull but essential donkey work of routine correspondence over supporters' enquiries, subscriptions and so forth; we were all intelligent and dedicated people with a strong personal concern for the campaign to succeed, and we not unnaturally felt that we ought to have a more direct say in policy-making.

The executive committee for their part were mostly not homosexual themselves; they were very conscious of the delicate, and in some respects potentially dangerous, nature of the task which they had taken on, and they were understandably nervous of being 'railroaded' by a group who, however well-informed and well-intentioned, were all personally vulnerable in the existing state of the law and might do irreparable damage to the Society's cause if they put a foot wrong, individually or collectively. They also had to negotiate with another group of would-be reformers who had some influential support and funding resources. Tony Dyson and Kenneth Walker were acutely aware of the potential damage which any competitive rivalry threatened, and fortunately their tactful diplomacy secured the other group's adherence to the HLRS.

Looking back, it amazes me that the Society survived its birth-pangs at all, let alone that it functioned so effectively for a decade. Tony Dyson went on to found a distinguished literary journal, the *Critical Quarterly*, to edit the controversial 'Black Papers' on education, and to become Reader in English Literature at the University of East Anglia; but if he had done nothing else, his brave initiative in launching the HLRS should earn him an honourable footnote in the social history of this country.

In May 1958, the Albany Trust was set up alongside the HLRS as a registered Charity whose objects were:

> To promote psychological health in men by collecting data and conducting research: To publish the results thereof by writing, films, lectures and other media: To take suitable steps based thereon for the public benefit to improve the social and general conditions necessary for such healthy psychological development.

The Trust's first secretary, Andrew Hallidie Smith explained its origins:

> From the start, those who were instrumental in creating the HLRS were conscious of the fact that a change in the law was only the essential first step towards a more constructive approach to the problem of homosexuality. Even when the law was changed, a larger and longer task of education and social work would remain if a healthier mutual relationship between the community and its homosexuals was to be brought about, and if homosexuals were to be helped to help themselves. . . . In order to make a beginning in fields which lay outside the scope of a law reform society, and to create an organisation which might continue doing this work after law reform had been achieved, the Albany Trust was formed. . . . Whilst it was created primarily in order to promote a beneficial solution of the difficulties confronting those who are concerned with homosexuality and homosexuals, the efforts of the Trust are not confined to this subject, but are potentially concerned with all problems of intolerance, persecution and social injustice.

The founding Trustees were A. E. Dyson, Jacquetta Hawkes, Kenneth Walker, the Rev. Andrew Hallidie Smith, and Ambrose Appelbe. The

Trust's name, which has often puzzled people who do not know its derivation, referred to the historic residential chambers in Albany, Piccadilly, where Jacquetta Hawkes and her husband, J. B. Priestley, had an apartment (B4) in which early Trustees and HLRS executive committee meetings were frequently held.[19] The Albany Trust speedily found itself as busy as the HLRS, and became the pioneer national counselling agency not only for gay men, but also for lesbian women and members of other sexual minorities, such as transvestites and transsexuals, who felt hesitant about approaching other, more conventional organisations, or even their own doctors or clergy.[20]

One of the most moving speeches in the Pakenham debate had been made by Lord Brabazon of Tara, who had the courage to break the ultimate taboo and to speak of homosexual love. He said:

> When we speak about the repugnance and disgust of the (homosexual) act, we have to face the fact that all sexual intercourse, be it heterosexual or homosexual, if it is looked at anatomically and physiologically, is not very attractive. But along comes the glamour of love; and that is a mystical, creative, Divine force which comes over two people and makes all things seem natural and normal. And what we have to get into our heads, although it is difficult, is that that glamour of love, odd as it may sound, is just as much present between two homosexuals as it is between a man and a woman. Perhaps that is a terrible thing, but it exists and we cannot get away from it. . . . Because we do not understand the mysteries of sex; because we do not understand the terrible handicap of an invert, it surely should not be in our tradition to beat our breasts and say, 'We are holier than thou', and to persecute.

I was much struck by the wisdom and compassion of this; and, as a friend of my father's knew him, I asked for an introduction to Lord

---

[19] It was an appropriate tribute. Jack and Jacquetta Priestley were two of the most stalwart and active supporters of the Homosexual Law Reform Society and the Albany Trust from the outset.

[20] Strictly speaking, the Trust was limited by its Trust Deed to promoting the psychological health of men only. We overcame this, somewhat casuistically, by telling ourselves that by improving the psychological health of the women who sought our help, we were indirectly contributing to the psychological health of men as well. The Trust only succeeded in obtaining registration as a charity, entitling it to claim tax rebate on deeds of covenant, in the autumn of 1965. Its track record as a counselling agency undoubtedly swayed the decision in its favour.

Brabazon. I was invited to see him at his office in Berkeley Square in February 1958. It was an occasion which remains etched in memory, not because I recall all the details of what was said but because of the stature and sheer humanity of this man. A younger contemporary and friend of Sir Winston Churchill (and wartime Minister of Transport and Aircraft Production), Colonel Moore-Brabazon had been an outstanding sportsman and a pioneer of aviation and motoring before the First World War, when he had been a friend of Edward Montagu's father, the second Lord Montagu of Beaulieu, who was also a pioneer motorist.[21]

In a typical gesture, 'Brab' had made a point of publicly associating himself with Edward Montagu as soon as the latter was released from prison. His powerful intervention in the debate impressed many. I wanted to tell him about the progress we were making with the Homosexual Law Reform Society, and to ask for his help. Although Lord Brabazon never became an Honorary Committee member of the HLRS, he gave active and immediate support by going with Lord Pakenham to see the Lord Chancellor (Lord Kilmuir) to urge him to adopt at least some of the Wolfenden Committee's recommendations.

After my visit he wrote to me:

> First of all I want to thank you very much for coming to see me and for giving me the opportunity of having such an interesting talk with you. I have already tried to galvanise Frank Pakenham into action and I ought to get hopping next week. . . . Please remember that you will always be welcome here and that I will do all I can to help over this difficult question.

A fortnight later he wrote at length, reporting on his visit with Lord Pakenham to the Lord Chancellor, who had not been very encouraging. Nevertheless, Lord Brabazon

> thought the interview was well worth while because it shewed that there were people who wanted to get on with the thing and [the Lord Chancellor] told me that [R.A.] Butler was very keen on doing something, but it does mean the introduction of a Criminal Law Amendment Bill. . . . I thought you would like to hear this as, although it is not very exciting, it does mean that the debate that took place is not just dead and buried.

---

[21] He wrote a characteristically vigorous and incisive autobiography, *The Brabazon Story* (Heinemann, 1956). He died in 1964, aged 80.

In the summer of 1959 I wrote again to Lord Brabazon, giving him details of a case of which I had personal knowledge where two young men, both over twenty-one, had been given a 'lenient' sentence of nine months' imprisonment each after pleading guilty on the basis of their own extorted confessions to a totally private, mutually loving relationship which, as the judge remarked, had not corrupted anybody. In the same court on the same day, the same judge merely bound over a man who had committed buggery with a stranger in a public lavatory. This, replied Lord Brabazon,

> made me boil with fury. It is difficult to know what we can do, but I am getting in touch with Frank Pakenham again to see if we can again go and see the Lord Chancellor to see if he could concentrate on one point which would be I hope that no proceedings could take place without the Attorney General's consent. This would considerably curtail local police 'witch hunts'.

The vision of 'Brab' boiling with fury filled me with awe!

IV

Getting Under Way

'Reform in general does not spring from the generous impulse of a politician or the zeal of a civil
servant but from an accession of public interest.
Most of the milestones on the road . . . mark the
spots at which the public had the problem thrust
under its nose.'

The *Economist*, 20 February 1937

At the beginning of October 1958 the Homosexual Law Reform
Society appointed a full-time salaried Secretary and opened an office
in the West End of London. The Secretary was a young married
clergyman, the Rev. Andrew Hallidie Smith, a friend of Tony Dyson's
since their university days at Cambridge. He had been closely associated with Tony in the early stages of the HLRS and, when sufficient
funds had been raised through advertising and from other donations
to pay a short-term salary, he gave up his curacy in Birmingham to
take on the job. The offices were at 32 Shaftesbury Avenue, on the
second floor of an outwardly imposing but inwardly squalid Victorian
block forming part of the Trocadero building, then owned by J. Lyons
the Corner House caterers.[1] The HLRS was to remain there for almost
a decade.

MPs did not tackle the Wolfenden Report until November 1958,
more than a year after its publication. So Hallidie Smith's first urgent
task was to circulate briefing material to MPs – a pamphlet, *Homo-*

---

[1] Despite the prestigious address and central location, there was no hint of luxury;
the lift was ancient and the single shared lavatories on each floor sordid – steeling oneself
to use them was an act of dedication in itself. The building has now been demolished
and the site redeveloped.

sexuals and the Law, mainly drafted by Peter Wildeblood.[2] The Society also sent its draft Bill, which had been drawn up in consultation with some eminent lawyers, to the Home Secretary, and Mr Butler agreed to receive a deputation. He left them with the impression that he personally would be glad to see the Wolfenden proposals implemented. He commended the HLRS' work of public education, and remarked that politicians too needed to be educated.

However, in the weeks before the debate it became generally known that the Government intended to legislate on prostitution in the sense that the Wolfenden Committee had recommended, but would use the Government whip to defeat any back bench amendment in favour of the homosexual part of the Report. A further setback occurred six days before the debate when a Junior Minister at the Foreign Office, Ian Harvey, was arrested in St James's Park with a soldier and charged with gross indecency. He resigned from the Government, and though the incident probably did not alter what was said in the House it added to the seriousness of the debate.

Opening for the Government, the Home Secretary, Mr Butler, while acknowledging the human suffering which the existing law caused, said that the Government did not as yet believe that they would be supported by public opinion if they legislated as the Committee proposed. He thought more time was needed for the public to be educated towards the type of reform which would be generally acceptable. Other speakers from both sides of the House echoed his view that, while reform might be desirable in principle it would be premature to attempt it yet, though some minor adjustments to the law's administration might be acceptable.

Inevitably there were a few hostile and more ill-informed speeches. Two Labour MPs, Frederick Bellenger and Mrs Jean Mann, lambasted the proposals; Mr Bellenger perceived homosexuality as a 'malignant canker in the community' which, if allowed to grow, would eventually destroy all normal life, and belligerently scorned 'this fancy talk – for that is all that it is – of love and affection for another man'. Mrs

[2] Unknown to the HLRS, two recent books on the topic, *Live and Let Live* by Dr Eustace Chesser and the Penguin edition of Peter Wildeblood's *Against the Law*, had also been widely circulated in the House, with the unfortunate result that hostile MPs were able to raise a plausible outcry that Parliament was being pressurised by a wealthy and powerful perverts' lobby. But no such thing existed: if it had, the Society's task would have been lighter and its coffers heavier.

Mann discerned 'a very limited but very powerful and influential body' behind the Report, with 'very wide international ramifications' – an 'evil thread' running 'through the theatre, through the music hall, through the Press, and through the BBC'. The Report would permit adult males to get other adult males to go to some private place – 'they can set up as lovebirds anywhere'.[3] She vowed to follow the discussions of the Report wherever they were, to show that the Wolfenden Committee sought 'to allow male adults to procure male adults and to allow male adults to set up house together'.

The most telling comment on the debate was that of Mr Leslie Hale: 'The *vice Anglais* is not buggery but humbuggery.' As Andrew Hallidie Smith commented:

> to those who live under the shadow of the law, and to those who have been its victims, the long discussions about public morality, the elaborate anxiety lest Parliament should appear to condone sin, the cautious suggestions . . . and the ambiguities of Mr Butler must have seemed unbearably cynical.

The debate made it clear that no early Government action was likely on the Report, and that the HLRS was in for a long hard slog. But Hallidie Smith's advent had inevitably disrupted the smooth pattern of administration which Len Smith had established at Liverpool Road. In theory, Andrew was to take all this over as soon as he had got himself installed in the new offices; in fact, from the moment the offices opened he was besieged by letters, telephone calls and personal visits from people offering, or much more frequently seeking, help. The HLRS swiftly and unavoidably became a 'casualty station' for homosexual men (and some women) in difficulty or distress, and there were plenty of them. My recollection of those early days is of Andrew restlessly pacing his small office, chain-smoking and incessantly interrupted by the ringing phones, and with no helper except his wife Betty who did some part-time typing.

So the routine administration stayed with Len Smith and the working party at Liverpool Road. And, while welcoming Andrew's appointment, I think that Len secretly preferred to keep charge of the books. Anyhow, when the point came at which Andrew was ready to take over, Len refused point blank to give them up. He was worried,

[3] 'Pairs of them on one's very stair', she gloomily reflected on another occasion.

he said, about security at the office. And he had become very critical of Andrew, whom he viewed as slothful and ineffectual. In fact, Andrew, despite his misleadingly diffident manner, was a tough and shrewd operator. He sensed a wish to oust him, and fought tenaciously for his job.

There developed a huge internal row of the sort which, though it may retrospectively be described as a storm in a teacup, whips up intense emotions and absorbs vast amounts of energy. Everyone concerned had the best interests of the Society – and even more of the cause – very much at heart: I think we were all terrified that the HLRS would blow itself apart, which would set back disastrously the prospects for law reform. The executive committee got drawn in, and for the first time some of them began having direct contacts with members of the working party. It was at this time that I first met Bill Hewitt (C. H. Rolph), whom I later came to know well. For most of the active law reforming period, he was Chairman of both the HLRS and the Albany Trust, and I was frequently grateful for his steadying touch on the tiller. A former Chief Inspector of the City of London Police, Bill was a staff writer on the *New Statesman*, where he had acquired (and still has today as a very active ninety-year-old freelance) an outstanding reputation as one of the foremost commentators in the country on legal and social matters. A man of great personal charm and exceptional human sympathy, and a gifted writer, Bill had not felt comfortable in the police; he identified much too readily and sensitively with the underdog. In this HLRS row, he worked hard to pour oil on the turbulent waters, and largely succeeded – though not before Len had written some very angry letters.

So Andrew Hallidie Smith stayed, and his workload rocketed. The Society was now being asked for speakers, articles and comment by MPs, the press and the public. It became the recognised authority on its subject, and some of its early pamphlets are still intrinsically valuable. Somehow Andrew found time to write a book, *The Right to Exist*. Unfortunately, this was never published; it should have been, because it was a cogent and very readable exposition of the case for reform. Luckily, I still have a manuscript copy, and rereading it brings back vividly the atmosphere and preoccupations of those days.

From the outset, Andrew emphasised that

The mainspring of the campaign for a reform of the law is not pity, but justice – the conviction that a persecution which cannot morally be justified, and which is based on nothing more than unreasoned prejudice, damages not only its victims but also those who impose it – in fact the whole community. The existing law went beyond its proper sphere. By invading what is properly the realm of moral choice, the law is itself morally unjustifiable. . . . Those who see the present law as a bulwark of morality have yet to show how morality can be preserved by the enforcement of a law which is itself immoral because it denies to the homosexual that freedom of choice which is itself the prerequisite of moral behaviour. . . . In the moral sphere it is important that people should make the most constructive possible use of the nature which is theirs. For a moral attitude to condemn the whole direction of a person's sexual nature, which cannot in any case be altered, can only breed a false sense of shame and an inadequate acceptance of real moral choice.

It was

about as convincing to defend this state of affairs on moral grounds as it would be for a pacifist to compel someone else to adopt the pacifist position by threatening them with death if they refuse.

Andrew had by now met and corresponded with several hundred homosexuals,

not one [of whom] has admitted to being deterred by the law from indulging in homosexual behaviour from time to time if he wants to. . . . It seems to me to be entirely right that people should refuse to allow the law to govern their private relationships. If we can imagine a state of affairs in which heterosexual intercourse was made illegal, I hope that those of us who are married would have the moral courage to continue to associate with our wives: and I believe that most of us would.

Indiscriminate police prosecutions and court convictions went on as if the Wolfenden Report did not exist, and Hallidie Smith listed several examples from the HLRS files. In December 1958 two middle-aged men gassed themselves in their Midland home after being questioned by the police in connection with 'certain unnatural sexual offences'. They left a note asking that they should be buried together. In the same month, seventeen men from Lurgan, Northern Ireland, aged between twenty-seven and sixty-four, were given sentences ranging from three years' imprisonment to 'recorded sentences' (equivalent to probation) for various acts committed with one another over a long period. The offences came to light through the police interviewing each of the accused in turn and getting him to implicate one or more of the others. The judge told the detectives that they had done 'a very useful piece of work in clearing up this mess in Lurgan'.

During the early months of 1959, inconsistencies in sentencing became more apparent. In contrast to the Lurgan case, thirteen men who appeared at Appleby Assizes in January were discharged by the Judge. He criticised the chain reaction of 'voluntary' statements on which the prosecution's case was founded, and expressed the hope that one of the men would be reinstated in the job from which he had been suspended. He wished also that he could right the injustice of another man's being deprived of the pension for which he almost due, and added:

> If anyone thinks that punishment is due to you for what you have
> brought on your own head by these lapses of personal morality,
> they are welcome to their opinion; but I do not share it.

The trail of personal disasters continued. In January 1959 a man killed himself while awaiting trial in a south coast town. In February a young soldier hanged himself in his barrack room in similar circumstances. At York, a man was sentenced to five years' imprisonment for offences with youths which came to light after he had reported that four youths were attempting to blackmail him; they had demanded the use of his car, and money to run it on, so that they could conduct various criminal enterprises. The blackmailers were also prosecuted, and their leader got a considerably shorter sentence than the man who reported him. Yet the Home Secretary continued to insist that no immunity could be guaranteed to homosexuals who reported blackmail, and such men continued to be prosecuted. Early in 1960, for instance, a man reported to the police that he was being blackmailed by his homosexual partner. No charge of blackmail was brought (the evidence may have been insufficient), but both men were prosecuted for homosexual behaviour.

The HLRS sent summaries of these and other cases to members of parliament from time to time, and I am certain that this information made a considerable impact on some MPs who had not yet decided to support reform. We also circulated several leaflets as widely as we could, even getting some of our voluntary supporters to leave them in cinemas, tube trains, buses and other public places.

> The attitude of mind which regards homosexuals as 'fair game' . . . is certainly held by a number of policemen [wrote Andrew Hallidie Smith]: 'I went out to hunt for homosexuals: to have some fun at these fellows' expense.' These words were used by a policeman at his trial for assault in 1958. He had beaten up a suspect to such an extent that [the man] had to spend eleven days in hospital. In this instance the policeman had picked on a man who was not homosexual and who therefore had nothing to fear in making a complaint: but one wonders how often he may have dealt in this way with men who really were homosexual. At Portsmouth in 1956 the magistrate did not think it strange that a policeman should have broken the arm of a man whom he was arresting for homosexual behaviour.

Though stories of police violence were not commonplace, those concerning the use of *agent-provocateur* methods were:

> Time and again [the HLRS] had been told substantially the same story by men who can have no conceivable knowledge of or communication with one another, but in almost every case it has been a question of whether to believe their word or that of the policeman who made the arrest. . . . I think it is likely that some policemen, if they see a man who they think is homosexual and he is alone for some time, arrest him and charge him with importuning for immoral purposes even if he has been doing nothing of the sort. The usual police story is that he approached a number of men and spoke to them or smiled at them suggestively; but I know of no case where the men who are alleged to have been approached have been produced as witnesses. Sometimes it is alleged that the man accosts the arresting officer and these stories are believed by magistrates with unfailing regularity.

A number of men who had been arrested in such circumstances had told him that the policeman had taken the initiative by smiling, making sexual remarks, or sometimes even by making physical advances. He became so familiar with these stories that while they were being told to him he could often correctly anticipate what he was going to hear next. However, he concluded charitably, if such police behaviour indeed occurred,

I do not think that [it] results from deliberate malice or love of perjury, but from the attitude of mind that homosexuals are criminals anyway, not too easy to lay by the heels, and so it doesn't matter too much how you catch them.

For the next eighteen months the Society developed its campaign and ensured that the Wolfenden Report was not forgotten. But we deliberately avoided further approaches to Parliament, as we felt that these would be premature in the light of the hysterical outbursts about 'sinister pressure groups' on the previous occasion. Then, in June 1960, Kenneth Robinson, the Labour MP for St Pancras, North, secured time for a debate specifically on the homosexual section of the Report (previous debates having also covered the prostitution section). The HLRS put itself into high gear, and arranged to hold its first public meeting at Caxton Hall on 12 May 1960, shortly after sending a deputation to see the Home Secretary.

The meeting amazed us. We had no idea who, if anyone, would turn up, or whether to book the small or the large hall. When the evening arrived, we discovered a seething mass of about a thousand people crowding into Caxton Hall, and Hallidie Smith had hastily to arrange an overflow meeting in the smaller hall. Even then there were many people standing. The audience, we afterwards gathered, including MPs, magistrates, doctors, lawyers, clergy and probation officers as well as many members of the general public, some of whom were rather bemused by the whole affair. Only recently, a friend recalled the meeting and told me that he sat next to a lady who looked increasingly puzzled and after an hour or so said: 'This isn't the Westminster Conservatives' meeting, is it?'

Kenneth Walker took the Chair, and the speakers were the Bishop of Exeter, Mrs Anne Allen JP, Dr Neustatter and Kingsley Martin, Editor of the *New Statesman*. Their attitudes to the nature of homosexuality were varied, but all were united in calling for reform of what the bishop called this 'monstrously unjust law' – though he also angered some of the audience by likening homosexual tendencies to a cancer which, if not controlled or eradicated, would be destructive of human personality and of society. Mrs Allen, a warm and lovely person and a well-known newspaper columnist (sadly, she committed suicide some years later in a fit of depression), spoke as an ordinary mother who would be appalled at the thought of her own sons being

41

dealt with as criminals if they had to face this problem in their lives. Dr Neustatter spoke as a forensic psychiatrist of the absurdities of the law and court procedure. Kingsley Martin said that of all the laws on the Statute Book, this was the one most clearly preserved by the primitive as against the civilised. Either the Home Secretary should proclaim his belief in the law, and enforce it rigorously, or else he should acknowledge that it was archaic, inhumane, bad, cruel, and ought to be abolished. There were some salty questions from the audience – one of whom responded to the bishop by remarking that 'to find a priest who can speak to a homosexual is to find an oyster in a field!'

The meeting closed with a vote in favour of reform of approximately one thousand, three voting against and only a handful abstaining. Immediately afterwards a letter signed by the Society's Chairman and Secretary was handed in at the Home Office, recording the result of the meeting and pointing out the predominantly favourable reception with which the Society's campaign was meeting throughout the country. In view of this, Mr Butler was asked to give his reasons for stating to the HLRS deputation only a few days previously that legislation would be premature. In his reply the Home Secretary adhered to his view, adding that he preferred not to anticipate what he proposed to say in the Commons debate on 29 June.

That debate was interesting, if predictable. Kenneth Robinson opened with a coolly judicious speech. Avoiding the moral issues, he said he regarded homosexuality as an undesirable way of life because of the unhappiness, loneliness, frustration, guilt and anxiety to which it so often gave rise. But many of its most objectionable features arose from the criminal stigma which our laws, unlike those of most other European countries, attached to it. As for public opinion, it was frequently a government's duty to lead it and to do what they knew to be right. But in this case, there was no evidence of widespread public opposition to reform – rather the opposite. Almost everyone had now expressed an opinion except the House of Commons, and it was time for them to do so; for 'if we are to retain the respect of the nation we cannot for ever emulate the ostrich on matters of social controversy'. In the final analysis, this was a matter of tolerance and common justice.

The simplicity and forthrightness of this speech was typical of Kenneth Robinson (now Sir Kenneth), one of the nicest and most straightforward people in politics that I have known. He later became a mainstay of the HLRS executive committee, giving sagacious advice on parliamentary tactics – always a minefield for the unwary would-be reformer – and in his subsequent career served with distinction under Harold Wilson, first as Minister of Health and later of Housing and Local Government, before leaving politics to become chairman first of the English National Opera and then of the Arts Council.

Several opponents of reform who spoke in the debate showed a grudging shift towards the logic of Wolfenden, saying that even though they did not wish to see homosexuality decriminalised, they did not think that imprisonment was the appropriate way of dealing with it. One[4] paradoxically tried to argue that a Wolfenden-type reform would be against the interests of homosexuals themselves, and in any event would leave their status in society largely unchanged (only from criminal to non-criminal, Kenneth Robinson drily observed), yet he was in favour of repealing the Labouchere Amendment. Another described 'the general run of homosexuals' as 'a dirty-minded danger to the virile manhood of this country'. And a Tory brigadier indignantly enquired: 'If we allow this sort of thing to occur, would (we) be happy to go into a public house and find a couple of hairy old males sitting on each other's knees and liking it?'

In his speech the Home Secretary managed to display sympathy with those affected by the existing law while giving no commitment to any positive action. He said several times that it was very difficult to get the best of both worlds, yet seemed content to offer nothing but the worst of either. He felt that in an age of weakening religious and ethical restraints the law had an important 'signposting' role to play. He did not believe that the full case for a change had yet been made; nor was he convinced that a final decision could yet be taken as to what the precise nature of any change should be. It was, as Anthony Greenwood, winding up from the Opposition front bench, wittily said, 'a characteristic speech, of the sort we are accustomed to hear from [Mr Butler] – the kind of speech in which he promises us every assistance short of actual help'. Years later, Lord Butler expressed hindsighted regret (in his memoirs *The Art of the Possible*)[5] that he did not take a more robust stance over implementing the Wolfenden rec-

---

[4] William Shepherd, Conservative Member for Cheadle, Cheshire – my birthplace, incidentally.

[5] Hamish Hamilton, 1971.

ommendations on homosexuality, as he had done with the prostitution section of the Report (by enacting the much-criticised Street Offences Act of 1959). But he did not grasp the opportunity provided by Kenneth Robinson, whose motion was defeated by 213 votes to 99.[6]

Despite R. A. Butler's ambition to be remembered as a great reforming Home Secretary, his passivity in this instance justified the old jibe that 'the snores of the Home Office reverberate up Whitehall and disturb the pigeons in Trafalgar Square'. The Parliamentary supporters of reform were in a dilemma. Knowing that the opposition stemmed largely from deeply irrational feelings of revulsion, they tacitly agreed to concentrate on the anomalies, injustices and unenforceability of the existing law, and were at pains to distance themselves from any charges of acting as champions or agents of the homosexual minority. This attitude was typified by Roy Jenkins, then a Labour backbencher (later the Home Secretary who gave the reform Bill a fair wind to help it pass into law, and now Lord Jenkins of Hillhead), who said in response to an opponent of reform:

> I wish that the Hon Member would not speak as though one were representing a pressure lobby of homosexuals. In considering this question, I am not concerned only with what homosexuals want or even primarily with what they want. I am concerned with what I think is a reasonable law for a civilised country.

It was also noticeable in this debate that the distaste shown by opposing speakers for anal intercourse (sodomy, or buggery as the law called it) was far stronger than for other forms of homosexual behaviour (lumped together by the Labouchere Amendment under the legal designation of 'gross indecency'). Indeed several speakers, including opponents, protested that if the removal of what was never intended by Parliament in 1885 was all that homosexuals really wanted, that could have been done a long time ago. Nevertheless, even this was well beyond the scope of Mr Butler, although he did say that if the Labouchere Amendment had never been on the Statute Book he would not have wished to put it there.

As Hallidie Smith commented:

> After the debate, the question was no longer *whether* the law would

---

[6] Among those voting in favour was a newcomer to the Conservative back benches, Mrs Margaret Thatcher.

be reformed, but *when*. In three years the word 'homosexuality' had ceased to be a dirty joke and had become a topic for serious discussion. The days when victims of prosecutions were disowned by their parents and friends are almost over, and an increasing number of employers are willing to re-engage convicted homosexuals. In 1895, the name of Oscar Wilde was unmentionable. In 1960, while the law under which he was condemned was being debated in the House of Commons, two of the most popular films in London were sympathetic documentaries of his trials.[7]

Kenneth Robinson's debate was the first big Parliamentary event of the campaign at which I was present, and I saw many of the protagonists in the flesh for the first time. I was to get to know several of them personally over the next few years.

One whom I soon encountered again, in a television studio, was Godfrey Lagden, the Conservative MP for Hornchurch, who had made the hostile speech about 'dirty-minded dangers' and had added: 'In my opinion, all right-thinking people would at best – and I put it at best – think of these homosexuals as people with warped minds who have little self-control.' When the television company approached the HLRS asking for a homosexual to appear (anonymously in shadow, back to the camera) in a programme with an opponent of reform, Andrew Hallidie Smith asked if I would do it. Rather recklessly I said 'yes', and set out to Cardiff. Our television confrontation over, Mr Lagden and I relaxed through sheer relief over drinks, and started talking quite amicably. We were lodged at the same hotel, and meeting again at breakfast we discovered that we were travelling back to London on the same train. So our conversation continued, and I flattered myself that I was doing some elementary education. But by the time the train reached Reading, I gave up. Lagden had leaned across to me and said, in a genuinely puzzled voice: 'Tell me, is it really true that these homosexuals find the idea of going to bed with a woman distasteful?' Wearily, I replied, 'Yes, some of us actually do,' and retired behind *The Times* for the rest of our journey to Paddington where Lagden left me, saying affably: 'I'm sure we shall meet again.' We never did – and, with poetic justice, his successor as constituency

---

[7] Another notable film treatment of a homosexual theme was *Victim*, starring Dirk Bogarde, released in the summer of 1961. The film's West End première aroused much interest, and HLRS supporters distributed leaflets to the waiting queues.

MP, Robin Squire, is now a very energetic Vice-President of the Conservative Group for Homosexual Equality.

There had been other bizarre encounters. By now I was the HLRS Treasurer, with a seat on the executive committee, and was speaking at meetings which Hallidie Smith could not attend. One which stands out in memory was of the Bow Group, then a flourishing branch of progressive Toryism. Though I had myself ceased to be a Conservative supporter since the traumatic days of the Suez crisis, I found myself in sympathy with the Bow Group's general approach. Their discussion of the Wolfenden Report was predictably enlightened until question time, when an elderly gentleman, quivering with passion, rose from his seat in the audience saying that he had come up from Tonbridge specially to beg the Conservative Party 'not to soil its hands with this pitch'. 'If we allow this,' he cried, his voice quavering with nausea, 'there are other, even worse, things. What is the age of consent for a goat?' Everyone howled with laughter. The brigadier (for such he was, presumably long retired) sat down discomfited.

Our supporters also encountered this type of crass homophobia in social situations. A woman barrister who enthusiastically advocated reform was talking to a Tory MP at an Oxford cocktail party, and asked his views on Wolfenden. 'If I had my way,' he replied, 'I'd castrate every single one of the dirty buggers.' 'So I opened my hand-bag', she told me afterwards, 'took out my nail scissors and handed them to him with a sweet smile, saying: "Well, there are at least two here in this room. Would you like to start now?" He turned puce.' I too had an amusing experience with a prominent Tory lady with whom I debated the issue at the Cambridge union (I won handsomely). Afterwards, having a nightcap together in our hotel lounge, she said: 'Do tell me why you chose to take up the cause of these unfortunate people? I would really like to know.' 'Because I am one of them,' I replied, to her genuine amazement.[8]

After the defeat of Kenneth Robinson's motion it was obvious that further parliamentary progress would not be speedy, and that the HLRS was in for a long haul until a new Parliament was elected, which

---

[8] I do not know what she expected one of 'them' to look like. She did become better informed on the subject, and some years later told me that she now had several homosexual friends. 'But what a pity', she lamented, 'that they sometimes form totally unsuitable liaisons quite outside their own class'.

would not be for another three or four years. So the executive committee did not meet again until November 1960. By that time Tony Dyson had resigned and Andrew Hallidie Smith had also left. He had originally undertaken the Secretary's job for a two-year stint, and this was now up. His successors appeared from out of the blue, just as he was wondering how to bow out. Venetia and John Newall were a wealthy and philanthropic young married couple who had decided to devote part of their time for the next two years to a 'cause'. Andrew invited them to become his assistants for a trial period. By November 1960 they were installed as Joint Secretaries. Their regime was very different from Andrew's; family and business commitments kept them in the north of England for a part of each month, and they also went on extensive overseas trips several times a year. But while they were in London they worked intensively for the Society, and kept up the momentum of its impact. They also acted as Secretaries of the Albany Trust, and undertook its growing counselling and advice work.

Initially there was some reserve – not to say suspicion – towards Venetia and John on the part of the working party and other longstanding HLRS supporters. But once I got to know them I found them sensible, dedicated and good to work with. We used to have lengthy lunches together in a crowded and noisy Chinese restaurant where we could, as Venetia put it, 'bellow about homosexuality to our hearts' content'. As Treasurer of the Society I was the most active executive committee member. This caused complications when the Newalls went abroad: they asked me to oversee the office, then staffed by an amiable elderly woman called Olive Brown.[9] Sadly, her notions of office management were as haphazard as the mix of colours in her name; my memory is of her sitting on the office floor surrounded by bundles of papers fastened together with metal bulldog clips, her rudimentary filing system. I used to go in periodically and ask Olive, who was officially Assistant Secretary, what she was doing and what was happening. She displayed a certain irritation at my curiosity, and

---

[9] When the question of appointing office staff had first arisen, the executive committee had stipulated that the person employed should be 'an obviously feminine woman of over forty'. This draconian rule was not adhered to in later years; at different times we had at least one transvestite working for us, and several extremely pleasant young women as well as some men.

it then transpired that the Newalls had forgotten to tell her that they had asked me to keep an eye on things!

A lasting innovation of the Newalls' time was the inauguration of the Albany Trust's journal, *Man and Society*, which ran to fourteen issues between 1961 and 1973 and had a very distinguished roster of contributors, none of whom took a penny. As its editor after the Newalls, I was proud of the fact that it commanded free contributions from, among others, J. B. Priestley, C. H. Rolph, Bertrand Russell, Lord Longford, the Bishop of Woolwich (Dr John Robinson), Angus Wilson, the Rev. Chad Varah, Iris Murdoch, the Rev. Norman Pittenger and Dr Charlotte Wolff. Although its name did not commend itself to feminists (innocent as we were about sexism in those days), *Man and Society* played a significant role in stimulating discussion of a range of social issues besides the one with which the Albany Trust was primarily concerned.

Its first issue was not an aesthetic success. The Newalls sent off the copy to the printers just before departing on one of their trips abroad. Several different, and some faulty, typefaces in each article and a higgledy-piggledy layout caused Venetia to weep when she saw the 'finished' product. Amateurish though it looked, this first issue was momentous for me because I published an article in it on Law and Morality as my contribution to what became known as the 'Devlin debate' which had arisen out of the Wolfenden Report.

In a British Academy Maccabean Lecture on 'The Enforcement of Morals', delivered in March 1959, Mr Justice Devlin had attacked the philosophy of the Wolfenden Report by declaring that the Committee's search for a single principle to explain the dividing line between crime and sin was erroneous. Memorably, he equated immorality with treason: 'the suppression of vice is as much the law's business as the suppression of subversive activities'. On the ground that the private morality of a country's citizens affected the health of its society as much as their loyalty, he claimed that there could be no *theoretical* limits to the State's power to legislate against immorality. Indeed, he discerned the ultimate source of the State's moral authority in the average citizen's sense of intolerance, indignation and disgust (which I dubbed the 'unholy trinity'). This doctrine had a long history going back to Fitzjames Stephen's attack along similar lines in his *Liberty, Equality, Fraternity* (1873) upon John Stuart Mill's classic exposition of libertarian social ethics in his famous essay *On Liberty* (1859). I preferred, and still do, the viewpoint which had recently been elegantly expounded by Sir Isaiah Berlin in *Two Concepts of Liberty*,[10] that genuine freedom entails respect for and mutual tolerance of pluralism of values, and that without such pluralism there can be no truly democratic society. So it was a great coup for me, a few years later, to secure Lord Devlin's signature to a letter published in *The Times* in May 1965, supporting Lord Arran's Bill to implement the Wolfenden proposals.

The period of the Newalls' secretaryship, which lasted until the end of 1962, was a time of consolidation rather than of advance. Their viewpoint, as heterosexual 'do-gooders', sometimes differed from mine; and possibly they considered that they were capable of greater clinical detachment. But working in a political and social vacuum, as we all were, they deserve much credit for their sustained endeavours to give the HLRS and the Albany Trust a forward-looking focus. They were particularly concerned to promote a socially responsible platform for the Trust, which would secure it the respect and co-operation of older and more orthodox social work agencies, as well as of Government. To this end they devised their three-stage plan for social action, comprising *prevention* of the homosexual problem (rather than of the homosexual condition) through education; *treatment* (again of the social consequences of the problem rather than an attempt to 'cure' homosexuals through conversion to heterosexuality) through the establishment of a specialist clinic; and *social adaptation* through a well-run social organisation such as already existed in the Netherlands with official encouragement there. Such an approach may seem stuffily paternalistic nowadays, but at that time we found that it was unacceptably too radical for most of the people whom we endeavoured to interest; the most we got from them was lukewarm lip-service.

The Albany Trust's customary fate down the years, indeed, was to be perceived as a prowling tiger by some and a toothless old sheep by others; maybe this meant that we often got it about right, but this was scant comfort in terms of the practical support and funds we usually lacked. Some of those we were endeavouring to help disapproved, maintaining that the sordid furtiveness in which homosexuals were

---

[10] Inaugural lecture as Chichele Professor of Social and Political Theory delivered before the University of Oxford, 31 October 1958 (Oxford University Press).

forced to live was 'more fun' than greater freedom under a reformed law and a more tolerant society would be.[11] At the other extreme, those who thought we were engaged in the work of the devil sometimes sent us lengthy, and frequently obscene, anonymous letters. One that I always remember with amusement concluded several pages of abusive scurrility with the priceless remark that 'I would sign my name to this letter, but people like us need protecting from people like you'.

The search for respectability was indeed not easy, and it led us to some strange byways. One bizarre series of discussions in which I and other Trust supporters became involved was initiated by Richard Hauser, an Austrian-Jewish sociologist who had come to this country in 1957 with an impressive reputation for varied pioneering work in a number of countries, and a charming wife in the person of Hephzibah Menuhin, the distinguished pianist sister of Yehudi Menuhin. Hauser announced his intention of investigating several neglected social problems in Britain, one of which was homosexuality, and he secured a research grant from the Home Office for this purpose.

Thereafter I went to his home for numerous individual and group discussions. These were always provocative, to say the least; Hauser saw his role as being to prod disadvantaged minorities out of their self-absorption into useful social activity. But much of the talk was, from my standpoint, maddeningly inconsequential – I never fathomed how much Hauser actually understood about homosexuality or about homosexuals (or, for that matter, about anybody); or whether his main, perhaps unconscious, impulse was to mystify and manipulate rather than, as he asserted, to promote effective self-help. Despite his advocacy of 'the Fraternal Society',[12] he was in reality extremely paternalistic in his attitudes, which exuded an air of: 'Do as you like, as long as it's what I tell you'. Other deprived social groups with whom he was concerned, I recall, were lonely and isolated widows

---

[11] The opposite viewpoint was eloquently expressed by one of the characters in Mary Renault's novel *The Charioteer*, first published in 1953 (Longmans, Green). 'It's only since it's been made impossible that it's been made so damned easy. It's got like prohibition, with the bums and crooks making fortunes out of hooch, everyone who might have had a palate losing it, nobody caring how you hold your liquor, you've been smart enough if you get it at all. You can't make good wine in a bath-tub in the cellar, you need sun and rain and fresh air, you need a pride in the job you can tell the world about. Only you can live without a drink if you have to, but you can't live without love.'

[12] The title of one of his books.

and women; gypsies; car thieves; and ex-prisoners. His big idea was that the most helpful way for the underprivileged to remedy their social disadvantages was by doing Good Works for other unfortunates which would gain them approving recognition from a grateful society. Thus, he urged homosexuals to decorate the homes of lonely women and to befriend ex-prisoners and gypsies. The fact that most of the men in his homosexual discussion group which I attended already did some voluntary work, including prison visiting, did not cut any ice with him. 'Why aren't you doing anything to help the homosexuals in Romania?' he once demanded. 'They are treated far worse than you are.' When we explained that we had our hands full dealing with the plight of those nearer home, he was not impressed. Nor were some of us very impressed with his lines of argument, and so some of our sessions with him were quite acrimonious.

When Hauser's report was published in 1962 as *The Homosexual Society*,[13] it proved to be, as I had anticipated, rather a hodge-podge,[14] although containing some shrewd insights and comments. But the overall tone was condescending; Hauser considered homosexuals to be the socially underdeveloped victims of a 'stress-disease' analogous to bed-wetting, and upbraided them for being self-centred, for living 'an eternal life of parties and excitement without any need to settle down', and for being mostly unwilling to make any contribution to society. He offered no supporting evidence for such sweeping generalisations, which rendered his book useless as serious social comment, and negated the few useful suggestions he made. He brushed aside the impact of the still unreformed law, although he did condemn the extreme bigotry of some anti-homosexual attitudes.

Hauser's central conclusion, eagerly relayed to the House of Commons by opponents of law reform, was that he knew no other minority among whom self-pity and self-righteousness were so rampant; which was so lacking in a sense of values outside its own circle, or so bereft

[13] Bodley Head, 1962.
[14] It contained a chapter listing over forty homosexual 'types', including the Demoralised Married Man, the Call-Boy, the 'Cottage' Type, Sugar Daddies, the Pub Type, the Club Type, the Prison Queer, the Ship's Queer, the War Queer, the Religious Homosexual, the Woman Hater, the Body-builder, etc. etc. and a weird glossary containing some words which I have never encountered elsewhere. I couldn't help feeling that some of the homosexuals Hauser had talked to had amused themselves by testing out how gullible he was.

of loyalty to its country[15]. An article to this effect which he contributed to *Man and Society*, published under the title of 'The Drug of Self-Pity'[16], in which he patronisingly referred to the break-up of homosexual partnerships as being followed by 'terrible tragedies of an adolescent type (which) shake otherwise mature people for about five days, depending on whoever loses most', and accused the great majority of homosexuals of lacking social responsibility, led to several sharp retorts from correspondents, printed in the subsequent issue under the heading 'The Drug of Self-Righteousness'. The writers pointed out that there was hardly any negative personality feature which Hauser did not try to foist disparagingly on homosexuals, and that his whole approach to 'social rehabilitation' through community service smacked of 'yesteryear's workhouse-and-poor-law mentality', and also of authoritarian demands on the individual like the 'Arbeitsdienst' of fascism or the 'voluntary week-end work' of Stalinism. What homosexuals actually wanted, one said bluntly, was 'to live their own lives just like everybody else, free from fear, from prosecution, and from the prying of self-appointed "social scientists". The homosexual in Britain owes his society no apologies and no penitent work along Mr Hauser's lines'. But one self-oppressed individual, writing anonymously 'since I am an established Civil Servant and, therefore, likely to be considered, automatically, a "security risk"', thought that Hauser's 'very excellent article' should 'be made compulsory reading' – an oppressive concept in itself! – 'for all homosexuals and those who work on their behalf'.

In March 1962, Leo Abse, the Labour MP for Pontypool, and a solicitor with a strong interest in social reform, failed to secure a Second Reading in the Commons for a Sexual Offences Bill to implement some of the minor proposals (but not the main recommendation) of the Wolfenden Report[17]. This roused just as fierce condemnation as Kenneth Robinson's motion had done; the Bill was talked out by opponents who were as vehement against it as if it had embodied the main Wolfenden proposal. They wanted none of what

[15] *Hansard*, Commons, 11 February 1966, col. 809.

[16] *Man and Society*, No. 6, Autumn 1963.

[17] The Bill sought to ensure that men complaining of homosexual blackmail should not themselves be prosecuted; that 'stale' charges relating to homosexual offences more than twelve months old should be prohibited; and that all cases against 'consenting adults in private' should be brought, if at all, by the Director of Public Prosecutions.

one of them called 'Wolfenden watered down'. Another objected to these 'abominable' offences being muddled up with 'more respectable' sexual offences in the Bill's title, and expressed the hope that neither that nor any future Parliament would go one inch along the path of legalising homosexuality, which he described as 'particularly repugnant to the vast majority of people in this country'.[18]

So it looked as if opposition to even small changes in the law remained as strong as it was to going the whole hog: and on the basis of that experience I am convinced that if you are ever afforded a realistic opportunity to get a reforming measure through Parliament you would be wise to make sure that it is as thoroughgoing and as radical as possible.

In the autumn of 1962, the Newalls told me that they wanted to give up the Secretaryship, having done their two-year stint, and the executive committee began looking for a successor. This involved sounding out a number of people who had been recommended or who offered themselves. None, however, seemed quite right for the job, and I was by now becoming increasingly convinced that I ought to take it on myself. During the Newalls' absences abroad, I had kept an eye on the day-to-day work, and was familiar with the Society's main tasks. I was increasingly restless with my job in public relations. The problem was that the HLRS did not have enough funds to offer me a full-time salary.

Unexpected rescue came from my former employers, the British Iron and Steel Federation, who asked me to be joint author, on a part-time basis, of a book chronicling the recent development of the steel industry. So it seemed feasible to propose to the HLRS executive committee that they should engage me, also on a part-time basis, and seek the necessary funding. In addition the Hon David Astor, who was already a generous supporter of the Society, very kindly offered me a Saturday sub-editor's post on the *Observer*, which he then owned and edited, as a means of supplementing my still meagre income. A six-day week was a strenuous option, but I undertook it for the next few years; and my Saturdays on the *Observer* turned out to be among the pleasantest days in the week; I shall always remember with pleasure the valuable journalistic experience I gained and the comradeship I

---

[18] *Hansard*, 9 March 1962, cols. 843–860.

shared there with the staff, who on Saturdays included several other part-timers with staff jobs on Fleet Street dailies – an interesting and friendly bunch.

V

Full-Time Campaigner

'What the public really loathes in homosexuality is
not the thing itself but having to think about it.'

E. M. Forster

At the beginning of December 1962 I took possession of the office
in Shaftesbury Avenue as Acting Secretary of the HLRS. I used my
pen name of Antony Grey – which I had chosen some while before
because of the conviction (which I still hold) that there are few entirely
black-and-white issues in life.

At this time, I looked upon my new post as a professional assign-
ment which would probably be of limited duration – perhaps two
years, as with Hallidie Smith and the Newalls; I did not, at that stage,
contemplate making the HLRS/Albany Trust the vocational career
which it subsequently became for me. Apart from my personal commitment to the cause, I believed that my previous working experience
had fitted me to run a small campaigning group. My twelve years on
the secretarial staff of a major national trade association, which had
involved being in close touch with parliamentary debates over nation-
alisation, and my recent stint with a large London advertising and
public relations agency, had taught me the essential need for high
standards of competence in the task of informing and influencing
public and political opinion.

I was determined to bring a higher degree of professionalism to
bear on the Society's work than hitherto. Pleasant and well-
intentioned as Olive Brown was, there was no more room for her
haphazard, bulldog-clip approach. At the advertising agency I had
made friends with a temporary senior secretary, Joyce Blanchard
(known to everyone as Joy) who was then in her late forties, and had
previously worked as personal secretary to several eminent busi-

nessmen – including David Astor of the *Observer*. I decided to offer her the position of Office Manager at the HLRS/Albany Trust offices, and she responded enthusiastically. Whether Joy was herself lesbian I never knew and never asked. I only know that she served the Society and the Trust with unstinting devotion for the next six years, made a host of friends who still remember her with affection, and gave me her personal loyalty.

The executive committee asked Olive Brown to stay on as Joy's assistant. Not unnaturally she viewed this as demotion from her nominal Assistant Secretaryship, and declined. She also refused to resign, saying that she enjoyed the 'human side' of her work;[1] so the committee felt obliged to terminate her employment. I was distressed that she felt so hurt, but I am sure I was right in believing that it was not possible to allow our genuine personal liking for her to get in the way of an essential reorganisation for the long, tough struggle that lay ahead. With a campaign so slenderly and precariously financed as ours, we owed it to our supporters to use every penny they gave us as effectively as we could.

Initially I had offered the Society my part-time services for 'one-plus' days a week for a fee of £500 a year until a suitable full-time (and preferably voluntary) successor to the Newalls could be found. The steel book would absorb three days a week, and I spent my Saturdays at the *Observer*. Inevitably the HLRS' 'one-plus' days were never less than two full days spent at Shaftesbury Avenue, and often considerably more than incidental time there on other days; frequent evening speaking engagements and the writing of many articles out of office hours were included in the reckoning. For the next five or six years I usually worked a fifty-hour week, and sometimes more. Luckily Joy proved a stalwart backstop, and I knew that while she was holding the Shaftesbury Avenue fort – and it often felt as if we were under siege there – I had no need to worry.

In a note which I circulated to the executive committee before they decided to appoint me, I set out my proposed strategy. Even if there were to be a general election in 1963 it was unlikely that there

---

[1] She was only the first of many staff members and helpers to feel this way. The volunteers, applicants for help, and casual callers who passed through the Shaftesbury Avenue offices included some varied and colourful strands from 'life's rich tapestry'.

would be an opportunity for a full-scale attempt to enact the Wolfenden proposals in the first session of a new parliament – i.e. before 1964.[2] I therefore calculated that we had between a year and eighteen months to build up our organisation and funds; and it was vital that we should use this time to the best possible advantage. Recruiting more supporters, and generating a larger guaranteed regular income, were the first priorities. Currently there was a steady income of around only £800 a year; we needed to increase this to £3000 or even £5000. This task, together with the promotion of research and educational work through the Albany Trust, would be the main focus of activity until mid-1963, after which I hoped the Society would be in a stronger position to mount a more specifically political campaign aimed at persuading the Government to legislate during 1964.

My appointment was not a foregone conclusion. I was asked to wait in Kenneth Walker's little Harley Street dining room while the committee discussed my offer. Besides Mr Walker, the others present were Dr Neustatter (the Society's deputy chairman), Kenneth Robinson MP, the Bishop of Woolwich ('Honest to God' John Robinson) and the Newalls. Apologies for absence had been received from Jeremy Thorpe MP, Ambrose Appelbe, C. H. Rolph and Jacquetta Hawkes, although I believe that most, if not all, of these had told Kenneth Walker of their views. The discussion seemed the longest half-hour of my life. They eventually agreed to appoint me as Acting Secretary for a trial period of six months. I don't think their prolonged deliberations were due to any serious doubts about my capability to do the work effectively, but rather because they felt the need to weigh the possible risks to the Society arising from my own sexuality; and the fact that, unlike my predecessors, I was unmarried and shared my home with another man. I understood their concerns; the main reason for the Society's existence, after all, was the vulnerability of men in my own position. However, their decision came as a great relief; I would have felt hurtfully discriminated against if they had not grasped the nettle, and shall always be grateful to them for having the courage, and the confidence in me, to do so.

Another decision at this committee meeting was that 'the present

[2] In the event the general election did not take place until October 1964, and the parliamentary campaign got under way in the spring of 1965.

policy of destroying correspondence was to be continued'. This practice had been instituted and adhered to by the Newalls so rigorously that I inherited a very scanty archive. While I appreciated the need to protect sensitive items relating to individuals' personal affairs or confidential political correspondence, it did not make sense to keep virtually no files at all. One of the early changes under my regime, therefore, was the amendment of this minute at the next committee meeting to read 'The present policy of destroying correspondence *at the Secretary's discretion* was to be continued'. My discretion was more liberal than John's and Venetia's, so the Society's main activities during the 1960s and 1970s can be traced through its surviving archives.[3]

The Newalls resigned as Trustees of the Albany Trust but were invited to remain members of the HLRS executive committee, and to continue as editors of *Man and Society*. But they soon resigned from these functions as well after differences with the Trustees which we sincerely regretted.

Man and Society continued to play a growingly influential role as the Albany Trust's major publicity vehicle. In addition, I instituted a newsletter for AT/HLRS subscribers, *Spectrum*, which appeared at least four times a year between October 1963 and October 1970. We called it *Spectrum* because its contents would not, we hoped, be uniformly sombre but would include some flashes of light relief and gems of wisdom.

In the autumn of 1963, with spy mania at its most feverish in the wake of the Vassall case and the Government ban on the posting of unmarried diplomats to certain foreign capitals, the eminent journalist James Cameron commented that 'with sane and humane legislation, queers would be no more vulnerable than teetotallers'; while the Government's Central Office of Information splurged £15,000 on a film whose plot included Nicolai Popov, 'a suave, well-connected Soviet agent' entertaining an unsuspecting Government official with homosexual tendencies in an unspecified part of Soho. One of the earliest calls for homosexual men and women to stand up and be counted was made by Alan Brien in the *Spectator*; but, as I enquired, who would be prepared to 'bell the cat' and come out first? Two young female correspondents of the *Daily Mirror* ('Bewitched and

---

[3] Now deposited with the British Library of Political and Economic Science at the London School of Economics.

58

Bothered') wrote: 'We have had dates with many men of executive class, but are amazed to find that although they appear to be perfect specimens of virile manhood, many of them have turned out to be "queer". Is there something wrong with us or aren't there any normal men left?' 'There are plenty of "normal" men around,' columnist Jane Adams tartly responded – 'Your trouble is that your judgment of character is at fault. Some women can spot a "queer" in a minute!' (I suggested that MI5 and the Foreign Office should seek out and recruit these lynx-eyed ladies.)

Clement Freud pointed out in an *Observer* article that 'While a Turkish bath could be said to be the epitome of the metropolitan man's world, it is not always advisable to talk to the other men there', while the *Listener* complained that a Third Programme feature on venereal disease, although a welcome breakthrough, was only likely to have reached highbrow homosexuals; the other two groups it dealt with (foreign immigrants and underpaid girls driven to prostitution by low wages) being unlikely culture-vultures. From Chester, a proto-Mrs Whitehouse complained that television ('a monster in the home') was filling her mind with suspicions of being surrounded by unnatural lusts. 'How can we love our neighbours if we suspect them of constant secret sexual orgies?' she plaintively enquired. (I did not venture to suggest 'by joining in'.)

An American psychologist complained that lie detectors were in-effective in weeding out 'homosexuals, drones and Communist agents' from the CIA because 'the genuine homosexuals, who lack even the rudiments of guilt feelings about their sex lives and actually may be proud of it [*sic*], probably will pass ... with flying colours.' (He should have seen our case files.)

Another naïve American, Mr George Meany, President of the giant trade union AFL-CIO, found himself in hot water when he described the Brussels-based International Confederation of Free Trade Unions as 'an ineffective bureaucracy, right down to the fairies'. *Time* Magazine commented: 'To anybody except small children and little old ladies, that meant only one thing'; ICFTU staff were reported as being 'deeply shocked'. 'It's all lies', protested a startled Mr Meany. 'I never used the word "homosexual". I am an Irishman, and we have a lot of stories about fairies and leprechauns, and we use the word "fairy" simply to say someone is an idle gossip.'

By New Year 1963, I was adjusting myself to my new threefold working life. It was a sad time of personal adjustment, too, as my father had died just before Christmas after several years' painful illness, and my mother was beginning almost a quarter-century's widowhood. Now that she and my aunt, both in their mid-sixties, were each living alone, I felt my responsibilities to them keenly, as well as those to my challenging mission for the Society. But in Shaftesbury Avenue there was little time for sad reflection. The office had always been busy, and with a more methodical full-time staff the tempo quickened. 1963 saw the start of a ceaseless round of meetings with potentially sympathetic individuals and groups, both in and away from the office – even on my industrial history writing days, I frequently visited Shaftesbury Avenue, or met a supporter or contact, at lunchtime. And for months on end I went to talk to numerous organisations who had requested a speaker, sometimes on two or even three evenings a week, returning home at midnight and even later from as far afield as the south coast or the midlands.

These meetings ranged from constituency associations and youth sections of all the major political parties to Church groups, university societies, Mothers' Unions and Rotary Clubs. The last two, especially, followed a pattern. The Mothers' Unions were a friendly and concerned bunch, genuinely interested and wanting to help to reduce the misfortunes of others. But they were understandably nervous of what I was going to say, and I always noticed that they settled back more comfortably in their seats and really began to listen once I had uttered the dread word 'buggery' (which did not seem to upset them nearly so much as it did the MPs and brigadiers). Rotary lunches, on the other hand, struck me as most odd affairs; the food was usually mediocre, and wolfed down rapidly so that the real business of the meeting could begin – this being not the speaker (who was usually merely an afterthought) but the announcements and discussions of their various local activities. I came to dislike these occasions, especially when I had to travel a long distance for the meeting, because of the cursory way my part in the proceedings was dealt with. On one occasion, I did succeed in galvanising their attention when in answer to a question as to what homosexuals were really like I replied: 'Well, not all that different from a gathering of Rotarians, actually!'

R. A. Butler had been succeeded as Home Secretary by Henry

Brooke, who seemed likely to be less sympathetic and not as anxious as his predecessor to give even verbal support to homosexual law reform. In correspondence with a constituent who was an HLRS supporter, and also at a small private lunch with Mr Rolph and myself which David Astor hosted in May 1963, Mr Brooke maintained the Home Office 'party line' that there was no evidence of a swing in parliamentary or public support since 1960 towards reforming the law; and that so long as it was impracticable to implement the main Wolfenden recommendation it would be very difficult to give effect to any of the subsidiary ones (such as placing 'consenting adult' prosecutions under some form of central control). However, in October 1963 the Home Secretary did inform Parliament that victims of blackmail concerning consensual homosexual practices who complained to the police need not fear that they themselves would be prosecuted except in 'grave or exceptional cases'.[4] Despite the assurance such prosecutions continued.

In the memorandum which I prepared for the Home Secretary before our lunch with him I emphasised the severe drain on the nation's mental health which the nervous stress caused by the existing law imposed; the unreality of the legalistic distinction between the *state* of being homosexual and homosexual *acts*; the bad social effects of the law in encouraging anonymous, furtive behaviour in public places in preference to more permanent private relationships; the questionable police methods employed in respect of both private and public offences;[5] and the lack of effective protection afforded to young people by such an indiscriminate law. 'We fully recognise,' the memorandum concluded 'that any reform of this nature presents a ticklish political problem which has to be approached circumspectly. We nevertheless feel that more could be done by the Home Office to help us pave the way for a wider degree of public understanding which is a necessary preliminary to

[4] *Hansard*, 24 October 1963, col. 242.

[5] The latter still continue, and allegations of the police behaving as *agents provocateurs* in public lavatories and parks are as frequent today as they were in the 1960s. The solution we recommended to Mr Brooke then – that such offences should be dealt with primarily as *nuisance*, and that the simplest way to prevent them was to provide adequate lighting in public conveniences and to have these regularly patrolled by uniformed officers – was the obvious one, and I cannot understand why it has still not been adopted.

reform.' Would the new Home Secretary be more helpful over promoting useful research than his predecessor?

Unfortunately, the answer turned out to be 'no'. We were still in the 'Catch-22' situation where a demonstrable shift in public opinion was required to prompt the Government to reform the law, yet the growing evidence of such a shift which our own work revealed was dismissed as special pleading. In these circumstances, the executive committee felt that if the Government would not commission such research themselves they might be favourably influenced by evidence produced by independent market research bodies. Such research was expensive, but even so the Albany Trust held discussions with the British Market Research Bureau and commissioned the first stage of a three-stage public opinion sample which the BMRB proposed. Their pilot attitude revealed 'a tentative picture of widespread confusion, uncertainty, outright misunder-standings and contradictory ideas'; they suggested that much of the hostility to reform was superficial and could be reduced by suitable educational programmes. These findings reinforced my own view that a campaign which focussed only on Parliament, and did not endeavour to reach influential 'opinion forming' sections of society, would be a waste of time; but the resources needed for such a broadly-based, nationwide campaign were beyond the means at our disposal.[6]

This was only the first of several research projects which the Albany Trust carried out itself, commissioned or sponsored, during the 1960s and 1970s. I had always been impressed by the ambitious projects and careful methodology of the American Kinsey Institute, and even more by the amount of publicity and discussion generated by the original studies of male and female human sexual behaviour by Dr Alfred Kinsey and his team in the 1940s and 1950s. I strongly believed – and still do – that this country would benefit greatly from the work of a similar UK-based research agency specialising in all aspects of human sexual behaviour; I realised that such a task was way beyond the tiny resources of the Albany Trust, but hoped that our advocacy

---

[6] So was the production of a film, which was several times proposed to us by would-be film makers who provided outline scenarios. Though these were interesting, none of them attracted the executive committee sufficiently to embark upon the major fund-raising effort needed for this purpose.

of it might help to bring it into being. With Gerald Sanctuary, who had been Secretary of the Marriage Guidance Council and had also worked with the Sex Information and Education Council in the United States, I drew up proposals in 1970 for a British Institute for the Study of Human Sexuality. We got the usual tepidly polite interest, but no practical support, from government and the wealthy medical and other research foundations. It is both sad and ironical that it was only the appearance of AIDS in the 1980s which at last made clear the urgent need to find out more about the British population's sexual habits and enabled a large-scale research into sexual behaviour to get under way.[7]

A second research effort which I initiated in the early days of my secretaryship was an endeavour to get the Home Office to produce a more adequate and informative breakdown of the statistics relating to homosexual offences. The chief and lasting value of this proved to be the friendly relations which it helped to establish between HLRS/Albany Trust and Home Office officials, who knew us well enough by the time the law reform campaign got into top gear a couple of years later to regard us as a responsible and useful, rather than a stroppy or nitpicking, pressure group.

In addition to our own interest in starting research projects, we were being approached at the Albany Trust increasingly often by academically based and other independent researchers wanting our help. One of these was Dr Eva Bene,[8] a Hungarian psychologist living in London who wished to meet homosexual men willing to help her with a research designed to produce a profile of their early family relationship patterns. We succeeded in finding over fifty volunteers who visited Dr Bene at her home in Wimpole Street for a short test. She later admitted to me that she had been rather nervous at first, as she had not knowingly met many homosexuals. 'But I needn't have worried,' she said, 'I've met some of the most charming men in London through this research!' She then went on to do similar research with a lesbian sample which we again helped her to contact through *Arena Three* and other sources. Both papers were published

---

[7] And even then, Mrs Thatcher's government prudishly declined to fund it on the pretext that it would be 'invasive of privacy'. How this could be, with the anonymity of participants rigorously safeguarded in the research method, escapes me.

[8] Pronounced 'Benay'.

in the *British Journal of Psychiatry*, and made a considerable impact.[9] Eva Bene was a most likeable person, and I was friendly with her for some years until she went to live in Canada.

Social action to support lonely and isolated homosexuals, of whose existence we were made only too acutely aware by an endless stream of appeals for help, was by now firmly on the Albany Trust's agenda, and I had already reached the conclusion that it would be wrong simply to 'shut up shop' after the law had been changed; indeed, the real longer-term work would only then begin. Since 1961, when I had first visited Holland and become friendly with the impressive people who had founded the Dutch homosexual organisation COC, I had urged upon the Newalls the need to prepare the ground for a self-help organisation which might ultimately achieve a similar degree of official support and recognition in this country. As a result of our discussions, they had drawn up a three-stage blueprint for social action which they presented to two meetings sponsored by the Church of England's Council for Moral Welfare.[10] Rereading it thirty years later, it inevitably has a paternalistic air about it which a young gay person of today might well find insufferably stuffy; but in the context of its time, I still think it was a brave and forward-looking document.

> Coming into contact, as we have done, ... with a very large number of male homosexuals [it said] we are conscious that the inconclusive public debate of the last ten years has done nothing to better their predicament. Demoralised already by what, it must be realised, seems to them unreasonable legal persecution, the increasingly academic argument about when, rather than if, reform should take place has encouraged a widespread attitude of

---

[9] *British Journal of Psychiatry* (Vol. 111, No. 478, September 1965): Eva Bene, MA, PhD: 'On the Genesis of Male Homosexuality: An Attempt at Clarifying the Role of the Parents'; 'On the Genesis of Female Homosexuality'. A sample of eighty-three homosexual men and eighty-four married men was used in the male survey. The results showed that significantly more of the homosexual men reported poor relationships with their fathers, but that there was no significant difference between the two groups in relationships with their mothers. The lesbian research (using thirty-seven lesbians and eighty married women) also showed far greater differences between the feelings of the lesbians and the married women about their fathers than in those towards their mothers. 'The lesbians were more often hostile towards and afraid of their fathers than were the married women. . . . The results . . . point towards a relationship between the parents' wish for a son and the homosexuality of their daughter.'

[10] Later Board for Social Responsibility.

despondency and cynicism. The homosexual feels himself made the whipping block for society's ills in general, and a sense of being irrevocably unacceptable to the rest of society is the result. . . .

Those who come into contact with homosexuals . . . will be well aware how disastrous their complete exclusion from society can be. It is their inability to establish normal human contacts as themselves [i.e. as homosexuals] that drives them to seek any way, however inadequate, out of their isolation. Often only the most unsavoury surroundings are available to them to do so. Dr Rodney Long [in 1957] mentioned the 'pathetic hells of existence endured by people living alone with their problem in shame, in fear and in despair'. Nothing has been done since then to mitigate the position. Indeed, discussion in Parliament and elsewhere, which has treated the homosexual as a nasty specimen under a microscope more than as a fellow human being, must have rather increased his fear, shame and despair.

The suggestion that an outpatient clinic should be established to specialise in the *treatment* of homosexuality[11] was first made by Dr Long, a general physician practising in central London who was very supportive to the Trust and many of its clients. The development of his idea formed the second phase of the Albany Trust's three-stage plan. The other stages were *prevention* (meaning the prevention, or at least alleviation, through education, of the social problems currently surrounding homosexuality, rather than the unrealistic goal of preventing homosexuality itself), and *social adaptation*. There was a need for education of the general public to an adequate understanding of the subject:

Not only are doctors and others whose advice may be sought often lamentably ignorant of the subject, but most parents are entirely unaware of the possibility of their bringing a potential homosexual into the world. Having ignored serious study of the whole question they are likely . . . to be appalled at any homosexual manifestation in their child, and to completely misunder-

---

[11] By which was meant constructive adjustment in the face of social and legal problems rather than 'cure'. Indeed, 'cure' in the sense of converting homosexuals into heterosexuals is both a misnomer and an impracticable goal, besides being ethically suspect. Where possible, and when desired by the person seeking help, a latent bisexual component may be activated and encouraged; but for most people, better adjustment to their innate homosexuality is the realistic aim.

stand its significance (if any). . . . Harm which will be extremely difficult to repair may be done by failure to understand the child's behaviour.

We called for an educational campaign on a scale requiring not only official collaboration, but the cooperation of as wide a range as possible of concerned organisations:

A proper understanding of the problem should enable the heterosexual and the homosexual portions of the community to achieve a mutually constructive attitude towards one another. . . . General ignorance of the problem – or even that a problem exists – is clearly the most serious obstacle. . . . Too little is being done, and practically no impact is being made.

This is still true today.

Dr Long believed that the very existence of a specialist outpatient and research clinic would go a long way towards achieving public recognition of homosexuality as a serious social and individual problem and towards removing the stigma attached to it. While I agreed with him about the potential usefulness of such a clinic, I realised that a lot of preparatory spadework would have to be done before it could be set up. By fortunate chance I had met, early in 1963, Hope Malik, an American woman living in London, who was experienced in public relations work and literary research and who had been involved in the United States in the pioneering birth control work begun by Margaret Sanger. Hope had later gone to India to help with the United Nations family planning initiative there, and had married an Indian journalist, Hitindra (Hitti) Malik. I met Hope when we were both giving some public relations advice to the Voluntary Hostels Conference (which later became the National Association of Voluntary Hostels), a body concerned with the already burgeoning problem of homelessness in London and other big cities. Hope and Hitti expressed strong interest in the Albany Trust's work and, as she had some spare time, Hope offered to undertake a series of meetings with individuals and agencies concerned with mental and social health to explore their reactions to, and possible support for, the proposed clinic. She carried out this complex task admirably over a period of some months, interviewed more than forty people, and prepared a thorough report which indicated broad support for our proposal. As a result of her involvement both Hope and Hitti later became Trustees of the Albany Trust for some years, and were a great help in many ways, as well as being good personal friends to Joy and myself.

The 'adjustment' which Dr Long envisaged the clinic providing might be needed in any one or more of the physical, psychological, spiritual, environmental and social spheres. It was in the latter of these that I personally most wished to see an advance, along the lines pioneered in Holland by the COC (Cultuur-en Ontspanningscentrum)[12] organisation. I had first been there, and met its founder, Bob Angelo (Niek Engelschman) in 1961. I had been greatly impressed by Bob's personality and achievements.[13] One of Holland's leading actors, who appeared frequently on television, he had founded a journal concerned with homosexuality, *Right to Live*, in 1940 but this was almost immediately suppressed by the German invaders. It restarted in 1946, when the prohibitive penal law imported by the Germans was abolished and the Code Napoleon restored. But the Netherlands remained socially and religiously conservative, and when a discussion group of fewer than one hundred members formed around Bob and the journal, they originally met discreetly as a literary circle, the 'Shakespeare Club'. As the range of social activities widened they adopted the name COC and sought permission from the Amsterdam police to open a non-profitmaking members' club. This was given, on condition that no-one aged under twenty-one or known to be a prostitute was admitted. A COC national office was opened in 1948 under Bob Angelo's direction, and soon afterwards branches were started in Rotterdam and The Hague, and later in other Dutch towns. The declared aim of the COC was that homosexuals must be integrated into the wider social community *as themselves*; they must be brought to understand and accept their own nature, and society must be brought to understand and accept them too. No other satisfactory solution to the 'homosexual problem' was possible.

In 1951 an international congress was held in Amsterdam and was so successful that an International Committee for Sexual Equality (ICSE) was set up to organise future events, at several of which partici-

[12] Cultural and Recreational Centre.
[13] Bob Angelo died, aged seventy-five, in 1988. A few years previously, he had been awarded the Grand Cross of the Order of Orange-Nassau (equivalent to a knighthood) in recognition of his services to the Dutch homosexual community. A street in Leiden has been named after him.

pated authoritative speakers on religion, law, psychology and sociology from a number of countries, including Britain.

By the time I first visited Holland the COC had over 4000 members (including 500 women) throughout the country, 1600 of them in Amsterdam. The main club premises had a dance floor, bar and meeting rooms, and a variety of discussion groups and social and artistic activities took place there. 'I want my friends to lose their cynicism,' Bob Angelo told an *Observer* reporter in 1963.[14] The journalist concluded that the COC's achievements in terms of relief of personal unhappiness and isolation were considerable, even though its impact on public attitudes had so far been slight.

Nowadays, after twenty years of openly gay organisations in Britain and with a variety of commercial meeting places which offer same-sex dancing, the COC with its dance floor sounds commonplace. But in pre-law reform days such a meeting-place 'not only where homosexuals gather openly but to which they are guided by the police . . . may sound unbelievable to English people' (*Observer*). The Albany Trust advocated this innovation for Britain in the third section of our Social Action memorandum, urging:

> Given that the condition of homosexuality exists, and that places will always be found where homosexuals congregate, it is surely better that such places should be well run, and conducive to a generally high moral outlook, than sordid and with no serious motivation.

While women were sometimes seen at public dances pairing off because they lacked male partners, the idea that two men might choose deliberately to dance with each other was, in those days, regarded as outrageous. One spin-off from the *Observer* article was that Bryan Magee, the popular presenter of the top ITV current affairs programme *This Week* (and later a Labour MP), approached the Albany Trust with plans to make a half-hour television documentary on male homosexuality which would include shots of the COC dance floor. Some of our regular helpers assisted by appearing in the programme (anonymously and in shadow, of course), and its success encouraged Magee to follow it up with a second programme on lesbianism, with which we also helped, putting him in touch with the newly formed

[14] 'A Club for Homosexuals' by Roy Perrott. *Observer*, 13 January 1963.

lesbian Minorities Research Group. Bryan subsequently wrote up his resulting knowledge and assessment of homosexuality in a successful and sensible book, *One in Twenty*. [15]

Other sensible books on the topic were now appearing. Gordon Westwood[16] followed up his 1952 pioneering study *Society and the Homosexual*[17] with *A Minority: Male Homosexuals in Great Britain*[18] in 1960, in which he too called for the integration of homosexuals into the community. In his introduction he observed:

> It is impossible to work on a research on this kind without becoming immediately aware of the repugnance with which homosexuality is regarded by many people. Trusts and Foundations which have given generously to other social researches promptly rejected requests for funds, sometimes before an explanation of the aims and methods could be given. . . . Two excellent organisations which have done good work in the fields of broken marriages . . . agreed to the hire of one of their spare rooms for interviews; but when they realised that this would mean that homosexuals would have to enter their premises, the offers were withdrawn.

It was a response with which we at the Albany Trust were wearisomely familiar. We were rejected by at least two potential landlords of office premises for the same reason. So we perforce stayed on in the crumbling Shaftesbury Avenue building.

In his Foreword to Westwood's book Sir John Wolfenden commented that

> very little is known about homosexuality or about those who commit homosexual acts. . . . There is no agreed definition of 'a homosexual'. . . . The 'surface morality' of our society today finds it hard to tolerate homosexual behaviour between men, though it is tolerant (some would say to a fault) towards other forms of sexual irregularity.

The 'surface morality' to which Sir John referred was indeed a major stumbling block to our work. Besides assisting outside researchers, journalists and broadcasters to collect material, which we hoped they

---

[15] Secker & Warburg, 1966, 1968.

[16] The pseudonym of Michael Schofield, who later published a third book, *Sociological Aspects of Homosexuality* (Longmans, Green, 1965) under his own name.

[17] Gollancz, 1952.

[18] Longmans, Green, 1960.

would use as building-blocks for enlightenment, we pursued our own educational activities as vigorously as we could.

One vehicle was the annual series of Albany Trust Winter Talks which for several years took place at approximately monthly intervals between September and March. The Winter Talks attracted consistently high-calibre speakers and an interested and attentive audience which sometimes exceeded one hundred and rarely fell below forty. There were always lively question-and-answer sessions after the talks.[19] The first (1962–63) season's speakers were C. H. Rolph on 'Homosexual Law Reform'; Dr W. L. Neustatter on 'Sexual Deviation from the Psychiatric Standpoint'; Kenneth Robinson MP on 'Parliament and the Wolfenden Report'; Gordon Westwood (Michael Schofield) on 'Sociological Aspects of Homosexuality'; Mrs Anne Allen, JP, on 'Sex and the Family'; and myself on 'Towards a Sexually Sane Society'.

These first Winter Talks, together with a summary of the questions and answers which followed them, were reprinted as an Albany Trust booklet – the only series which were; it is a pity that the later ones were not similarly preserved. The booklet is still worth reading, not least for the atmosphere it conveys that those of us who were dedicating our efforts to secure reform still regarded this as a very uphill task, even after the Wolfenden Report. Mr Rolph spoke of 'something in human nature (particularly in the English brand of it, it seems to me) that inhibits all rational behaviour in relationship to sexual questions', and recalled that after presenting a radio programme about homosexuality in 1954 he received hundreds – and maybe thousands – of letters, seventy-five per cent of which were couched in 'that peculiar poison-pen abusiveness that makes you wonder whether people are not driven into literary composition by an unconscious reverence for the fountain-pen as a kind of phallic symbol.' 'I don't believe for a moment,' he added, 'that they represent anything significant in English life: they come from a sort of stuttering lunatic fringe that keeps for its bedside book the eighteenth chapter of Leviticus.' I wish I could echo his

---

[19] I shall never forget the superb aplomb with which Anne Allen instantaneously fielded a question, which was obviously designed to test her supposedly 'white liberal' tolerance, as to what she would do if she found her son in bed with another boy one morning by replying, 'Well, I hope I'd have the presence of mind to ask "Do you prefer tea or coffee?"!'

optimism today, when far too many of these 'biological cavemen' (and cavewomen) are still braying away loudly.

Mr Rolph rightly saw the Society's central task as moulding public opinion – and especially the opinion of the 'small c conservatives' who were influential in law-making. Such people were prone to inertia, Kenneth Robinson thought: 'This whole area of socially controversial legislation is looked upon by Governments as a kind of minefield, dotted about with sectional pressure groups, which a false step may at any moment explode.' To what extent was this fear of legislating ahead of public opinion justified? 'It is never easy to define what public attitudes are, but it is at least questionable whether public opinion on these matters is always as illiberal as Parliament, and Governments, appear to assume.' He thought this was the case with regard to homosexuality. Whenever reform did come, there was likely to be 'a short, sharp outcry; but I think this will soon die away, and the new situation will be as readily accepted as the present one' – another forecast which has ultimately proved to be too rosy.

In his talk, Gordon Westwood prophetically emphasised what are still, in the 1990s, twin drawbacks of homosexuality: the social harm caused to individuals by hostility and prejudice; and the negative ingredient of the resulting minority group culture: 'A union against the dominant majority . . . is not in itself a constructive entity. It is more likely to be an irritant than an aid to the well-being of the community.' Notwithstanding all the subsequent positive achievements of Gay Liberation, the ultimate challenge, it seems to me, is for everyone to move on beyond the ghetto culture.

My own concluding talk of the series attempted to put the sexual aspect of life (grotesquely mismanaged as it is by the English) into some sort of wider perspective. A sexually saner society, I suggested, required honest self-criticism from everyone, which might be a refreshing change from some people's incessant criticisms of everyone else except themselves. I spoke of the progressive endeavours of the Dutch COC to effect their members' personal integration into the wider community, and the integration of their sexuality into the rest of their lives, instead of withdrawing into a gay ghetto. I affirmed that law reform by itself was not enough; indeed, that it was merely a preliminary to what I was already envisaging as the Albany Trust's ultimate task: that of helping everybody in this country who has a sexual problem, whether a heterosexual one or a homosexual one, to find the way towards a happier, a healthier and a fuller life. And I concluded with words which I still profoundly believe are true:

> After all, our lives here on earth are very short, and we should not be having to waste a minute of them on unnecessary or artificially created problems.

VI

Some Enthusiasts

'Nothing great was ever achieved without enthusiasm.'

R. W. Emerson

These Winter Talks, like a great many other HLRS/AT activities, were only possible because of the devoted help of several of our regular volunteers.[1] Although we now had a competent paid staff in the person of Joy Blanchard and a succession of her assistants – notably Jocelyn Cummins, Frances Regan, Eileen (Lee) Charles, and Val Preece – there was always far more paperwork than they could cope with by themselves;[2] and just as the Liverpool Road working party had supplemented the endeavours of Len and Reiss, so now we had a number of people who came more or less regularly to Shaftesbury Avenue and freely gave their time and skills.

One of the most constant and loyal of these was Marian Dutta, a professional librarian who for years came over from Bloomsbury almost every lunchtime and masterminded the vital task of keeping our supporters' address and subscription lists up to date. As she usually

---

[1] One of our volunteers tape-recorded nearly all of them; the original tapes are now deposited with the National Sound Archive. Another volunteer, who was an audiotypist, painstakingly transcribed the whole of the first series (including the questions and answers) so that these could be published as an Albany Trust booklet.

[2] Reporting to the executive committee in January 1964, Joy Blanchard said that with the help of only one part-time paid assistant, she had typed and despatched 900 letters in less than six months; prepared numerous articles for publication in *Man and Society* and elsewhere, as well as stencils for *Spectrum* and other circulars, including internal memoranda. There were currently 1300 subscribers on the mailing list. Callers were numerous, and often time-consuming. They included at least one a day on average in the 'case' category, who had to be referred to suitable legal, medical or spiritual counsellors. There was also a great deal of unavoidable routine paperwork to do with financial and other office matters.

spent more than an hour with us, in addition to the travelling time involved, it was not surprising that her superiors at the library where she worked hauled her over the coals at times! Another of Marian's functions was to act as doorkeeper and ticket seller at the Winter Talks. She had been married to an Indian Parsee which in those days was sufficiently unusual to have incurred the strong disapproval of her conventionally English family. Perhaps for this reason, she had a strong sympathy for the sexually unorthodox and had many gay friends, for whom she used to give bibulous parties. I remember at one of them she anxiously said to one guest: 'I do hope everyone is behaving exactly as if I weren't here. Are they?', only to receive the rather crushing reply: 'Well, I don't know about anyone else, Marian, but *I'm* not!' She assured another of her friends that they needn't be the least bit worried about telling her whatever they liked about themselves, as she always wrote her diaries on rice paper so that they could be instantly eaten in case of emergency. Comic as this may sound now, such mild paranoia was by no means unreasonable then; the precarious atmosphere in which we operated is not widely realised these days. And I do not want to give the impression that Marian was merely a figure of fun, even though her intense earnestness amused us at times. She was an exceptionally hard worker and loyal friend, and was devoted to Len and Reiss, helping them for several years with their weekly antiques stall in Portobello Road as regularly as she did the HLRS. Sadly, she died recently, soon after starting a well-earned retirement.

Among others who gave valuable voluntary help were John Alcock, David Allen, John James, and Graham Melville. It would be impossible to mention everyone, and I can only apologise to those who feel left out because unnamed here: I can assure them that they are still remembered with warm gratitude. The office was a brighter, livelier and more efficient place because of them.

Inevitably, however, there were some visitors to Shaftesbury Avenue who were not so welcome. If Joy had a weakness, it was a fixed conviction that, because we needed help so urgently, we should not turn any offer down. Consequently, we sometimes found ourselves giving soup-kitchen hospitality, or at any rate tea and sympathy, to people who were ostensibly offering help while actually needing to kill a few hours of loneliness. Some of these were gossipy time-wasters, and when I saw them coming into the office I would give an involuntary scowl which Joy and the staff thought most undiplomatic. But having the need to use our time as effectively as we could always uppermost in my mind, I was unrepentant.

In the spring of 1963 my appointment as Secretary of the HLRS and of the Albany Trust was confirmed, and the executive committee and Trustees determined to raise sufficient funds to employ me on a full-time basis as soon as possible; this proved to be from June 1964. Fund raising accordingly became a constant preoccupation. Numerous schemes were proposed and explored; in the end, the money to keep us going came mainly from our existing supporters, or through them – and a few large donations (sometimes arriving unexpectedly at critical moments) played a crucial role. Lack of funds, the short-term nature of most of our income, and the threat of enforced closure within a few weeks, became a constant worry. Even during the most strenuous periods of intense parliamentary activity I was rarely able to report to the executive committee that we had more than a few hundred pounds in hand; and though periodic special appeals brought in sufficient to keep us in existence they never achieved our modest target for an assured annual income. The appeal money we did receive came from only a minority of those who subscribed a minimum £1 a year[3] to be on our mailing list, most of it in comparatively large amounts of £100 or more from a handful of generous people.

So we were continually worrying our heads over survival and searching for effective ways of raising more money.[4] Several discussions with professional fund-raisers proved abortive; they were either unrealistically optimistic or, more usually, extremely pessimistic. All, without exception, were far too expensive for a small, precariously financed operation such as ours.

A fruitless scheme for an art sale came from Alfred Hecht, a Chelsea picture framer who knew many people in the political and artistic worlds. Hecht had been one of those with whom Tony Dyson negoti-

[3] Increased to £2 in 1966! But even £1 had been too much for one lady to stomach in 1963. 'I'm afraid I can't afford to belong to a charity that insists on a minimum subscription of £1', she wrote. We regretfully concluded that we could not afford to keep her on our mailing list for less.

[4] We even explored the possibility of forming an American arm of the Albany Trust, to be called the Albany Foundation. This was enthusiastically proposed to us by an American supporter, but came to nothing.

ated in the earliest days, and he and his friends had generously contrib-uted several hundred pounds. He was always holding out impressive but vague promises to recruit influential supporters and raise large sums of money for the HLRS in return for the seat on the HLRS executive committee which he coveted. An energetic and imperious man whose strong-headedness was not always matched by sagacity, he did not seem likely to us to be a reliable and level-headed colleague, and so to his chagrin he was never invited to join the Society's inner circle. But he behaved as if he belonged to it, and was one of those who campaigned vigorously to get rid of Andrew Hallidie Smith. I think he would have liked to get rid of me, too, because when I became Secretary I did not take much notice of his bossy interference. He once peremptorily demanded my immediate return from a much-needed Mediterranean holiday to deal with some item in the news-papers which had displeased him: I stayed put.[5]

Professor A. J. (Freddie) Ayer, who became our President in Sep-tember 1963, was a great asset to the Society, not only because of his academic and intellectual distinction and his popular image as a broadcaster and enthusiastic football supporter, but also for his committed support for our cause, his wise advice, and his willingness to use his extensive contacts on our behalf. I had first met his then wife, the American journalist Dee Wells,[6] some years before, and her own enthusiastic support supplemented his. One of his first acts as President was to launch an appeal for the necessary funds to appoint me as full-time Secretary. We were successful in raising two-thirds of the £10,000 appeal target, and I took up my full-time post on 1 June 1964.

Some large donations arrived out of the blue. One day early in 1964 I was visited by an elderly gentleman from the Channel Islands who spent half an hour endeavouring to persuade me that the single most important thing we should be doing was to initiate research into animal behaviour, because if we could demonstrate that homosexual

---

[5] When Hecht died early in 1991 an obituary notice solemnly stated that he had been the 'moving spirit' behind the HLRS, and that it was 'greatly through his effort and his tireless lobbying of the powerful, the great and the good' that the law was eventually changed. He had evidently convinced himself, and given his friends the impression, that he masterminded the Society. In fact, Hecht had little to do with the HLRS after 1964.

[6] At that time she was his second wife; later they were divorced, and remarried after the death of his third wife in 1985.

activity was widespread in a variety of species (especially monkeys) the argument that it was 'unnatural' would collapse.[7] Somehow I managed to convince him that, while I could not guarantee that this would be our immediate priority, we had the point very much in mind; and to my amazement he left me a four-figure cheque. At that time we had a young man working in the office whose talent for instant light verse kept us amused. After banking the cheque he provided the following salute to our benefactor:

> Great Pompey![8] To thy Channel Isle
> Where sapient simians know thy smile
> And even the baboons are gay,
> Our thanks for princely gifts we pay.

Another casual caller, after asking a few questions about what we were doing, and saying: 'I suppose you could do with some money?', wrote out a cheque which I thought would probably be for £5 or £10, but which also turned out to be in four figures. He proved to be a distinguished retired colonial civil servant with both literary and sporting interests. He kept in touch with us and contributed to later appeals – though he once upbraided me (after law reform) by quoting St Paul: 'If the trumpet give an uncertain sound, who shall prepare himself to the battle?'[9] By then the battleground (not to mention the trumpeter) had become more confused and the choice between alternative strategies less obvious.

A memorable meeting which I had in the mid-1960s with an even more distinguished benefactor was at King's College, Cambridge, where I had been invited to visit Dr E. M. Forster. Though I knew of his great eminence as a novelist, I was (like most people then) unaware of his private life and the extent of his circle of homosexual friends, knowledge of which has since been publicised in his own biography[10] and those of others such as Joe Ackerley[11] and William

---

[7] The point was admirably made a few years later by Dr Wainwright Churchill in his impressive book *Homosexual Behavior Among Males: A Cross-Cultural and Cross-Species Investigation* (Hawthorn Books Inc., New York, 1967).

[8] I have changed his name. I never saw him again, but several years later, when holidaying on his Channel Isle, I passed by his house. There were no signs of life – not even a chimpanzees' tea party.

[9] I Corinthians ch. 14 v.8.

[10] P. N. Furbank, *E. M. Forster. A Life* (Secker & Warburg, 1979).

[11] Peter Parker, *Ackerley: A Life of J. R. Ackerley* (Constable, 1989).

Plomer.[12] When I met him, he was at least eighty-five, and physically frail. I remember vividly the sweetness of his smile and his at once gentle and acutely perspicacious conversation. He questioned me minutely about the HLRS. My answers apparently satisfied him, for he got up and walked slowly over to his desk, saying: 'I would like to give you something – luckily I've just had some royalties from America.' His cheque was for quite a few thousand pounds – enough, in those days, to keep us running for several months. I was overcome with gratitude.[13] Perhaps I would not have been quite so surprised if I had known, as I do now, how generous he was financially throughout his life to those worse off then himself (shrugging this off by remarking: 'I am the only bugger of us all who has any money').[14] Nor had I then seen his sage comment in the terminal note he had written in September 1960 to his still unpublished homosexual novel, *Maurice*, that, while he and Edward Carpenter had looked forward to an evolution in public opinion which would bring the generous recognition of an emotion and the 'reintegration of something primitive into the common stock', they had not realised that 'what the public really loathes in homosexuality is not the thing itself but having to think about it'. The profound truth of this insight is borne in upon me again and again, not least in the present-day context of AIDS.

Most 'buggers with money' lacked Forster's generosity. Some were positively stingy. I remember one private dinner party, at a select address near Harrods, where I had been invited to meet some wealthy gay men all of whom were in a position to give the HLRS and Albany Trust substantial help. It was during the busiest period of our campaign, when we were working flat-out to assist the progress of Lord Arran's Bill through the Lords and were besieged by an overflowing tide of casework. There were as many servants as guests at the dinner, and two or three (perhaps more) chauffeured limousines

---

[12] Peter F. Alexander, *William Plomer. A biography* (Oxford University Press, 1989).

[13] I still am, and recall my meeting with him as one of the memorable days of my life. I greatly regret that the otherwise admirable pamphlet *With Downcast Gays* (Pomegranate Press, 1974), written by my friend the late David Hutter, a talented artist, and Andrew Hodges, biographer of Alan Turing, is marred by a vitriolic attack on Forster as a traitor to his sexual orientation. If, being of his generation and class, Forster felt obliged to stay in the closet and do good works behind the scenes, that surely does not of itself constitute treachery.

[14] Peter Parker, op. cit., p. 351.

waiting outside. The half-dozen or so guests listened spellbound while I recounted what we were doing, and told them of some of the miserable court cases and other personal tragedies we were being faced with almost daily. But I don't recollect even one of them donating as much as £50. The mythical well-funded lobby of influential perverts perceived by the paranoid opponents of reform remained mythical.

Nor were the proprietors of the gay 'pub and club' scene any more generous. One Brighton club did make periodic collections for the HLRS, but it was the exception. In London, our supporters who frequented 'the scene' could arouse little interest in our work – most people who went out once or twice a week simply wanted to enjoy themselves, and did not welcome 'serious' topics like law reform. When some of our supporters urged the proprietor of one of the most popular drinking clubs to make a donation, he held a lengthy committee meeting and eventually produced the princely sum of £5!

So we followed up all possible leads to funds. One effort was our participation as a collecting agency in the 1964 Greater London Mental Health Flag Day. About twenty of our supporters put in many hours between them, but at the end of the day our percentage of takings amounted to little more than £1 a head, not the most productive investment of their time and energy. The insight which this little exercise gave me into the labyrinthine organisation of flag days led me to vow never to get entangled again (much as I admire the stamina of those who do); and when Mr Rolph flatteringly though too generously referred to me in his autobiography as being capable of running 'anything from a flag day to a Federal Parliament',[15] I was sure the second would be far the easier.

The variety of callers arriving unexpectedly at the Shaftesbury Avenue office never ceased to surprise. One of the more memorable visitors was Dr Rachel Pinney, whom I found in the office one lunchtime in the spring of 1963 expounding Creative Listening and its possible application for our cause. Although a Quaker, Dr Pinney had a distinctly military bearing (her father was a general). She also used to suffer, she told me, from a tendency to interrupt people – a lucky fault, as it happened, since her invention of Creative Listening had an element of personal therapy at its root.

[15] C. H. Rolph, *Living Twice* (Gollancz, 1974), p. 230.

Dr Pinney's principle was that in the customary sort of discussion or argument, each participant is so busy formulating his response while the other is still speaking that neither gives their full attention to what is being said. So before world peace, or any improvement in the condition of humanity, can be secured we need to aim deliberately at understanding our adversaries' viewpoints, instead of concentrating on 'winning' our side of the debate. And we must also aim at getting our opponents into the same frame of mind, so that they will – perhaps for the first time in their lives – really understand what *we* are saying.

What she proposed, and was then dedicating her life to putting into practice, was a sort of verbal unilateral disarmament. She had been touring the country using her method, which she called 'Listening for Peace', to generate new thinking about nuclear weapons; at this time 'the Bomb' was uppermost in almost everyone's consciousness. What she did was first to ascertain that the other person disagreed with her on the issue (i.e. that they were opposed to unilateral nuclear disarmament). She then invited them to explain to her, as fully as they desired, why they adhered to this view. She, for her part, promised them before they began to do so that she would not argue back, or take a turn to state *her* point of view, because the object of the exercise was for her to understand *them* as completely as she could. She would only ask an occasional question if this was necessary to clarify something they had said which she did not understand. 'In this way' (her leaflet describing the process explained) 'the listener really hears and understands the speaker, and the speaker is confident of being really listened to by his opponent. *This enables both people to change slightly and get a little nearer to understanding each other*'. (My italics.)

Initially I was a bit sceptical. Wouldn't a contract along Dr Pinney's lines, with a built-in promise 'not to answer back', give the listener a moral advantage that was a bit smug? Wasn't it turning the other cheek to unfair excess? No, said Dr Pinney, that would be 'aggressive listening'! The key to the whole thing must be the listener's honest search for a sympathetic understanding of his adversary; Listeners for Peace must really strive to be *sympathetic* listeners, even if they violently disagreed with the views being expressed. 'Anyhow,' she said, 'why not try it out for yourself? Come and "Listen for Wolfenden" with me on the knocker tonight!'

So I did; and that evening provided both Dr Pinney and myself with considerable food for thought. We set out from Earls Court Station to hear what we could get passers-by to say about homosexuality. It was, in fact, Dr Pinney's first 'Listen' in London; she had previously been Listening only in the provinces. Usually, she told me, people never refused to talk; and I would not have thought that homosexuality was an especially closed subject in Earls Court, even for those who disapproved. But hostile talkers proved difficult to find, despite Dr Pinney's winningly persuasive sales pitch. Marching up to front door bells or accosting ladies tending their front gardens, she would explain that she had been touring Britain Listening for Peace, but '*tonight*' (emphasised in a delightfully 'you are especially privileged' tone of voice) – '*tonight* I am Listening on homosexual law reform!' A few of those thus addressed hastily bade us good evening, looking as if they consigned us to the depths of depravity. But most of them never batted an eyelid at the dread word, smiling as unconcernedly as if we had been selling washing powders or canvassing for local council elections.

As most were on our side, Dr Pinney varied her routine with Listening on the Bomb, which gave her all her longest listens that evening. We encountered only one forthright opponent, and he predictably said he was not prepared to discuss homosexuality in the street (or, I suspected, anywhere else). When pressed by Dr Pinney to give a reason, he replied, 'I was forty years in the navy, madam, and that's quite good enough reason. Good day to you!' Our most informative Listen was with a taxi driver at West London Airport Terminal. As soon as Dr Pinney announced her topic, he waxed voluble. 'Yes,' he said, 'me and my mates knows all about these homosexuals. Some of them are all right, perhaps. I know some quite well-known people who are that way – and a few may be born like it. But for most of them, it's just something they do for an extra sensation. There's none in the working classes, of course.' (The working classes, presumably, not providing many late night taxi fares).[16] His main

---

[16] But, like syphilis (and nowadays AIDS), homosexuality always *is* somewhere else, and to do with somebody else, than 'us'. An amusing example of this was when someone asked the Newalls what the law about homosexuality was in Abyssinia. Helpful as always, they telephoned the Imperial Ethiopian Embassy, and were asked to hold on while a somewhat nonplussed official, consulted, for some obscure reason, the Commercial Attaché. After about quarter of an hour, they were assured that there was no homosexuality in Ethiopia; it was a *European* vice.

grudge appeared to be that the activities of 'these homosexuals' had led to the closing down of nearly all the overnight public conveniences which he and his mates used for more orthodox purposes.

Although this evening encouraged me to toy with the idea of establishing an Albany Trust 'Listening for Wolfenden' team, like so many other potentially worthwhile plans it never got off the ground; there simply was not enough time to follow up every initiative. And so far as I know, Dr Pinney did not repeat the experiment; she went on Listening for Peace, and this eventually took her as far afield as Moscow.

More effective, if less entertaining, inroads into public opinion were achieved during 1964 when within a short space of time several prominent women journalists, including Anne Sharpley of the *Evening Standard*, Monica Furlong of the *Daily Mail*, and the already veteran Marje Proops of the *Daily Mirror*, approached us for help in compiling factually accurate articles intended to 'open up' the topic of homosexuality – not least for women readers. I had some most interesting discussions with them, especially with Anne Sharpley, a charming and brilliant woman who was at that time the *Standard*'s ace reporter and a personal friend of its formidable octogenarian proprietor, Lord Beaverbrook. She wrote a series of five articles entitled 'London's Hidden Problem' which were originally scheduled to appear in the spring but were shelved, or at least postponed, because of Beaverbrook's death. For a while their fate hung in the balance, but they finally appeared during July 1964 when thousands of extra copies of the paper had to be printed to meet the demand which they generated. They were, I believe, a lastingly influential turning point in making sensible discussion of homosexuality easier.

Not all press attention was so helpful. An exceptionally silly article called 'How to Spot a Possible Homo' appeared in the *Sunday Mirror* in April 1963, at the height of the furore over the Vassall spy case, and so irritated the executive committee that we wrote personally to Mr Cecil King, chairman of the Mirror Newspaper Group, enquiring whether this 'reactionary and ill-informed' piece on the difficult and often tragic problem of homosexuality reflected a new departure from his papers' progressive social policies and his own 'well-known humanity of outlook'. He did not reply.

I also made a point of following up all the published hostile comments from opponents of reform which came to my attention, and a high proportion of my numerous letters to the press were printed. There were also growing radio and television interest from such programmes as the BBC's 'Woman's Hour' and ABC's 'Sunday Break'. While such small successes were not individually very significant, they all added to the steady impetus towards reform which we now began to detect. This was also evidenced by the vocal support we were receiving from sympathetic bodies such as the National Council for Civil Liberties, Justice, and the Howard League for Penal Reform.

VII

Genesis of a Bill

'I believe these laws will be changed and that when
my children are grown up they will be amazed that
laws of this sort could have existed in the middle
of the twentieth century.'

Marquess of Queensberry
24 May 1965

In October 1964 there was a change of government, when a general
election put Labour into office with an overall majority of only five.
This encouraged our parliamentary supporters to plan an early debate
on homosexual law reform, even though another general election was
unlikely to be long delayed. The HLRS had ready a draft parliamentary Bill, which we kept constantly updated, and we were on the
lookout for possible sponsors in both Houses, besides making contacts
with members of the new Government whom we knew to be friendly
to our cause. We also recruited more MPs and Peers from all three
major parties to the executive committee. After the hysterical reaction
of our opponents to the modest lobbying which had preceded earlier
debates we decided upon a more circumspect approach to the new
Parliament, such as a mildly worded Motion in the Lords which could
be withdrawn without a vote if this appeared tactically necessary.
Although most members of the executive committee believed that the
Wolfenden recommendations were too cautious – and in particular
that the proposed age of consent was too high – we agreed not to
change our official policy of standing in line with Wolfenden but to
ask some of our parliamentary supporters to move amendments at an
appropriate time when a Bill was in progress.

Even before the change of Government there had been attempts,
not initiated by us, to bring the matter before Parliament. In the
spring, I had been approached from an unexpectedly right-wing

84

quarter – by Sir Thomas Moore, the high Tory MP for Ayr and 'Father' of the House of Commons, who was usually regarded as an extreme social reactionary and an ardent hanger and flogger. But it turned out that he was also a supporter of the Wolfenden proposals because (he told me) he had known some men of upright character whose lives had been made miserable because of this law, which he regarded as unjust. When he received a summary of case histories which the HLRS circulated at the end of 1963 Sir Thomas asked the Home Secretary, Mr Brooke, whether he proposed implementing the Wolfenden Report; and on receiving a negative reply he tabled a Motion in April 1964 calling on the Government to legislate, on the grounds that this 'would tend to prevent much blackmail and many personal tragedies'.

Sir Thomas Moore requested the Society to ask those MPs who had supported Kenneth Robinson in 1960 to sign his Motion, but only about two dozen did so: several of them considered that it was too near the end of Parliament's life for such a gesture to be fruitful while others were possibly unwilling to march under Sir Thomas's banner. He himself was disappointed at the scant support, and privately expressed the view that with a general election in the offing those with marginal seats were unwilling to sign anything which might have been used against them in the forthcoming campaign. As he was retiring from Parliament he had no need to worry about this for himself. His Motion did, I believe, play some part in bringing about the administrative changes which followed shortly afterwards. Whether this was so or not, Sir Thomas Moore deserves an honourable mention in the annals of homosexual law reform.

In July 1964 it was unexpectedly announced that the Director of Public Prosecutions had 'requested' chief constables to consult him before prosecuting men for homosexual acts committed in private with another consenting adult, and also in respect of offences more than twelve months old or revealed because of blackmail complaints. It was pointed out by the Attorney General at the time, and also by Home Office spokesmen in later parliamentary debates, that this did not imply that any substantive change in the law was being introduced through administrative action, or that the law was never again to be applied against consenting adults in private. (As a matter of fact it was, subsequent to the Director's 'request'.) The aim was merely to achieve greater uniformity. Nevertheless, this directive was a sign of official concern at the operation of the existing law – a concern which I like to think our campaign, and particularly the summaries of recent cases which we circulated to MPs from time to time, helped to generate.

Our other active pre-election supporter was a member of the Upper House, the Earl of Arran, whom I first met in July 1963 when he informed me of his determination to get the Wolfenden proposals made law. As it was not the first time that a parliamentarian had said this to me, with little if anything resulting, I did not at first take Lord Arran more seriously than the others. Indeed, he seemed a somewhat unlikely champion of social reform. The eighth Earl of Arran (known to nearly everyone as 'Boofy' – a babyhood pet-name that had stuck) was a small, brick-red faced and snow-white haired man who talked volubly and excitedly, frequently ending his remarks with a 'what, what?' reminiscent of George III. He wrote an idiosyncratic weekly gossip column in the London *Evening News*. He struck me as too politically marginal and personally eccentric to be an effective champion. In fact he turned out to be a shining specimen of *noblesse oblige*.[1]

During the next four years I came to know Lord Arran a great deal better; though I can't honestly say that I ever got to know him well. Kind and friendly though he always was to me, and often full of humour, he always called me 'Mr Grey' and treated me rather like a professional factotum – the family solicitor, perhaps. He was a curious mixture of schoolboyish informality and aristocratic hauteur. I once visited his office at the *Evening News* to find him lying full length on the floor on his tummy in his shirt sleeves, wearing vast red felt braces, chewing a pencil as he composed his column 'Lord Arran Writes'. I discovered that despite (maybe because of) his eccentricities Lord Arran was a popular and respected member of the House of Lords, about half of whose active hereditary members seemed to be his more or less distant cousins – a fact which proved of inestimable value for his political activities. At the time I met him he was a Conservative, but after he had successfully piloted his homosexual law reform Bill (which in his column and elsewhere he quaintly christened 'William')

[1] Lord Arran did not tell me why he was so passionately determined to change the law; Leo Abse has suggested (*Private Member*, p. 150) that he was spurred on by a family tragedy. Whatever his reasons I warmly admired his good-humoured courage, and respect his memory.

through to the Statute Book he switched to the Liberal benches.[2]

At the beginning of 1964 Boofy wrote to the new Conservative Prime Minister, Sir Alec Douglas-Home, announcing his intention of seeking to implement 'Wolfenden Part II' either by putting down a Motion for debate in the Lords or introducing a Private Member's Bill, and seeking Government support.

> I have long felt that action towards this end would not only be humane, but the sensible thing to do. And I also feel that public opinion is now ready for this step forward. [He added that, whilst a Labour Government might be more likely to support the reform,] might it not be better if the change were brought about under a Tory Government? Many people tend to regard the Labour and Liberal Parties as the parties of compassion, and it would be useful, I feel, if the Tories were to give their blessing to this major piece of social legislation.

The Prime Minister's reply was a damper:

> I don't really share your confidence that the balance of Parliamentary and public opinion is now in favour of amending the law [he wrote]. I cannot feel that amending legislation would have much prospect of success in the present Parliament, nor can I give any undertaking about the Government's attitude.

It was the same old 'party line' again. But with the autumn change of government Lord Arran was raring to go, and the HLRS felt that our previous six years' hard slog had done much to lay the ground for a successful parliamentary campaign.

On the afternoon of 12 May 1965 Lord Arran rose in the House of Lords to call attention to the recommendations of the Wolfenden

---

[2] Homosexual law reform was not the only topic which engaged Boofy's legislative energies. He was ardently fond of badgers, which were becoming an increasingly threatened species, and after his Wolfenden success he piloted another Act through Parliament to protect them from unauthorised trapping. He kept a tame badger at his country home as a household pet, and on the only occasion I visited him there, on a rainy Sunday when our Bill was in committee stage and he wanted to discuss amendments with me, it was disconcerting to have this large and, to my mind, uncertain-tempered animal lumbering around the drawing room and snuffling suspiciously at my ankles as Lady Arran served tea and cake. And I nearly leaped across a Soho restaurant where Boofy and I were having lunch one day, seated cosily side by side on a narrow settee, when he suddenly pulled up his nearest trouser leg and said: 'Look at my ringworm! I got it off the badger.' He had indeed.

Committee on homosexual offences; and to 'move for Papers[3].' The debate had been preceded by a great deal of activity on his part, and he had rallied some formidable support. He said:

> I have read much on this subject – so much, indeed, that at times the issues became blurred, and I no longer knew what it was all about. But, in the end, having read all, or most, of the books, and absorbed to the best of my ability all the clever arguments and counter-arguments, I found myself back where I started, and with these conclusions: that, in accepting the law on homosexual practices as it now stands, we are persecuting a minority and we are being unjust. And these things, I think, are unbecoming to our country.

There were no clear-cut answers to questions such as what causes homosexuality, can it be cured, how many homosexuals there were in Britain – though the best guess, he thought, was somewhere between half a million and a million men, 'a frighteningly great number of souls', who lived in shame and in fear. 'They are the odd men out: the ones with the limp.' He believed they were born rather than made, and that nothing and nobody was going to change a man's basic desires, his erotic make-up, so that fears of the corruption of youth – 'the nub of the business' – were largely groundless.

> We talk about homosexuality as unnatural (Lord Arran continued) but the truth is that whatever a man or woman does, unless they are paid for their services, is natural to him or to her. They would not do it if it were not. There is no ultimate standard of natural behaviour. Nothing is more unnatural than Nature herself. In defiance of her own laws, she delights in producing sports and deviations; she does it with plants, with flowers and with animals; and, most cruelly – and most incomprehensibly, if one is a Christian – she does it with human beings. As with the animals, we do not like these sports; and although we do not mob them and peck them to death like the birds, they embarrass us; we wish they were not there. And in the ultimate cases, where

---

[3] 'Moving for Papers' is a procedural device by which peers can introduce a debate on a topic of their choice. There is not usually a vote on such a motion. When Lord Arran expressed his intention of pressing his motion to a vote, a former Leader of the House (Lord Swinton) pointed out that this was 'an entirely novel idea'. He could only remember one occasion when such a motion had been carried; nobody knew what to do next, and an official 'found a lot of papers and put them in a box and sent them along to the Clerk of Parliaments, who had not the faintest idea what to do with them'.

the deviations result in gross mental malformations which to us are loathsome, we put them away in silent places and pretend they do not exist.

It is much the same, I believe, with homosexuals. To normal people, to the very great majority of whom life has no such problems, these men are unpleasant. We do not want to think about them; we try to regard them as evil; our instinct is to want to stamp them out. We use all kinds of moral and high-falutin' language about them, and we send them to prison. We talk uninformedly about the empires which are said to have crumbled because of this appalling vice.

If, as he believed, homosexuals were what they were by birth, or through early environment, and were not in themselves deliberately vicious men, they should not be punished for indulging in what were to them their natural desires, so long as they did not do harm to others, and particularly to young people. 'To punish in such circumstances is to persecute: to persecute a minority: to persecute as others have persecuted Jews and Negroes.' It was time to remove this relic of barbarism. He believed that reform of the law would remove the glamour of forbidden fruit, and that homosexuality would become uninteresting overnight: 'What is there to say on this most grey and drab subject, except in its present context of injustice?'

It was a powerfully moving, noble speech, striking a note of enlightened compassion which Lord Arran for the most part sustained throughout the long series of debates that followed, with only a few unfortunate lapses into bathos. He had seized the moral high ground, and the tone which he set was followed by his supporters.

Lord Arran was supported by the Archbishops of Canterbury and York, two other bishops, and a cross-section of the House including the Earl of Longford (the former Viscount Pakenham), Baroness Gaitskell (widow of the former Labour Party leader) who became one of the reform's staunchest and most articulate supporters, the Marquess of Lothian (who had been a member of the Wolfenden Committee) and (on a personal basis[4]), the Lord Chancellor, Lord Gardiner. Lord Stonham, Joint Parliamentary Under-Secretary of State at the Home Office, made it clear on behalf of the Government that in their view there was no satisfactory compromise between acceptance or rejection

[4] i.e. Not as a member of the Government.

of the main Wolfenden recommendation. It was a clear moral issue for the House. If reform was to come it had to be by Private Member's Bill, with the final decision left to a free vote of Parliament. 'This Administration will not attempt to drive your consciences into one lobby or another on this issue.'

The Archbishop of Canterbury (Dr Michael Ramsey) said that while homosexual acts were always wrong, in the sense that they used in a wrong way human organs for which the right use was intercourse between men and women within marriage, the case for altering the law in respect of consenting adults in private rested on reason and justice, and would benefit the community. There was real cogency in the plea of the Wolfenden Report that not all sins should properly be given the status of crimes. 'To say this is not to condone the wrongness of the acts, but to put them in the realm of moral responsibility.' The proposed reforms would help to bring about a greater balance between the forces of law, morality, remedial science and the cure of souls.

Michael Ramsey, the one hundredth Archbishop of Canterbury, was one of the most eminent and best loved holders of his office in this century, ranking for me, and I am sure for many others, with the great William Temple. His major speeches on the Arran Bill were a model of temperate wisdom and charity, although he was, from the HLRS' standpoint, unreliable on detail, and supported some unhelpful amendments. His bulky appearance and rather hesitant manner always reminded me of the Tenniel illustration in Lewis Carroll's *Alice Through the Looking Glass* of the sheep knitting in the railway carriage. But his ponderous form was invested with a sharp brain and a strongly liberal social conscience as well as transparently sincere piety. He commanded a respectful hearing from everyone. Boofy Arran told me that after one of the debates, when the Bill's opponents had rumbled on and on and on about the horrors of buggery and the nastiness of all homosexuals, he gave the Archbishop a lift back to Lambeth Palace and on the way Dr Ramsey said with obvious concern: 'Oh dear, oh dear! What a terrible time the poor things must have had at their public schools!'

Out of twenty-two speeches only three were totally hostile to the main Wolfenden recommendation. After more than five hours of debate Lord Arran expressed himself 'surprised and delighted by the virtual unanimity of opinion', and said that, 'overwhelmed by the support for the change in the law', he would definitely introduce a Private Member's Bill.

Immediately after the debate ended I sat with Lord Arran on one of the red leather benches in the Peers' lobby and drafted the substantive clause of what ultimately became the Sexual Offences Act 1967:

> Notwithstanding any statutory or common law provision, a homosexual act in private shall not be an offence provided that the parties consent thereto and have attained the age of twenty-one years.

We straightway took this to Peter Henderson, one of the Lords' Clerks,[5] who was to be unfailingly helpful in guiding Lord Arran through the procedural thickets of promoting his Bill, and it was formally printed next day and tabled for Second Reading less than a fortnight later – on 24 May. Encouraged by Lord Arran's success, Leo Abse MP gave notice that he would introduce a 'Ten Minute Rule' Bill into the Commons on 26 May.[6]

Piloting a Private Member's Bill on to the Statute Book is no easy task, and Lord Arran was new to it. Once a Bill has been introduced in either House it is printed and deemed to have been given its First Reading. A full discussion of its broad principles follows in the Second Reading debate. Unless the Bill is voted down at this stage it then goes into Committee, where its detailed provisions are discussed, and possibly amended, clause by clause. (In the Commons, Committees detailed to scrutinise Bills usually sit 'upstairs'; in the Lords, the whole House takes the Committee Stage.) The Bill, with amendments, is then reported back to the whole House, and further amendments may be debated and voted upon at the Report Stage. There follows a Third Reading debate, when the final draft of the Bill is voted on. If the Bill receives a majority on Third Reading it is then sent to the other House, and has to go through all the same stages there before the end of the same Parliamentary Session in which it was introduced (i.e. it must pass completely through both Houses within what is usually a twelve-month period between November and October of the follow-

---

[5] Later Clerk of the Parliaments, and now Lord Henderson of Brompton.
[6] This is a procedure under a Standing Order of the Commons whereby a Member can seek the permission of the House to introduce a Bill by making a ten-minute speech, followed for a similar time by an opponent, after which a vote is taken.

ing year). Any amendments made to a Commons' Bill by the Lords, or to a Lords' Bill by the Commons, are sent back to the other House for acceptance or rejection, and only when a Bill has successfully passed through all these stages does it receive the Royal Assent and become law. The availability of sufficient parliamentary time is crucial. In the case of the Sexual Offences (homosexual law reform) Bill, official Government neutrality was benevolently interpreted by the Home Secretary, Roy Jenkins, so as to ensure that sufficient time was made available for the Bill to proceed to its next stage after each favourable vote in either House. In return, the Government conveniently ensured, through the provision of official drafting help, that the terms of the Bill were to its liking.

By 24 May the opposition in the Lords had rallied their forces, with Field-Marshal Viscount Montgomery of Alamein in the vanguard declaring that Lord Arran's Bill would be 'knocked for six'. He had formidable support from two former Lord Chancellors (the Earl of Kilmuir and Viscount Dilhorne) and an ex-Lord Chief Justice (Lord Goddard). It was therefore with some trepidation that Lord Arran rose to move the Second Reading of his Bill.

It was, he said, 'an expression of opinion – if you like, an expression of faith'. It was a simple Bill, indeed, over-simple, and would require expansion and amendment in Committee. But Sir John Wolfenden had written to him saying: 'It must be clear to everyone that (your) Bill lays down the basic principle which is recommended in our Report'. The issue, said Lord Arran, was: 'Are we or are we not in favour of homosexual law reform?'

Speaking for the Government Lord Stonham again emphasised their collective neutrality, and the freedom of ministers to vote as they personally wished. He came down even more squarely than he had done in the previous debate against the administrative practicality of repealing the Labouchere Amendment while leaving the law against consenting homosexual buggery intact; 'it would make the already difficult task of the police in enforcing these laws quite impossible.' They had gone to the limit of what could properly be done to mitigate the effect of the existing law by administrative action. It was encouraging to hear that the Government favoured the full 'consenting adults' reform rather than a half-way house. Finally, Lord Stonham announced his own intention of voting for the Bill:

I have reached this decision as a result of the close study which I
had to give to this subject in order to speak to your Lordships
about it. I certainly approached it with no predisposition in favour
of legalising homosexual conduct in any circumstances. But I am
satisfied that the injustice and the evils of continuing the present
law are greater – very much greater – than the risks involved in
making the proposed change.

This too was encouraging; I had already formed an admiration for
Lord Stonham, which was fully borne out by his handling of the
subsequent debates on the Government's behalf. Quietly spoken,
patient, always clear and concise, he was a doughty foil for the opposition heavyweights.[7]

Next, the former Prime Minister, Earl Attlee, made a typically
pithy four-minute speech. The time for change had come, he said.
'Today we have the chance of getting rid of an evil of which far more
is said than need be.'

'Monty' then took the field with reckless panache. To condone
unnatural offences would be utterly wrong: 'One may just as well
condone the Devil and all his works.' Any weakening of the law would
strike a blow at all those devoted people who were working to improve
the moral fibre of the youth of this country. 'And heaven knows! It
wants improving.' What effect would it have on the minds of school-
boys and undergraduates if they knew that their masters and tutors
were indulging in these unnatural practices and that the law of the land
allowed it? And that suddenly, on the morning of their twenty-first
birthday, they too could do what they liked?

At this point, Lord Arran interjected: 'Does this not apply equally
to the age of consent for girls? Suddenly, over the age of sixteen, it is
all right.'

> Viscount MONTGOMERY of ALAMEIN: 'I am not very expert
> on girls. No doubt the noble Earl knows more about that than I
> do.'

The proposed reform, he continued, would strike a blow at the discipline and morale of the armed forces. Instead of helping these unnatural practices along, they should

---

[7] As Victor Collins, Lord Stonham (1903–1971) had been Labour Member of
Parliament for Taunton from 1945 until 1953. He was created a Life Peer in 1958.

build a bulwark which will defy evil influences which are seeking
to undermine the very foundations of our national character –
defy them; do not help them. I have heard some say . . . that such
practices are allowed in France and other NATO countries. We
are not French and we are not other nationals. We are BRITISH,
thank God! . . . I appeal to all . . . who have at heart the best
interests of the young men of Britain, to go with me into the
Not-Content Lobby and knock this Bill for six right out of the
House.

This rumbustious stuff did not have quite the effect the gallant field
marshal intended. Indeed, he provoked considerable amusement. And
he was visibly nettled by Lady Gaitskell's stinging observation later in
the debate that while he had been

in brilliant command of millions of men, and he did a wonderful
job, I was amazed that he did it with, in a way, so little knowledge
of the sex habits of the men under his command.

Lord Montgomery was followed by an impressive maiden speech from
the Marquess of Queensberry – current holder of the title which
graced Oscar Wilde's persecutor, and therefore, perhaps, conscious of
a special burden of atonement. This was, he said, a matter about which
he had felt strongly for many years. The existing laws had helped to
produce a nasty, furtive underworld that was bad for society and bad
for the homosexual. The debates so far had been impersonal, but many
peers must have some first-hand knowledge from a homosexual of his
predicament.

I have certain friends with whom I have [discussed] this, and I
do not think that they are in any way more depraved or immoral
than either myself, or any other normal man of my acquaintance.

Most British citizens believed that one of the important principles of
freedom was that a man should have the right to choose to do something that was morally wrong, provided that it was not antisocial.

I believe these laws will be changed and that when my children
are grown up they will be amazed that laws of this sort could
have existed in the middle of the twentieth century.

Another opposition 'big gun', the Earl of Kilmuir, upheld society's
right to maintain minimum standards by the sanction of the criminal
law, and alleged that reform would lead to 'proselytisation . . . from

sodomitic societies and buggery clubs, which everybody knows exist'. Challenged by Lord Arran and others to produce details of these fraternities, he did not do so but stuck to his guns. Indeed, he added the accusation that the Bill would permit army officers, senior policemen and prison officers to go to bed together and so forfeit the respect of their subordinates.

> Toleration of actions of lying and cruelty and indecency can never be right. It then becomes indifference, and indifference to the spread of actions which the vast majority of people think wrong, unnatural and degrading is something which the legislators of a country cannot afford.

Finally, and a bit desperately, he appealed to the 'humbler and more democratic viewpoint' that 'the dead are the great majority, and many of the dead were not fools'. The debate was certainly producing some curious arguments. The eighty-year-old Lord Goddard confirmed with all the authority of a former Lord Chief Justice the existence of 'buggers' clubs'. Every circuit judge had found them from time to time, in various – quite different – parts of the country; 'associations or coteries of people who are given to this particular vice'. At these coteries of buggers, he explained, 'the most horrible things go on. As a judge, one has to sit and listen to these stories which make one feel physically sick'. The Bill would be a charter for these buggers' clubs – they would be able to spring up all over the place. Once, on circuit, he had sixteen people in the dock at the same time, none of whom would have been guilty of a criminal offence at all if this Bill had been law. 'If you had seen them, perhaps your Lordships would have agreed that they ought to have been put out of circulation.' There might have to be some amendment of the law; but not this Bill, which posed a threat to family life. 'If it is known that there is a bugger in the family and that he cannot be dealt with, one need not wonder very much at what will happen.'

Despite ridicule of the belief that any relaxation of the existing law would produce 'an immediate rush on the part of tutors, lecturers, professors and Army officers into a sort of mass buggery' (Lord Francis-Williams) or 'a sudden and large defection from heterosexual ranks to join homosexual brigades' (Lady Gaitskell), the opponents continued to voice their apprehensions that these disgusting, horrible activities would spread like wildfire if the law was changed. It was obvious now, if it had not been before, that rational argument would find little place in the parliamentary struggle, and that few MPs or Peers would be as scrupulous as Lord Stonham in making up their minds after studying the evidence. I braced myself for many more hours of emotional rhetoric. Eva Bene, for whom I had obtained a visitors' pass for this debate, said to me afterwards that she had been fascinated by the psychology of these eminent, elderly Englishmen expressing their fear and horror of buggery at great length in such vivid terms. 'How they loved talking on and on about it!' she said. The Earl of Iddesleigh, recounted how, as a young man, 'I walked through Soho with a knowledgeable friend who pointed out to me the door of a well-known buggery club'. (What, I wondered, did he fantasise had been going on behind the green door?)

If the Bill was passed, they would have to consider whether clubs where men danced with male partners and saw 'the kind of cabarets that homosexuals want to see' were private places. And what did 'consenting' mean? The Bill would make it easier for older men in positions of authority to put pressures on sexually innocent youths.[8]

The debate continued along now familiar lines, with consistent support for reform being voiced from the bench of bishops and consistent opposition from the lawyers. The Bishop of Southwark (The Rt Rev. Mervyn Stockwood) appealed for an appreciation of the pastoral aspects: the existing law was not only immoral in the negative sense of making no distinction between different categories of behaviour; it was also positively immoral, leaving a trail of unhappiness, and sometimes tragedy, not only among those directly affected by it but also among their families, parents and friends. 'I wonder

---

[8] This canard of the 'buggers' clubs' was an early example of homophobes' fertile talent for inventing mythical aunt sallies. Repeated letters (on our grandest writing paper, festooned with the names of our very distinguished one-hundred-strong Honorary Committee) to Lords Kilmuir and Goddard, requesting solid information about these elusive organisations, remained unanswered. Lord Iddesleigh did have the decency to reply, naïvely repeating his story of the door in Gerrard Street pointed out to him by 'a journalist on the *Evening News* (Lord Arran's paper!) who had a considerable knowledge of the seamy side of London life'. 'I should imagine', I wearily replied, 'that the establishment which your friend pointed out was most likely just a drinking club, and not a scene of more lurid activities'. Lord Annan reports another peer as declaring that he had seen a member of one of the buggers' clubs 'shamelessly flaunting the club tie'. (*Our Age*, p. 134.)

whether those who theorise about the role of the law in upholding moral standards in this matter have ever had to deal with its results in shattered lives?' It was the majority view of Church Assembly that this law was one of the most misguided, most vicious and most evil in its consequences of any law upon the Statute Book.

Such compassionate views did not mollify Viscount Dilhorne, who wound up for the opponents. Formerly Sir Reginald Manningham-Buller (once aptly dubbed by Bernard Levin 'Bullying-Manner'), this former Attorney General and Lord Chancellor looked and sounded like a rhinoceros on the charge. I never failed to be surprised by the vindictive vehemence which he brought to the task of opposing Lord Arran's Bills.

> If this Bill receives a Second Reading tonight [he declaimed], it will be taken throughout the country that this House approves in principle of sodomy between consenting males. That is what we are voting for. . . . The Bill will be taken as permitting any form of gross indecency between male persons.

He regretted that sodomy was no longer described as 'the abominable crime'. If the Wolfenden test of consent in privacy was accepted, how could incest remain a crime? Or bestiality? But their legalisation was not being advocated. Why not?

> In my belief, the answer is that incest and sodomy with animals are so abominable, so disgusting and so degrading – and, I would say, such a grievous sin – that it is accepted as right that they should be regarded as criminal. In my view, sodomy with a human being comes in the same category.

And to define a homosexual act 'in private', as the Wolfenden Committee had done, as not in a place 'where members of the public might be likely to see it and be offended by it' did not cover the case of a considerable number of homosexuals engaging in these practices in the same premises or in the same room. In that case 'the way is open to the kind of clubs to which Lord Goddard drew attention'. In contrast to the Archbishop of Canterbury he could not believe that for the State to appear to condone gross indecency and sodomy between consenting adults would promote what was good and right.

In the face of this broadside Lord Arran said he had been impressed by the arguments brought forward for rejecting his Bill, but not unduly impressed. The issue remained a simple one, and no amount of smokescreens could confuse it. What the vote would say – contrary to Lord Dilhorne's assertions – was simply that the House wanted, or did not want, homosexual law reform.

By 94 votes to 49, the House of Lords decided that it did.

Two days later, the Commons refused, by 178 votes to 159, to allow Leo Abse to bring in a Bill to amend the law relating to homosexuality, even though in outlining its terms he sought to cover the objections raised in the Lords to the Arran Bill.

His Bill, Mr Abse said, would ensure that the maximum penalty for buggery committed by a man against a boy under sixteen would continue to be life imprisonment. The Bill would ensure that an indecent assault upon a boy would attract a penalty of ten years' imprisonment.[9] It would make a public act of indecency liable, as now, to a penalty of two years' imprisonment. It would increase the existing penalty of two years' imprisonment for an act of gross indecency[10] committed against a youth aged between sixteen and twenty-one to five years. It would protect military discipline, and would treat premises used for homosexual practices as a brothel.

> It cannot possibly be in the minds of any except those who wilfully refuse to know our proceedings that the Bill would in any way mean that this House approved or condones homosexual practices, or will countenance any act of indecency against youngsters or any public display of homosexual conduct.

He outlined the now familiar case for reform, saying that in his view,

> by far the worst feature of the law is that the preoccupation with the punitive proceedings leads the community to avoid searching for the genesis of the homosexual condition and, by so doing, failing to take the preventive action which may save a little boy from the terrible fate of growing up to be a homosexual [which he oldfashionedly described as 'the curse of a male body encasing a feminine soul'].

A criminal code opposed by so much informed opinion could not be indefinitely sustained. 'Those of us who are possessed of the normality

---

[9] The technical term 'indecent assault' applies to mutually consenting behaviour with a boy below the age of sixteen.

[10] I.e. a homosexual act other than buggery.

which makes us look with revulsion at homosexual conduct must surely want an end to this continuing public discussion.'

He was opposed by Sir Cyril Osborne, the Conservative MP for Louth, who epitomised the crusty High Tory Right. I had imagined Sir Cyril to be large, grave and magisterial, but on this occasion, at least, he appeared small, anxious and twittery – possibly because his speech, in contrast to Mr Abse's, was received with some derisive interruptions. ('This is not the Reichstag yet,' Sir Cyril peevishly retorted to his hecklers.)

The proposed reform, he said, would offend the nonconformist conscience of the country. 'The vast majority of our people consider, rightly or wrongly, that sodomy is wrong, unnatural, degrading and disgusting; and I agree with them.' Those who voted for this proposal ought, in fairness to their constituents, to say clearly in their next election addresses that this is what they advocate and agree with. What was required was sterner discipline, not more licence. The gravest harm that the Bill could do to the country would be to send out a message from the House to our friends and allies abroad that somehow the character of the English people was going wrong. (Hon. Members: 'Really!')

But Sir Cyril narrowly won the vote, and Lord Arran's Bill was left to proceed through its remaining stages in the Lords with a smaller chance than we had hoped for of its endorsement by the Commons.

VIII

Lords' Marathon

'Good Lord! In what different orbits human souls
can move. He talks of sex out of legal codes and
blue books. I talk of it from human documents,
myself, the people I have known, the adulterers
and prostitutes of both sexes I have dealt with over
bottles of wine and confidence.'

John Addington Symonds (1890)

Lord Arran's Bill now entered upon a marathon Committee Stage in
the Lords. The Bill which had been given a Second Reading still
consisted only of the one short clause Boofy and I had drafted on the
envelope:

> ... a shockingly drafted Bill (Lord Stonham had called it),
> because it is simple, it is clear, and it is short. No reputable
> Parliamentary draftsman would have allowed a measure to emerge
> in a form which a child could understand, so it must be full of
> legal loopholes.

When its Committee Stage began, on 21 June, there were twenty-one
amendments on the Order Paper – most of them tabled by Lord
Arran, the Archbishop of Canterbury and other supporters of the
reform, but several from Lord Dilhorne.[1] All related to issues which
had been raised in the previous debates. Should buggery remain
criminal in all circumstances, and the reform limited to repeal of the
Labouchere Amendment? What should be the age of consent? Should
the armed forces be excluded from the Bill's operation? How should
'in private' be defined? What constituted 'consent'? The bishops tabled
clauses incorporating the increased penalties which the Wolfenden

[1] Lord Arran's amendments, and those of other HLRS supporters, were based on
the HLRS draft Bill. The Archbishop had his own drafting advice.

100

Report had recommended for offences committed by men of over twenty-one with youths below that age. Other supporters sought to limit the circumstances in which prosecutions could be brought, to equate homosexual brothels with heterosexual brothels, and to penalise homosexual pimps. Lord Arran and Baroness Wootton moved the earliest version of a clause, which the HLRS considered of extreme importance, aiming to prevent the bringing of conspiracy charges in relation to homosexual activities legalised by the Bill.

It was obvious that there would be a strenuous struggle over all these details. Lord Dilhorne had mustered his supporters in strength, and after their demoralising and unexpectedly heavy defeat on the Second Reading vote, but encouraged by the Commons' narrow rejection of Mr Abse's Bill, they were determined to kill the Bill dead in its tracks now if they possibly could by winning some 'wrecking amendments'.

The debate lasted for more than nine hours on the first day – when the House did not adjourn until just after midnight – and for almost a further two hours a week later. It would be tedious to recount all the discussions in detail; and they are available for scrutiny in the *Official Report* for those who are interested. Here, I shall simply pick out a few highlights and record the fate of the major amendments. It is important to know the course these debates took in order to understand how some of the contents of the Bill which I and most of the reform's supporters have then and ever since considered to be unjust and objectionable came to be part of the 1967 Sexual Offences Act.

Lord Dilhorne kicked off by moving an amendment designed to retain consenting buggery as a crime. Unmoved by Lord Stonham's repeated protestations that this would make the work of the police impossibly difficult, he yet again held forth about the abominableness of such behaviour (demanding that the bishops should testify as to whether or not they too considered it to be abominable), and maintained that it was so repulsively different in kind from other homosexual crimes as to justify its exemption from any relaxation of the law. He was supported, surprisingly, by Lord Boothby – a strong, but capricious, supporter of reform,[2] who voted for this amendment as well as (more regrettably) for the Dilhorne definition of 'privacy' –

---

[2] As a Conservative MP he had been one of its earliest advocates. But his interventions in the Lords' debates were unpredictable, and not always helpful.

and also by Earl Attlee. But Lord Arran successfully opposed the amendment as being emotional and illogical, as well as unenforceable.

Lady Gaitskell made another of her inimitably succinct and pithy speeches, saying that to listen to Lord Dilhorne and Lord Kilmuir

> one might think that all the sex habits between men and women were confined to a kind of platonic friendship with a plastic model of Brigitte Bardot, all wrapped up and hermetically sealed, not with the temptations of the flesh.

It was a great pity that Nature had made childbirth an entirely female function, she tartly added;

> if men had babies, they would be less squeamish about their own bodies and perhaps less insistent about their disgust about homosexual behaviour.

The amendment was defeated by 86 votes to 52.

The House then moved on to amendments fixing the age of consent. Opponents of the Bill wished to substitute twenty-five for the age of twenty-one recommended by the Wolfenden Committee; the Earl of Huntingdon (unofficially encouraged by me and other members of the HLRS executive committee) proposed eighteen; and a last-minute handwritten amendment tabled by 'Monty' plumped for eighty, 'because after that age it does not really matter what we do'. Lord Huntington's case for eighteen, based upon a careful analysis of the various sets of arguments set out in the Wolfenden Report (which had itself only hesitantly opted for the higher age), was, Lord Arran admitted, logically strong; but Lord Arran preferred at this stage to stick with the Wolfenden Committee, saying – too sanguinely as it later proved – that if they were being over-cautious, and the reform did not open those dreaded (and, he thought, imaginary) floodgates, there could be further legislation. All three amendments were withdrawn.

The next amendments concerned the Bill's application to the armed services. The drafting points raised were technical, and as all concerned, including the Government, were agreed that even consenting homosexual activities between serving members of the forces should remain prohibited as contrary to good order and discipline, and the only point at issue was the most appropriate way of dealing with them, the amendments were withdrawn so that further discussion could take place between the various parties.

The debate next turned to how 'in private' was to be interpreted. This revealed deep divisions of view, and led to the most serious defeat which the Bill's opponents managed to inflict on its promoters. In its report the Wolfenden Committee had said:

> Our words 'in private' are not intended to provide a legal definition. Many heterosexual acts are not criminal if committed in private but are punishable if committed in circumstances which outrage public decency, *and we should expect the same criteria to apply to homosexual acts*. It is our intention that the law should continue to regard as criminal any indecent act committed in a public place where members of the public may be likely to see and be offended by it, *but where there is no possibility of public offence of this nature it becomes a matter of the private responsibility of the persons concerned and as such, in our opinion, is outside the proper purview of the criminal law*. It will be for the courts to decide, in cases of doubt, whether or not public decency has been outraged, and we cannot see that there would be any greater difficulty about establishing this in the case of homosexual acts than there is at present in the case of heterosexual acts. (Para. 64. My italics.)

It is clear from this that the Wolfenden Committee had uppermost in their minds a concept of 'in private' which hinged upon the presence of consent and the absence of public indecency. It was along these lines that the HLRS draft Bill had been framed, and Lord Arran proposed to enact that, '"In private" means in a place which is not a public place', adding a definition of a 'public place' based upon that contained in the Public Order Act 1936.

Lord Dilhorne, however, had a different attitude. No doubt stimulated by the lurid stories of 'buggers' clubs', he wished to provide that 'the commission of (a homosexual) act when more than two persons are present shall not be deemed to be in private'.

> To me (he said), the commission of a heterosexual or a homosexual act in private means something quite different from applying the test whether any member of the public is available to see it or whether it is committed in a public place.

Conveniently ignoring later amendments relating to brothels, he asserted that if Lord Arran's definition was preferred to his own 'it

103

will mean that buggers' clubs can operate with complete impunity'. Surely, he continued,

> the right test is this: that the conduct shall be deemed to be in private unless more than two persons are present when the homosexual conduct takes place. . . . If that test is taken, then it prevents this Bill from becoming a charter for these buggers' clubs which really do exist.

He was supported – inevitably, I suppose – by the Archbishop of Canterbury, who, throwing any subtle distinctions between law and morality to the winds, and scuttling right away from the Wolfenden principle of consent, said that Lord Dilhorne had hit upon a workable definition which 'will clearly bring clubness, and anything approaching clubness, still under the condemnation of the law'. The Archbishop's naïve notion that this punitively moralistic approach was 'workable' displayed complete ignorance and lack of concern over the practical consequences of thus empowering the police to continue keeping the private homosexual behaviour of consenting adults under special scrutiny, with its horrific prospect of many further interrogations to establish whether more than two men had been 'present' on otherwise private, consenting occasions. Besides being a gross breach of the consent principle, such investigations would surely be open to precisely the same objection of administrative impracticability which Lord Stonham had raised against the proposal to repeal only the Labouchere Amendment.

But on this occasion, despite having been unable to unearth any convincing evidence in Home Office files of the existence of the notorious 'buggers' clubs', Lord Stonham did not stand squarely against Lord Dilhorne's novel interpretation of 'in private'. Its sinister implications were also blithely ignored by Lord Boothby, who promptly jumped on the Dilhorne bandwagon and expressed his 'total agreement' with it (on the dubious ground, as he later explained, that a 'moderate and reasonable' Bill would stand a better chance of passage into law). Despite Lord Arran's plea for the House to adhere to the Wolfenden line of defining 'in private' as being not in a public place, and Lady Gaitskell's strong distaste for this move towards 'a Puritan police state', Lord Dilhorne carried his amendment into the Bill by 41 votes to 26.

Sitting in the guests' seats below the Bar of the House, I was downcast by this new and unexpected vista of a future bedroom gestapo. But as the debates proceeded it was becoming increasingly obvious to me that the terms of any reform which finally emerged were going to be more punitive in several respects than Wolfenden's proposals. Most of the Bill's supporters (with a few shining exceptions such as Baronesses Gaitskell and Wootton) were throughout at pains to emphasise their aversion from homosexual desires and their antipathy towards homosexual practices.

The outlook for any candid acceptance by the politicians of those of us who happened to be homosexual as simply ordinary human beings with socially harmless minority sexual interests and affections seemed bleak. Indeed, I was struck by the debaters' capacity – particularly marked amongst the Law Lords – to discuss increased maximum terms of imprisonment for those who breached the 'age of consent' provisions in an abstract way which reflected their own moral indignation (or physical nausea?), but with no apparent comprehension of what it actually meant to serve a long prison sentence – especially as a 'sex offender'.

This lack of humanity was, indeed, heightened by the saloon bar jocularity of some of the after-dinner speeches (punctuated by the customary bleats from Lord Kilmuir about these 'horrible, unnatural and beastly acts', and the refreshing observation from Lady Wootton that 'the morals of this matter have a fascination for many of your Lordships which I do not share'), when Lord Dilhorne's proposal to exclude from the consent provisions a homosexual act induced by payment of money or a gift was discussed. Fortunately, this further attempt to discriminate in law between heterosexual and homosexual situations was defeated by 37 votes to 18.

Although the HLRS had consulted an eminent Queen's Counsel with parliamentary drafting experience, to assist Lord Arran and his supporters in framing amendments to the Bill, several of these amendments were withdrawn after criticism of their wording from Lord Stonham and others, which led Lord Arran to complain that he was in 'severe technical trouble'. Pressed by Lord Boothby for official drafting help, all Lord Stonham would say was that the Government would consider the position of the Bill on completion of the Committee Stage. This undertaking resulted in the provision, before the

Report Stage, of drafting assistance from the Government's parliamentary draftsmen – an invaluable coup for Lord Arran, but one which meant that once the principle of a clause had been agreed by the House the Government would be in a position effectively to determine the precise wording of the Bill.

For those of us who were 'shadowing' Lord Arran at the HLRS, it became from now on more difficult to get him to pay attention to our views on points which, though presented as drafting details, often involved crucial issues of principle and practice. Although I requested him to do so, he never arranged a meeting between the HLRS and the Government draftsmen, and he did not discuss with us the latter's draft amendments before tabling these. Nor did Leo Abse pay much attention to our views on drafting when the Bill was passing through the Commons.[3] So we virtually lost any effective influence over the Bill's contents, except insofar as we could persuade our sympathisers in each House to move amendments and raise debating points which at least got an airing for the matters which concerned us. Those who imagine that the Sexual Offences Act 1967 as it finally reached the Statute Book was framed along the lines desired by the HLRS, or that we were in some way responsible for its objectionable and discriminatory features, are totally mistaken. The Bill's chief sponsors – Lord Arran in the Upper House and Leo Abse in the Commons – firmly believed that it was so vital to get the behaviour of consenting adults decriminalised, even in a limited way, that they at times bent over too far backwards (in my opinion) to placate their opponents, and were not prepared to stick out for anything which went beyond – or in some respects even as far as – Wolfenden. Boofy was fond of reiterating to me that 'politics is the art of the possible'. I agreed; but at times his view and mine of what was in fact politically possible diverged sharply.

While we were still discussing our drafting proposals for that first Committee Stage, I visited Lord Arran at his country home one wet Sunday afternoon (his pet badger joined us for tea). The occasion produced a memorable boofyism. He had tried several times, without success, to telephone the Archbishop of Canterbury's Lay Secretary, Mr Robert Beloe, to discuss some of the points in the Bill which

---

[3] Humphry Berkeley did; but, sadly, he lost his seat in the Commons at the general election which soon followed the successful Second Reading of his Bill in February 1966.

concerned the Archbishop. Getting no reply, he stalked impatiently back into the room, looked out of the window at the pouring rain, and said: 'He's out. He must be taking his wife and daughters for a tramp through Richmond Park. Strength through misery!'

This certainly evoked a comic vision. Mr Beloe was a tall, gaunt man of grave and dignified demeanour and speech. I immediately pictured him marching his ladies, doubtless in an orderly crocodile, through the dripping foliage. After one of the debates as Mr Beloe and I were leaving the Houses of Parliament through the precincts of Westminster Abbey and he was bemoaning the attacks which were being made upon the Archbishop over his unwavering support for law reform, I attempted to comfort him by remarking: 'Well, Mr Beloe, this is one of those occasions when the doctrine of the lesser evil must be applied.' He retorted, with vehement gloom, 'I can assure you that it has been – copiously!'

Over a dozen amendments had been tabled for the Report Stage on 16 July, mostly by the Bill's supporters. These, Lord Stonham revealed later, had been prepared with the assistance of the parliamentary draftsmen. But discussion of them was preceded by a rerun of the 'consenting age' amendments seeking to substitute twenty-five, or eighteen, for twenty-one. On this occasion there was a vote: forty peers voted to substitute twenty-five and sixty-two to retain twenty-one.

Lord Arran then moved a revised subsection defining privacy:

> An act which would otherwise be treated for the purpose of this Act as being done in private shall not be so treated if done –
> > (a) in the presence of persons other than the parties to the act; or
> > (b) in a lavatory to which the public have or are permitted to have access, whether on payment or otherwise.

This, said Lord Arran, was intended to meet the wishes of the House that a homosexual act should not be deemed to be in private if committed in the presence of others.

> I am advised [he continued] that the wording here in no way alters the sense of the amendment moved by [Lord Dilhorne] in Committee . . . indeed it subsumes it. Perhaps I should say that this and most of the other amendments before [you] today have been drafted by Parliamentary experts. . . .

107

This goaded Lord Dilhorne to fury; it was indeed an eyebrow-raising example of the prowess of the 'parliamentary experts'. Lord Dilhorne described it as 'most astonishing' – not least because of the incorrect claim that it made no difference to the sense of the Bill. What it had, in fact, done (presumably inadvertently) was not only to remove the limitation to '*two* persons', but also to permit, by inference, the presence of at least one non-participant. As Lord Dilhorne proceeded to point out, with extreme indignation,

> what [Lord Arran] is now suggesting is that we should agree to a provision which would make it possible to have a homosexual party, without any limit as to numbers, provided that they are all participating in the acts and provided that there is not more than one spectator. And he has the nerve to come and say that this amendment, drafted by parliamentary experts, makes no difference. . . . I must say that it seems to me rubbish. . . . I will reserve my fire to the later stages.

I could not help being a trifle amused (not maliciously, I hope) by Lord Arran's obvious discomfiture. Having twitted me with providing him with technically incompetent drafting, he had thrown himself headlong into the arms of the experts proffered by the Home Office, only to come an inglorious cropper. Though I did not like Lord Dilhorne's line of argument, his impersonation of a furious buffalo was diverting. Lord Stonham then stood up and took him on the chin, coolly, competently and deflatingly. While remaining neutral on the policy issues of the Bill, he said, the Government had thought that it would be appropriate to help with the redrafting of the amendments so that the House could reach a decision without the frustration of drafting difficulties and the waste of time they might well involve. In response to Lord Dilhorne's enquiry as to what was wrong with his original amendment which had been voted into the Bill, Lord Stonham pointed out that this implied that not more than two persons could lawfully be 'present' when a homosexual act was committed – the implication being that those 'present' might be additional to those 'participating'. Increasingly abstruse argument crystallised around the point that, whatever the precise final wording, there was now majority support in the House for what Lord Dilhorne advocated. Even Lady Gaitskell made the uncharacteristic remark that she agreed and sympathised with the

view that homosexual privacy should be more stringent than heterosexual privacy, because

> when I see two young people embracing on the moving stair-
> case on the Tube I am not outraged myself, but I should be
> outraged if I saw two homosexuals doing just that.

(I wondered why.) The new amendment was voted into the Bill by
59 votes to 32.

Successive amendments were then accepted to preserve all the
existing powers under the Army, Air Force and Naval Discipline
Acts to punish homosexual offences by court martial (including
offences legalised for civilians by the Bill); to provide that men
suffering from severe mental subnormality could not consent in law
to a homosexual act; to implement the revised (in some cases,
higher) penalties for offences recommended by the Wolfenden
Committee; to penalise anyone procuring a homosexual act between
others, or living off the immoral earnings of a male prostitute; and
to place a time limit of twelve months on certain prosecutions. The
Bill thus emerged from its Report Stage in a much more comprehensive form, approximating to its final shape when it reached the
Statute Book two years later.

On 28 October, just before the end of the session, the Lords
gave the Bill a Third Reading by 116 votes to 46, and passed it
at the end of the debate by 96 votes to 31. There was again a
lengthy debate, opened by Lord Arran, who confessed that

> frankly I admit that many times I would gladly have been shot of
> the whole wretched business. There is no fun in it, and sometimes
> one feels desperate at some of the letters one receives. Most of
> my post is anonymous nowadays and such letters do not exactly
> encourage one to continue. They are full of the most fearful con-
> demnation. Curiously enough, they all seem to quote *Deuter-
> onomy* and *Leviticus* but never the Sermon on the Mount, except
> one letter from a man who calls the Sermon on the Mount 'that
> masterpiece of appeasement'. The obscenity of some of these
> letters passes all belief. . . . But . . . just as one is thinking of
> chucking it, one gets another of those ghastly letters from some
> man who is being blackmailed or who is facing criminal pros-

ecution, or from parents who are terrified on behalf of their homosexual son. . . . So of course one has to go on.[4]

And he was encouraged by the findings of two national opinion polls
(Gallup and NOP), both within the previous two months, which
showed that by a majority of five to three the public now supported
homosexual law reform. This reinforced his plea to the Government
to grant the necessary time and facilities for the Bill to be debated in
the Commons.

In the debate which followed, thirteen Peers supported the Bill
(not counting Lord Stonham, who spoke for the Government), and
four opposed. Though inevitably going over much well-trodden
ground the debate was of high quality, and included a notable supporting maiden speech from Lord Annan and a characteristically caustic
intervention from Lady Wootton. She was, she said, 'completely
puzzled' by the discriminations between one form of abnormal intercourse and another, and 'could only conclude that this was a queer form
of physical geography with which I was unacquainted'.

The Archbishop of Canterbury deplored the 'really lopsided presentation of morality' which took the line that sexual sins were apparently the worst of all sins, and that homosexual sins were invariably
the worst sort of sins among sexual sins. A more balanced, Christian
and rational presentation of morality was needed to win the respect
and allegiance of the younger generation, he said. This irked Lord
Dilhorne who retorted that supporters of the Bill might just as well
argue that to legalise murder would promote morality. Praising Lord
Arran's courage and dogged persistence, Lord Stonham said that,
while the Government could make no promises as to the allocation of
time and business in the Commons, they recognised the importance
of this issue, which was the very essence of a Private Member's Bill.
He thought it would be quite remarkable if an MP who was fortunate
in the Ballot[5] could not be found to sponsor it.

With that the Bill was passed – and died with the Session.

---

[4] He was indeed having a grisly time, with obscenities about him being painted
outside his London clubs, and human excrement being sent to him through the post. His
splendidly stalwart secretary, Stella, opened such a package one day, and told Boofy
afterwards: 'I threw it away, Lord Arran – it wouldn't keep.'

[5] The annual Commons Ballot for Private Members' time to introduce Bills.

IX

On to the Statute Book

'The *vice Anglais* is not buggery but humbuggery.'
– Leslie Hale MP

Lord Stonham proved right. Humphry Berkeley, the Conservative MP for Lancaster, won second place in the new Session's ballot for Private Members' Bills and announced his intention of introducing a homosexual law reform Bill into the Commons. His Bill, when published, was – inevitably, from a tactical point of view – worded identically to that which had just received its Third Reading in the Lords. He had mustered an impressive array of all-party support, the Bill's other sponsors being the Liberal Party leader, Jo Grimond; Christopher Chataway, Lord Balniel, Nicholas Ridley and Peter Kirk (Conservative); and G. R. Strauss, Shirley Williams, Dick Taverne and Arthur Blenkinsop (Labour).

Humphry Berkeley was the most helpful and congenial of the parliamentary sponsors with whom I worked. We had been contemporaries at Cambridge, where we had both been active in the University Conservative Association, and Humphry had been President of the Union. He was now prominent on the progressive wing of the Conservative Party and an outspoken opponent of colonialism in Africa and elsewhere.[1] He knew more about the personal and social aspects of the homosexual issue than either Lord Arran or Leo Abse, and would, I believe, have disputed the Home Office's somewhat ivory tower approach to the Bill's contents, and confronted the opposition in the House, more effectively than either of them. His defeat in the general election of March 1966, after successfully securing the

---

[1] He later left the Conservative Party for Labour – but not before taking a leading part in formulating the Conservative Party's new leadership election rules.

Second Reading of his Bill in the Commons, was a blow to our cause.

The five-hour debate on 11 February 1966 was the first occasion that the Commons had had a full-length discussion of homosexual law reform for six years, and the first time a fully drafted Bill had been before it. It was, therefore, an important occasion which would reveal the strength of support for, and opposition to, reform. The HLRS office was extremely busy during the period between the ballot and the debate, answering requests for information from numerous MPs who wished to speak – including some opponents as well as supporters of the Bill.

Mr Berkeley spoke ably and with restraint, asking opponents to recognise the sincerity of the sponsors' motives, as he acknowledged theirs. After rehearsing the now familiar arguments for reform, and outlining the detailed provisions of the Bill, he concluded that sufficient time had elapsed since the Wolfenden Report, and the matter had been sufficiently debated in the country, to give no further grounds for delay.

He was opposed by Sir Cyril Black, Conservative MP for Wimbledon and a leading Baptist layman. He claimed that the Bill would lead to a great increase in unnatural vice, and accused the HLRS of swamping the country with its misleading propaganda – a tribute of sorts, I suppose, to our efforts. The distinction between sin and crime was not understood by the man in the street, Sir Cyril said; homosexual law reform would give 'a new view of this form of sin to the great mass of the nation'. Another persistent opponent, William Shepherd, attacked the HLRS's 'propaganda' as 'nonsense' and 'wildly distorted', citing Richard Hauser's views as 'proof' of the essential nature of homosexuals. He was, he said, convinced that homosexuality was environmentally determined, and 'something to which any of us can succumb if the circumstances of our lives or the weakness of our outlook make us susceptible'. Homosexuals were 'seeking sexual gratification without responsibility'. Blackmail was not the consequence of criminality, but of social disapproval. If the House wanted to get rid of that, they would have to 'approve of buggery as a social act'. Homosexuals were promiscuous proselytisers, but he would nevertheless be prepared to accept repeal of the Labouchere Amendment in order to remove some of their sense of grievance.

My dealings with Mr Shepherd were always personally pleasant, even though he was so critical of the HLRS. Shortly after the Commons debate he and I were the chief opposing speakers at a London School of Economics Students' Union debate – or should have been, but he left in the middle of his opening speech because he was upset by some jocular interruptions from the audience. Mr Shepherd also contributed an article to *Man and Society*, at my invitation, accusing homosexuals of 'glorifying' their conduct as 'a superior way of life' and of wanting to 'turn the rest of society upside down so that it faces the same way as he does'. Every homosexual, he believed, was a potential danger to young persons. It was in the public interest to discourage as many as possible from this way of life. This broadside produced predictable reactions from our readers, one saying that he thought the article was a comic parody until he checked that Mr Shepherd really was an MP. In the next general election, Shepherd lost his seat to a Liberal, Dr Michael (later Lord) Winstanley, who became a staunch supporter and trustee of the Albany Trust.

Mr Shepherd was followed by Leo Abse, who pointed out that a decision to keep the existing law was a decision to enforce it; otherwise it was meaningless.

> Let those who want to retain the law as it stands face up to the fact that if it could ever be enforced at all it could be done only by the most massive recruitment of police ever envisaged and by the invasion of privacy in a way which all of us would find utterly intolerable.

To send a homosexual to an overcrowded male prison was as therapeutically useless as incarcerating a sex maniac in a harem.[2] Someone who demanded total and permanent abstinence from 'those whose terrible fate it is to be homosexuals' reminded him of William Blake's saying that 'the only people who condemn passion are those who are deficient in it'. Continuing discussion of punishment diverted attention from the real challenge of 'how we can reduce the numbers of faulty males' in the community.

Sir Cyril Osborne then contributed the helpful observation, from his point of view 'as a straightforward, simple square' that he was 'rather tired of democracy being made safe for the pimps, the prostitutes, the spivs, the pansies and now, the queers', with much more in

---

[2] A distinctive Absean variation on the familiar 'alcoholic in a brewery'.

this vein. Fortunately not all Conservatives were as reactionary or homophobic in those days as the two Sir Cyrils, and three of their number spoke strongly in support of the Bill: the Hon. Richard Wood (Bridlington), Norman St John-Stevas (Chelmsford), and Christopher Chataway (Lewisham, North).

The Home Secretary (Roy Jenkins) began his speech by praising the quality of the debate. He reaffirmed the Government's attitude of neutrality towards the principle of the Bill, which should be decided by a free vote of the House, while offering further drafting assistance if necessary. He personally intended to vote for the Bill, and so, 'by an entirely personal process of decision', did the other three Home Office ministers. The majority of homosexuals, said Mr Jenkins, were not exhibitionist freaks but ordinary citizens doing normal jobs, in many cases usefully and unobtrusively, and sometimes with great distinction. Most did not choose their inclinations, which were a grave disability for the individual, leading to a great deal of loneliness and unhappiness and to a heavy weight of guilt and shame, and greatly reducing their chances of finding a stable and lasting emotional relationship. If the law were to be changed there could be no compromise such as a repeal of the Labouchere Amendment only: 'that halfway house would have no basis either in logic or in morals'. He did not think they would gain by further postponement or get a better Bill on which to face this difficult issue.

When the House divided 164 MPs voted for the Second Reading and 107 against. 111 Labour, 48 Conservative and 4 Liberal members supported reform, while 11 Labour and 96 Conservative Members opposed. But with the dissolution of Parliament shortly after the debate the Bill was stillborn. And, most unfortunately, Humphry Berkeley lost his parliamentary seat in the March General Election when Labour increased its majority from three to ninety-seven.[3]

Spurred on by the brighter prospects for reform in the new Parliament, and with the prospect of an early Commons ballot for Private Members' Bills, Lord Arran reintroduced the Bill into the Lords at the beginning of the new Session, and it passed through all its stages between 10 May and 16 June. Inevitably, the debates were repetitive,

---

[3] Berkeley afterwards blamed his defeat on his sponsorship of the Sexual Offences Bill, although William Shepherd and several other Tory opponents of the Bill also lost their seats by a similar margin in the national swing to Labour.

with the by now familiar supporting and opposing casts doggedly sticking to their scripts. Lord Arran told the House that the Lord Chief Justice, Lord Parker, now broadly approved of homosexual law reform, so long as there was no question of corruption, though he was 'far from certain what the age of consent should be'.

As the opponents reiterated their forebodings of the dire consequences of passing the Bill, and made great play with apprehensions voiced by the Merchant Navy as to the 'considerable problems' which a reformed law would create on board ship, Lady Gaitskell wearily enquired whether there was a psychoanalyst in the House, and commented that a short course in physiology might enlighten them as to how diffused sexual pleasure could become, and possibly shake their convictions about what was 'natural' or 'unnatural'. Far from having a corrupting influence, the Bill would create a much healthier attitude to sex in general and alleviate much persecution and suffering. She believed that 'the dangers of facing the facts about human nature are less than the dangers of denying their existence'.

The Bill received its Second Reading by 70 votes to 29. In Committee, Lord Saltoun pressed his '25' amendment to a vote, and was defeated by 77 votes to 16; Lord Huntingdon then lost '18' by 78 votes against 12. His proposal, prompted by the HLRS, to replace Lord Dilhorne's definition of privacy by a stipulation that 'a homosexual act shall not be deemed to be done in private if done in a place where members of the public are likely to see and be offended by it' was withdrawn after Lord Stonham had poured cold water on it, and Lord Arran, though in 'moral sympathy', thought it unwise to reopen the issue at that stage.

There was an interesting discussion on conspiracy. Lady Wootton had once again agreed to move an amendment making it clear that it would not be a common law offence to conspire or attempt to commit a homosexual act legalised by the Bill; I had asked her to do this because of the HLRS' concern at the possible effect of the Law Lords' judgement a few years previously in 'the Ladies' Directory Case',[4] reviving (or inventing) the Common Law crime of 'conspiracy to corrupt public morals'. Lord Conesford foresaw a quite different sort of conspiracy which he wished to guard against: 'We may be giving

[4] *Shaw v. DPP*, 1961.

protection to the propagation of a cult'; a club formed for the purposes of promoting homosexual practices, saying that they were a desirable form of activity, or publishing a directory of practising homosexuals, ought not to be tolerated. Lord Stonham said he had been advised that

> broadly speaking . . . an agreement to promote homosexual acts would not amount to an offence of conspiracy unless there was some public affront involved. If the arrangement were such as to create a public scandal or a public outrage then this would amount to an offence of conspiracy, but not otherwise.

A private agreement between adult males to commit homosexual acts in private would not constitute an offence if the Bill became law. On the basis of this assurance Lady Wootton withdrew her amendment.[5]

The Bill was reported without amendment, and given a Third Reading on 16 June by 83 votes to 39. Lord Arran began the debate by moving yet another Home Office-drafted amendment to the 'privacy' clause. This became the final wording, providing that a homosexual act shall not be deemed to be done in private 'when more than two persons take part or are present.'[6] Such complete capitulation did not mollify Lord Dilhorne, who ungraciously retorted that, while he supposed it was an improvement, 'the best improvement to this Bill would be to cut its throat'.

The debate also featured a sulphurous eruption of vintage homophobia from the Earl of Dudley:

> I cannot stand homosexuals. They are the most disgusting people in the world, and they are, unfortunately, on the increase. I loathe them. Prison is much too good a place for them; in fact, that is a place where many of them like to go, for obvious reasons.

This, and a further declaration of abhorrence from Lord Saltoun, prompted Lord Arran to declare, rather smugly, that

---

[5] I thought at the time that Lord Stonham's reassurances were over-sanguine; the *International Times* and *OZ* cases a few years later showed that my forebodings as to the use of conspiracy charges in respect of homosexuals seeking partners for activities decriminalised by the Bill were well-founded.

[6] Or (as before) in a public lavatory.

in all the discussions we have had, and in all the speeches, no single noble Lord or noble Lady has ever said that homosexuality is a right or a good thing. It has been universally condemned from start to finish, and by every single Member of this House.

This remained the predominant tone, although Lord Snow (C. P. Snow, the novelist) expressed incredulity at the 'curious unworldliness' of some of the discussion.

It has seemed to me, occasionally, that some noble Lords speak as though they have never met a homosexual, as though these were something like the white rhinoceros – strange animals, difficult to observe. Yet every noble Lord here must have met many homosexuals . . . some of [them] the most distinguished and, if I may say so, worthy of Englishmen.

Another note of unrealism was struck by Lord Stonham's inability to give any firm assurances of the Bill's further progress in the Commons. But it was, he said, a most unusual Private Member's Bill; there was a general feeling in the country that it was going to become law sooner or later – the only question was in which Session? On this inconclusive note, the House again passed the Bill by 78 votes to 60.

The Bill's final entry into the Commons was not long delayed. Less than three weeks later, on 5 July 1966, Leo Abse rose to move, under the Ten-Minute Rule, 'that leave be given to bring in a Bill to amend the law of England and Wales relating to homosexual acts'. This Bill, the one which finally passed into law, was known in its early stages as the 'Sexual Offences (No. 2) Bill', because of the other Sexual Offences Bill (Lord Arran's) which had already passed the Lords in this Session.

Outlining the Bill's now familiar provisions, and emphasising their restrictive nature, Mr Abse claimed that 'only those wilfully blinding themselves to the nature of our proceedings could suggest that the Bill would assist or approve of homosexual practices, or would condone any act of indecency against a youngster, or any public display of homosexual conduct'.

After Mr Abse had spoken, Sir Cyril Osborne rose (Hon. Members: 'Oh, no.') to assert that there was no mandate for the Bill. He denied the claims that there were about one million 'homos' in Britain: 'I do not believe that our country is as rotten as all that.' It would mean that there were at least thirty 'homos' in the House, but in all his twenty-one years as a member, he had never come across a single case. The House's response to this was to give Mr Abse leave to introduce his Bill by 244 to 100 votes.

As the new Session had a full year to run the Bill now stood a good chance of passing into law, provided that sufficient time was available for all its remaining stages in both Houses. This was by no means assured; there was no prospect of the Government itself adopting the Bill, so it was dependent in the Commons upon the hazards of Private Members' time, which was very limited. However, the Home Secretary, Roy Jenkins, who was a strong supporter of the Bill, managed, with the help of the Leader of the House, Richard Crossman,[7] to persuade his Cabinet colleagues (some of whom, including Prime Minister Harold Wilson, George Brown and Jim Callaghan, were reluctant to abandon the Government's traditional posture of neutrality) that it was tactically desirable to provide limitless – though inconveniently late-night – Government time for the Bill so long as its supporters continued to muster a majority in the House. The Cabinet also agreed that, while its members would be free to *vote* for or against the Bill as they wished, the Home Secretary could also speak in its support 'with all the briefing and such authority as (he) could command as Home Secretary'.[8] The first of these factors proved crucial to the Bill's success; otherwise, the 'frail craft' (as Lord Jenkins has since described it to me) would have foundered.

The Bill's Second Reading was on 19 December. Mr Abse had again obtained strong cross-party support, his co-sponsors being the Hon. Richard Wood, Sir Peter Rawlinson, Mr Hugh Fraser, Mr Ian Gilmour and Mr Norman St John-Stevas (Conservatives); Mr Charles Pannell, Mr G. R. Strauss, Mr Michael Foot, Mr Eric Varley and Mr John Horner (Labour); and Mr Jo Grimond (Liberal). Significantly, the reasoned amendment for the Bill's rejection was narrowly based upon the fears of the Merchant Navy that they were not being afforded

---

[7] Although Crossman 'strongly favoured' its Second Reading in December 1966, by the Third Reading in July 1967 he had decided that it was 'an extremely unpleasant Bill' which 'may well be twenty years ahead of public opinion. . . . It has gone down very badly that the Labour Party should be associated with such a Bill'. (Richard Crossman, *The Diaries of a Cabinet Minister*, Volume Two (Hamilton/Cape, 1976) pp. 172, 407.) Yet he was a longstanding member of the HLRS Honorary Committee!

[8] Roy Jenkins, *A Life at the Centre* (Macmillan, 1991) pp. 208–9.

the degree of protection and exemption which the Bill provided for the Armed Forces, so that it could create circumstances which would lead to corruption of young seamen.

Opening the debate Mr Abse, who in his appearance[9] and manner struck (as an opponent[10] put it) 'the perfect balance between stolid normality and flamboyant eccentricity', commented that

> we are prone in this country to extend our national debates on legislation touching on human relationships to the point at which they sometimes verge almost on farce, and sometimes they are taken to the point of morbidity.

It was time to conclude this one. The existing law was unenforceable, and had no rehabilitative element. Its effects were stigmatising and alienating; it was not surprising that, in such a climate of opinion, not a few homosexuals lapsed into near paranoia, or sometimes protected their self-esteem by

> absurdly proclaiming their superiority intellectually and artistic-ally to those of us who are mere heterosexuals. This is the reaction which we as a community almost provoke. . . . Then when they make such statements we accuse them of being proselytisers.

Turning to the details of the Bill Mr Abse said that he could not accept the amendment, but that after two long meetings with the National Maritime Board (representing the shipowners and all the seafaring organisations, including the unions) he would accept an amendment in Committee founded on the principle that a merchant seaman should be in no worse or no better a position than a naval rating.

The debate followed predictable lines. One opponent[11] feared more books and plays about homosexuality, more clubs, and that 'the vice would be looked upon as a normal and natural part of our daily life, and all checks would be gone'. The mover of the amendment[12] said that, without the sought-for protection, the Merchant Navy could become 'an attractive venue for homosexuals . . . (their) presence could give rise to serious conflicts at sea and jealousies could even lead

---

[9] He frequently wore strikingly colourful clothes, and always made a point of pride in being foremost in this respect on Budget Day and other special parliamentary occasions.

[10] T. L. Iremonger. (Cons.)

[11] Captain Walter Elliot. (Cons.)

[12] Simon Mahon. (Lab.)

to violence.'[13] Another[14] said he would prefer to see the law wither away through the disinclination of chief constables to prosecute rather than pass the Bill. He did not at all relish the thought of coming-of-age ceremonies being performed 'with pederastic celebrations in university colleges'. The Bill, he surprisingly added, would make the situation for homosexuals neither better nor worse; he did not think the homosexual population were people for whom one could do a lot. Supporters condemned the existing law as unjust, unenforceable, hypocritical, illogical, and an invitation to further crime.[15] The Bill would promote public morality by limiting itself to practical objectives and providing homosexuals with standards of behaviour which there was some prospect of their keeping.[16]

The debate was not about approval or disapproval of homosexual practices; any Bill along those lines would be overwhelmingly defeated in the foreseeable future. The issue was whether or not homosexual behaviour in private between consenting men should be within the same area of private moral choice and judgement which a man or a woman exercised when he or she committed or refrained from committing adultery or fornication.[17]

It was a temperate, low-key debate – perhaps because, as the Home Secretary (Roy Jenkins) said, the House recognised that over the previous decade there had been a massive and decisive shift in parliamentary feeling on the subject. He believed this was evidence of a growing recognition that, whatever their views about particular forms of conduct, 'there has to be a very clear social purpose served before it is right to subject private conduct to the rigours of the criminal law.' After voting by 194 to 84 to continue the debate after the adjournment was moved at 10 o'clock, the House gave the Bill an unopposed Second Reading.

The Committee Stage was a surprise. The prospect of this had given Mr Abse and his supporters some anxiety on at least two counts – first, because the Bill would normally have to take its place in the queue for a Private Members' Bills Standing Committee, giving

[13] Ian Gilmour retorted that he was quite unable to see why, if homosexuality were legalised on land, that should drive homosexuals to sea.
[14] T. L. Iremonger.
[15] Ian Gilmour.
[16] Norman St John-Stevas.
[17] Hon. Richard Wood.

opponents the opportunity to filibuster on earlier Bills so as to deny Mr Abse sufficient time to get his Bill through Committee and its remaining stages on the floor of the House; and secondly, because the Abortion Bill (which had been running neck-and-neck with ours through the House and also depended on the Government's goodwill over time) had become bogged down for several weeks in its Committee Stage – two of its most dogged opponents being Mr Abse and Mr St John-Stevas. So we feared a similarly long and hard-fought Committee Stage for the Sexual Offences Bill.

In the event Mr Abse secured the appointment of an additional Standing Committee specifically to consider the Sexual Offences Bill; and the Bill unexpectedly passed through its entire Committee Stage in a single morning, on 19 April 1967. This was partly because the opponents did not anticipate such an occurrence, and several of them did not make a point of attending the Committee's first sitting; it was also due to a self-limiting strategy by the Bill's supporters, who did their best to keep discussions of amendments as brief as possible.

Nevertheless, some interesting points were raised over important amendments – some of which were tabled by supporters of the Bill at the HLRS' request. But first the Merchant Navy again took centre stage. Since the Second Reading debate Mr Abse had held further consultations with the seafarers' representatives and the Home Office, and now produced a new clause – which became Section 2 of the Act – whose strange effect was that a homosexual act between two consenting adults in private on a United Kingdom merchant ship remained an offence if committed between a crew member of that ship and another crew member of the same or of any other United Kingdom merchant ship, but not if done on board such a ship by a member of its crew with a passenger or a *foreign* merchant seaman! Once again, the demon draftsman had triumphed; as Mr Ben Whitaker pointed out, the illogical absurdity of this new clause was such that it would bring the whole of English law into ridicule. However, the clause had the blessing of the Merchant Navy, the Home Office and Mr Abse, so it went into the Bill unopposed. The HLRS remained a passive and somewhat bemused spectator of this seafaring skirmish, which was conducted virtually singlehanded by Mr Abse without consulting us; it was a sophisticated tactical foray on his part which, though illogical, successfully drew the sting of opposition.

The Committee then discussed the 'Dilhorne' definition of 'in private'. Despite strong objections to this from Mr St John-Stevas who pointed out, quite rightly, that 'buggers' clubs' or orgies were in any case ruled out by the provisions in the Bill relating to brothels, and the word 'present' was too vague – did it mean in the same room or the same house? – Mr Abse and the Home Office advised the Committee to stick with Dilhorne.

They also refused to budge over the age of consent, although Nicholas Ridley made a cogently argued speech saying that he thought they should consider very deeply whether it was right to fix an age even as late as eighteen. He wondered whether the principle of legalising homosexual acts in private between consenting adults was the right one? 'Surely, it should be between consenting people of any age.' They ought to make the law clearly understandable to those who would be affected by it; setting an age of consent of twenty-one

> can make no sense at all in the minds of young men who will grow
> up having to observe this law . . . which will affect generations to
> come who will be afflicted by this problem, and if we get it wrong
> we will not be doing a good service.

'I do not think it can be doubted', Mr Abse responded, 'that there must obviously be an element of arbitrariness in any decision on this point': but this time, he urged the Committee to stick with Wolfenden. And they did, after George Strauss, the Father of the House, had reminded them how precarious the life of a Private Member's Bill was and urged them to 'suppress their doubts and worries about some of the details and give wholehearted support to the Bill as it appears before us today'.[18] So the Bill returned to the full House substantially unaltered, with the addition of the new 'merchant shipping' clause and a few drafting amendments.

The final battle was fought out on the floor of the House in a five-hour Report Stage on 23 June which was concluded, together with the Third Reading, in an all-night session lasting from 10.15 p.m. on 3 July until 5.50 a.m. on the 4th. This was an endurance test for all concerned – not least for Mr Abse, who had to keep a minimum of 100 Members available in the House to vote for the closure which ended the filibustering debates on amendments. This he managed to

---

[18] A view which Lord Jenkins still believes to have been tactically correct.

do, largely thanks to the assiduous whipping carried out on his behalf by Dr David Kerr, Labour MP for Wandsworth, Central. In the nine divisions during the final night, Mr Abse's vote stayed safely above 100, while the most his opponents mustered was 40. The Bill was finally given its Third Reading in the small hours by 99 votes to 14. Congratulated by the Home Secretary on the passage of 'an important and civilising Measure' (though not 'a vote of confidence or congratulation to homosexuality'), Abse was 'too emotionally drained to react to praise or blame.'[19]

The opponents were a small but dogged bunch who did their best to spin out the discussion with a sustained display of tremendous outrage and sought to insert some peculiar amendments into the Bill.[20] The first of these – moved by Sir Cyril Osborne, who confessed that he had never done such a thing before in all his twenty-two years in the House – sought to punish the promotion of homosexual acts between consenting adults 'through the publication of lists of names and addresses of known homosexuals or otherwise' with five years' imprisonment or a fine of £5,000. Sir Cyril was frequently ruled out of order by the Speaker for remarks irrelevant to the clause, such as that a doctor in his constituency had written to him wishing him success 'in your efforts to get Leo Abse's Bill for spreading filth chucked out'. Another opposing Tory, Sir Gerald Nabarro, expressed his extreme surprise that at many of the sixty public meetings he had addressed during the general election campaign he had been questioned on his attitude to 'this odious topic of homosexuality' (another inadvertent tribute to the HLRS' efforts). A third[21] read out advertisements for 'gay bachelors interested in male only activities' and offering 'cosy lodgings with meals'. The general public, he said, considered this sort of thing such an abomination that they were not prepared to talk about it, and could not understand why others did.

Yet another opponent was 'extremely shocked and disturbed with the whole atmosphere that [the Bill] conjures up'. But the atmosphere which was now being conjured up by these MPs was as shockingly exaggerated and fantastic as the Lords' rampage about the mythical

---

[19] *Private Member* (Macdonald, 1973), p. 158.

[20] Over fifty were tabled, although of course not all of these were selected by the Speaker for debate.

[21] Ray Mawby.

'buggers' clubs' had been. The former Solicitor General, Ian Percival, who now performed with gusto as a Commons 'mini-Dilhorne', said he increasingly wondered whether the Bill's promoters realised the disgusting and degrading nature of what they were talking about – 'what has been for centuries called the abominable offence of buggery'.

And so they went on and on, intent on proclaiming that, whatever the immediate detail of the amendment they were ostensibly discussing, any homosexual behaviour was appalling, filthy, degrading and disgusting; and all those who chose or wished to engage in it were utterly beastly, horrible, degenerate and depraved people. This atmosphere of exaggerated outrage, with its strong whiff of 'the lady doth protest too much', was later characterised by Leo Abse as 'the disgust and horror which some men need to express as their defence against admitting the existence of their own homosexual feelings'. Abse accordingly believed that, although he himself wholly accepted the Freudian belief in the universality of bisexuality,

> only by insisting that compassion was needed for a totally separate group, quite unlike the absolutely normal male males of the Commons, could I allay the anxiety and resistances. . . . Homosexuals had to be placed at a distance, suffering a distinctive and terrible fate so different from that enjoyed by Honourable Members blessed with normality, children and the joys of a secure family life.[22]

Having passed all its stages in the Commons, there remained for Mr Abse's Bill a final, rapid canter through the Lords. Lord Arran must have had a sense of *déjà vu*, but this time it was for real. While respecting his opponents and their point of view, he said, 'the more I have come to learn of the plight and the unhappiness of homosexuals, the more I have become convinced that this Bill is necessary'. Many of the now familiar cast of supporters and opponents reiterated their now familiar lines. So much so that Lady Wootton sardonically enquired:

What are the opponents of this Bill afraid of? They cannot be

---

[22] He added that 'judging from a bizarre conversation I once had privately with [Sir Cyril Osborne] . . . the curbs placed on his infantile masturbatory activities were so intimidating that he was thereafter compelled to protect himself from further danger by removing all temptation from the British scene. This was a formidable task. . . .' (Leo Abse: *op. cit.* pp. 147–8, 153.)

afraid that these disgusting practices will be thrown upon their attention, because these acts are legalised only if they are performed in private. They cannot be afraid that there will be a corruption of youth, because these acts will be legalised only if they are performed between consenting adults. . . . I can only suppose [she concluded with withering disdain] that the opponents of this Bill will be afraid that their imagination will be tormented by visions of what will be going on elsewhere. Surely, if that is so, that is their own private misfortune, and no reason for imposing their personal standards of taste and morality on the minority of their fellow citizens who can find sexual satisfaction only in relations with their own sex.

The Lords gave the Bill a Second Reading by 111 votes to 48.

On Third Reading Lord Arran – because, he said, it was 'a little occasion' – made a speech of which he was very proud. I know, because when he showed it me in his handwritten draft, and I tried to dissuade him from saying some of the things in it, he was quite hurt. Of course he deserved his valedictory moment, after all his prodigious and exhausting labours; but the purple plushness of his prose, as Lord Annan has said,[23] made some of his supporters wince. Because of the Bill, he said, perhaps a million human beings would be able to live in greater peace. 'I find this an awesome and marvellous thing.' On his release from Reading Gaol, Oscar Wilde had said: 'Yes, we shall win in the end; but the road will be long and red with monstrous martyrdoms.' He was right: the road had been long, and the martyrdoms many, monstrous and bloody. 'Today, please God! sees the end of that road.'

Listening to this effusion, which sounded even more embarrassing than it had looked on paper, I was already feeling queasy. Worse was to come:

I ask one thing and I ask it earnestly. I ask those who have, as it were, been in bondage and for whom the prison doors are now open to show their thanks by comporting themselves quietly and with dignity. This is no occasion for jubilation; certainly not for celebration. Any form of ostentatious behaviour now, or in the future, any form of public flaunting, would be utterly distasteful and would, I believe, make the sponsors of the Bill regret that

[23] *Our Age* p. 135.

they have done what they have done. Homosexuals must continue to remember that while there may be nothing bad in being a homosexual, there is certainly nothing good. Lest the opponents of the Bill think that a new freedom, a new privileged class, has been created, let me remind them that no amount of legislation will prevent homosexuals from being the subject of dislike and derision or at best of pity. We shall always, I fear, resent the odd man out. That is their burden for all time, and they must shoulder it like men – for men they are.

I did not merely wince at this frightful stuff; I almost puked, and scarcely heard Boofy's generous tribute to myself 'as having done more than any single man to bring this social problem to the notice of the public',[24] together with Leo Abse 'the lion-hearted', Sir John Wolfenden, Kenneth Robinson, Humphry Berkeley and other parliamentary campaigners for the reform.

The Lords passed the Bill without a division, and it received the Royal Assent on 27 July 1967.

---

[24] Did he, I wondered, think of himself as having done more than any other married man?

X

'Meanwhile, Back at the Ranch . . .'

'Nothing fails like success.'

Leo Abse

'When success comes, something is sure to go which leaves success a different thing from what was dreamt of.'

J. M. Robertson

The law was changed at last. Homosexual law reform had reached the Statute Book. Naturally we were elated, and only insulated temporarily from the physical effects of exhaustion by the heady wine of victory. But for the HLRS it was a limited victory; the Act as drafted departed restrictively in important respects from the Wolfenden recommendations, and all our efforts to secure its liberalisation had been firmly squashed by Leo Abse, who was convinced that the changes we sought would jeopardise the Bill's chances in the Commons. While acknowledging some of the new law's shortcomings, he wanted no more public discussion or action on what he felt was now an overworked topic. Lord Arran, notwithstanding his 'victory speech', told me that he saw the new Act as a holding measure to be improved upon.

As the late Professor Peter Richards pointed out,[1] it had been a feature of the debates that

> the fundamental moral issue was consistently avoided. Why have homosexual acts been regarded as abominable and depraved? . . . Clearly, it was not in the interests of the reformers to raise contentious issues of this sort. Their task was to arouse Christian compassion, not Christian controversy. Their tactic was to keep public

[1] Peter G. Richards, *Parliament and Conscience* (Allen & Unwin, 1970) p. 82.

and parliamentary debate as rational as possible because of the danger that an upsurge of emotion and prejudice would ruin their chance of success.

Certainly, where the HLRS was concerned, we were a 'single issue' organisation, our widely dissimilar supporters uniting only in their conviction that – whatever their favoured reasons – the existing law was bad and needed to be changed. There was no 'party line' as to the nature of homosexuality, or the 'correct' attitude towards it; nor could there have been.

My own view was that a better piece of legislation could have been achieved in the 1960s as easily as the Arran/Abse Act, because the vehemence and volume of opposition to any reform at all remained constant, regardless of the detail of what was being proposed. Once assured of a parliamentary majority for the principle of change, Arran and Abse could have secured concessions from the Home Office on a number of the points which worried us, if they had been so inclined. But they were too busy placating the implacable. I knew that some provisions of the new Act were severely disappointing to most of our supporters, and feared that the new law, if restrictively applied, would prolong social difficulties and cause some individual tragedies. I also foresaw that many homosexual people, then and later, would lay much of the blame for this at the HLRS' door. I was to be proved right in all these respects.

These, however, were matters for the future. Before turning to post-1967 events, I will briefly retrace my steps through the peak campaigning years of 1965–1967, in case anyone gets the impression, from the two previous chapters, that all we were doing in those days was talking with MPs and Peers and sitting in the public galleries of Parliament twiddling our thumbs as the lengthy series of debates proceeded.

Nothing could be further from the truth. Looking at my diaries for those years gives me a sense of breathlessness, even now. Almost every day was crammed with a succession of appointments, meetings, and formal and informal discussions with a wide variety of people, not only about law reform but concerning the growing interests and activities of the Albany Trust, which did not stand still during this time. Joy Blanchard and her stalwart staff, which for a few months in the winter of 1965–1966 numbered seven, worked at a cracking pace to keep abreast of the constantly rising volume of work. While some of this resulted from our own initiatives and efforts, much was generated by the high level of media and public interest in homosexuality sparked off by the parliamentary debates.

Keeping our supporters informed of what was going on, and how they could help, was one high priority. *Spectrum* frequently exhorted supporters to speak or write to their MPs about the Bill, both at general election times and while the debates were in progress. They were regularly appealed to for money, our finances remaining in a constant state of crisis throughout the campaign. And their criticisms of the details of the Bill, often couched quite fiercely, had to be heard and responded to as emolliently as possible – sometimes with an effort, when we personally agreed with them! Some were so disgusted with what they rightly saw as typically British sloppy thinking and absence of integrity in dealing realistically with sexual matters ('a tradition of hypocrisy and sadism, masquerading under the guise of piety', said one) that they urged the HLRS to disown the Bill, which we obviously could not do. But, as I have described, we did press Leo Abse strongly, though unavailingly, to improve the provisions relating to the age of consent, privacy, procuring and the danger of conspiracy charges.

It was galling to be working flat out to mobilise Abse's vote, acting as his unofficial whips' office, analysing MPs' voting records and so forth, while he turned a deaf ear to our pleas for a better Bill. But we had no alternative. Abse himself actually made a virtue of his unsympathetic treatment of us. In his political autobiography *Private Member*[2] he asserts that

> the legislator is inviting failure, or, worse, a disastrous piece of legislation if he becomes the puppet of any lobby, even one as sophisticated as the Homosexual Law Reform Society whose strength is dependent upon its blinkers: total vision would weaken the will of any organised lobby.

There are blinkers and blinkers. Without claiming 'total vision' for myself, Abse's use of what were on his own admission some 'highly selective' psychological arguments in making his case (without, he hoped, embracing 'intellectual corruption'), and his constant insist-

[2] p. 154.

ence that MPs' 'irrational fears which otherwise could have overspilled and totally engulfed the Bill'[3] could only be overcome by a policy of retreat, appeasement and compromise, smacked somewhat to me of what Freudians call projection.

Yet another set of blinkers impeded many of our supporters; far from recognising the difficulties of our position vis-à-vis the parliamentary sponsors, or the tact we had to muster in dealing with them, the troops fondly imagined that all the HLRS had to do was zoom through the opposition like a hot knife through butter. Would that it had been so! In fact at this stage our main arguments were with our sponsors. For all Leo Abse's superior tactical knowledge, and Lord Arran's overanxious deference to the Home Office, the HLRS and the Albany Trust, by virtue of the human documents who continually approached them for help, undoubtedly knew far more than either MP or Earl did about the actual impact of the law on people's lives; and some of our ideas for improving matters, legislatively and otherwise, were sounder than theirs.

Yet in the circumstances all we could do was to stifle our chagrin at a lost opportunity that was unlikely to recur in the foreseeable future, and buckle to in drumming up support. One way in which we did this was to enlist the signatures of more than 500 senior members of leading institutions in academic and professional life to a short memorial to the Prime Minister, urging the Government to implement the recommendations of the Wolfenden Committee without further delay. This sounds a simple task, and the resulting document looked unpretentious. In fact, we hired two extra pairs of secretarial hands for about six weeks to devote themselves exclusively to the massive chore of mailing hundreds of letters to this distinguished array. These two ladies were, I remember, quite impressively efficient and enthusiastic people, and we were only sorry that when their allotted task was complete we could not afford to keep them on the staff permanently. The memorialists included Church leaders of several denominations; Fellows of the Royal Society and the British Academy; University Vice-Chancellors, Heads of Colleges, and departmental Professors (especially in departments of law and criminology, sociology, psychology and psychiatry); and staff at many medical teaching and

[3] Leo Abse, *British Journal of Criminology*, January 1968, pp. 86–87.

research institutions. We had hoped to be allowed to present the memorial to Harold Wilson in person; however, it was graciously received from us on his behalf in February 1966 by the Home Secretary, Roy Jenkins, who used the occasion to express his pleasure at the near prospect of homosexual law reform. An inter-university students' petition in favour of reform, bearing several thousand signatures, was also presented to the Commons.

Throughout the parliamentary debates of 1965–1967 public discussion of homosexuality steadily increased in volume, with resulting heavy demands upon the HLRS for speakers, articles and television and radio broadcasts. I undertook much of this work myself, although other executive committee members also participated from time to time, especially Mr Rolph and Dr Neustatter. It was strenuous, but worthwhile; we never lost a single university union or other debate, usually winning the vote by handsome majorities. Editorial support also grew. As early as July 1964, the *Daily Telegraph* considered that

> there can be no longer be any doubt that the moral corruption which follows from the attempt to punish homosexual vice between consenting adults is greater than that which would follow from the abolition of this law. It should be abolished.

This theme was taken up and reiterated by the great majority of national and provincial newspapers as the campaign went on. The growing intensity of the publicity we were receiving resulted in an upsurge of casework which became increasingly time-consuming for Joy Blanchard and myself as the parliamentary campaign reached its climax. Although funds were still inadequate – in 1966, at the height of the parliamentary work, the Society and Trust together were assured of only a third of their modest £9000 budgeted annual expenditure – the executive committee and Albany Trust trustees decided that it was essential to appoint a full-time social caseworker, and in April 1967 Mrs Doreen Cordell joined the staff. She had training and experience in welfare and youth work, and had just returned with her husband from a period in Australia. An energetic and tireless worker, Doreen soon raised the Albany Trust's casework to a new pitch and made it even better known amongst social workers than it already was, with the result that after the law was reformed the numbers approaching the Trust for help more than doubled, from 240 people in 1967 to over 500 in 1968.

Our settled policy was to act solely as a referral agency, and not to become involved in long-term counselling with our clients. But we frequently found that there was no suitable referral resource available, and so we did have a sizeable proportion of people who were repeatedly visiting or otherwise in touch with us. Unfortunately, Doreen's zeal was not always tempered with a realistic grasp of the Trust's precarious situation; she perceived the needs of her clients as so pressing that she refused to contemplate the very real danger of overstretching our inadequate resources, and would never willingly agree to limit her caseload. Consequently my relations with her were not always as smooth and mutually supportive as those which I was accustomed to have with Joy, and this caused severe difficulties for the Trust at a later stage.

The growing caseload added urgency to our quest for support for the psychosexual clinic project originally proposed by Dr Rodney Long and developed by Hope Malik's research. She had industriously interviewed a wide range of professionally interested people and groups in medicine, psychiatry and the churches, and had assembled an impressive array of verbal support for the idea. In August 1965 Mr Rolph and I had a friendly meeting with Douglas Houghton,[4] the Chancellor of the Duchy of Lancaster, who expressed his strong personal support for the idea and promised to commend it to the Minister of Health, which he duly did; but they were unable to hold out any prospect of Government funding. As proved to be the case with so many of the Albany Trust's socially useful projects, all these fine words buttered no bank accounts, and the solid cash support required to launch the clinic never materialised. So we soldiered on, gradually creating a national network of friendly professional contacts, many of whom generously saw our out-of-London clients at no charge outside their working hours. Eva Bene offered to undertake another research project, at no cost to us, into the experiences of men and women who had undergone various types of medical and psychological treatment because of their homosexuality. The results of this would, we thought, be of significant help in planning the priorities for a clinic.

The social side of the Albany Trust's work led to my involvement

---

[4] Later Lord Houghton of Sowerby, and in his nineties still the doughtiest libertarian in the House of Lords.

in a variety of sympathetic outside agencies. Meetings with the Vicar of St Martin-in-the-Fields, the Rev. Austen Williams, resulted in my joining the executive committee of the Voluntary Hostels Conference[5] which was concerned with the homeless, and it was through VHC that I met Hope Malik. Another local involvement was with St Anne's, Soho, where Fr Kenneth Leech[6] was resident curate. Exceptionally erudite, and also very humane and approachable, Ken was (and is) one of the best informed people in this country about drugs and the drug-using culture, and his job in Soho was no sinecure, even in those days. With Ken, his future wife Brenda Jordan, and Judith Piepe, a church social worker attached to St Anne's who had a warm sympathy towards young people (and not least young homosexuals), I spent many late nights into the small hours sitting talking and sometimes dancing in the Soho coffee clubs – usually 'Le Duce' presided over by the mysterious Geoffrey Worthington – frequented by the much-maligned 'permissive young'. Far from being the selfish, callous and amoral lot depicted in the 1980s by jaundiced politicians as the cause of all Britain's subsequent ills, they struck me (with a few exceptions) as friendly, gentle, sincere and caring girls and boys who were mercifully far less conventional, censorious and prim than my generation had been.

Another dear friend whom I made through involvement in Soho was Anna Harper. She materialised in the Shaftesbury Avenue office one day early in 1967 – and 'materialised' is the word, as Anna never weighed less than seventeen stone while I knew her, and at one time tipped the scales at over twenty stone. (She was a 'food junkie', and become diabetic, dying in 1983 at the early age of sixty-three.) Anna was a remarkable person in many respects. Married to a cheerful though chronically unwell husband, Hughie, she lived in a large house in Sussex Square, Brighton, where she had quite by chance – or, as she would say, led by the Lord – become involved in rescuing young heroin addicts from a drifting life on the beach, providing accommodation for them in one of her flats. She led her life entirely by impulse, and her 'God-guided' climb up the stairs to our office began one of the most loving, supportive mutual friendships I have experienced outside my immediate family. Anna was up in London that day for

[5] Which later became the National Association of Voluntary Hostels.
[6] Who was later to be Race Relations Officer to the Church of England's Board for Social Responsibility, and Director of the Runnymede Trust.

a meeting of an anti-drug abuse group which contained some very straitlaced members, including Sir Cyril Black, so it is not surprising that I treated her a bit warily at first. But we soon discovered a deep appreciation of each other's personalities and mutual social work interests. Anna was entirely sympathetic to young gay people, as was Judith Piepe; they were two of the kindest and wisest of our 'resource people' for those beset by personal unhappiness – in both cases not so much because of any formal qualification, but because of the sort of people they *were*, and their wide experience of life.

Through St Martin-in-the-Fields and my membership of VHC's Council I made other valuable new religious and social work contacts, among them the saintly Anton Wallich-Clifford, who had left probation work to serve society's drop-outs more directly through the Simon Community he had founded; Mary Hamilton, the formidable, warm-hearted Bow Street senior probation officer; Austin Williams of the Roman Catholic St Martin of Tours House; the Methodist minister, Martin Atkinson; and Dr Erica Jones, whom Martin later married. All were supportive of the Albany Trust's work, as was a gentle, kindly Salvation Army colonel, Col Bovan. Through him, I was invited to address the senior officers of the Salvation Army, headed by the Commissioner, at their Broadstairs retreat in the autumn of 1966. The 'Sally Ann' was not noted for its tolerance of homosexuality, though I had found its members taking their collecting boxes through the crowded Amsterdam gay bars one Christmas, and I was rather nervous as to the reception which awaited me. However, I was entertained to a most pleasant lunch – after which the Commissioner suggested to the ladies that they 'might care to take a little walk along the front,' while I talked about a topic unsuited to their ears! I glanced out of the window; lowering black clouds were gathering over the cliffs, and I could not help thinking that the rainstorm which obviously awaited the ladies might discomfit them more than my highly dangerous plea for Christian understanding and compassion for homosexuals.

Another newly developing area during these years was the emergence, in 1964, of a fledgling 'homophile'[7] movement. Since the early 1950s organisations of openly homosexual men and women had

---

[7] 'Homophile' is a term which came into favour amongst gay rights activists during the 1960s and 1970s, in preference to 'homosexual', because its use of the Greek-rooted suffix '-phil' emphasised the loving nature of same-sex relationships.

existed in the United States, although American laws were as prohibitive as ours in almost every State of the Union. But their different legal and political traditions made it possible for such groups to organise and publish their viewpoints in ways which I do not believe would have been legally possible or politically tolerated in Britain before law reform became a live issue.

The first openly homophile group to be started in Britain was for women. In March 1964, *Spectrum* welcomed the appearance of a new monthly magazine, *Arena Three*, dealing with various aspects of lesbianism.

> So far [we commented], female homosexuality has received scant attention in public discussion of the homosexual situation – and when it is referred to, one is frequently assured by the 'experts' that it scarcely exists. The 'public images' of the lesbian, according to *Arena Three*, are varied and mostly somewhat bizarre; the truth, it suggests, is that lesbians are both more common and less freakish than most people imagine.

Arena Three had been launched by Esmé Langley, a middle-aged, wiry, grey-haired, bespectacled woman with a pawky sense of humour whom I came to like very much. By a coincidence Esmé and her then partner, Diana Chapman, lived in the same road that my partner and I did – Broadhurst Gardens, West Hampstead. We inhabited opposite ends, and in the middle had lodged at the turn of the century (in a house demolished by bomb damage during the second world war) Frederick Rolfe, 'Baron Corvo'. So with some justification Esmé and I used to say that we lived in Queer Street; Broadhurst Gardens certainly deserves at least one pink plaque, if not three.[8] Some mornings on my way to Shaftesbury Avenue I would call in on Esmé, to find her in her basement flat typing busily away surrounded by piles of letters from '*A3*' readers seeking advice and help; although unpaid and single-handed, she was soon running an advisory service for lesbian women practically full time, as well as producing *Arena Three*.

Such a state of affairs could not continue for long. Doreen Cordell and I did our best to help Esmé out; although the Albany Trust's scope of work was, strictly speaking, limited to promoting the psychological

---

[8] At nos. 47, 69 and 121. Indeed, there should be a fourth, at 119, where the late Laurence Collinson lived for some years.

health of *men*, we had never been able to restrict ourselves to this entirely, and there had always been a small proportion of women amongst our caseload. Now the arrival of *Arena Three* pointed up the need. Not being hamstrung, as were homosexual men, by the law, *A3* soon developed into a social group, and the 'Minorities Research Group' was also formed to encourage research into lesbianism, assisting Eva Bene, Charlotte Wolff and other researchers with volunteers for their projects and in other ways. MRG was the earliest gay women's group, and also the earliest overtly homophile group of any kind, in this country; other lesbian groups, such as Kenric and Sappho, which became larger and longer-lasting, soon appeared, but it is to Esmé Langley that the trail-blazing accolade is due.

In October 1964 the first local group supporting law reform was established in Manchester. The North-Western Homosexual Law Reform Committee came into being largely through the personal initiative and persistent efforts of Allan Horsfall, a Labour councillor in Bolton,[9] who was fortunate in obtaining an able chairman for the group in the Manchester Diocesan Social Worker, Colin Harvey.[10] Though it had a similarly wide-ranging list of local patrons to the HLRS' Honorary Committee, nearly all NWHLRC's active committee members were homosexual, among them some young men who were impatient with what they regarded as the pussyfooting of the HLRS. The emergence of the NWHLRC evoked an ambivalent response within the HLRS executive committee. Leo Abse, always alarmist about the counterproductive effects of any attempts by homosexuals to take their fate into their own hands, was hostile to any such development. I felt that it was better, at this stage of the law reform campaign, to encourage the North-Western group to affiliate to the

[9] In *Radical Records*, ed. Cant & Hemmings (Routledge, 1988), Allan Horsfall tells how he pioneered the NWHLRC's campaign from his Lancashire miner's cottage home. His neighbours in the local mining community took it all quite calmly; the Labour Party's Miners' Union-sponsored MPs were a lot more nervous.

[10] Colin was an extremely courageous person. Severely lame, he never allowed his disability to impair his energy and good humour. His presence as Chair in the early days of NWHLRC was invaluable, because his conventionally acceptable manner cloaked a strongly radical approach to social problems; he was in advance of his time in believing in an 'enabling' attitude to self-help, in contrast to the prevailing paternalism and 'soup-kitchen' stance usually adopted by heterosexual professionals towards homosexuals. After leaving Manchester for Glasgow, Colin performed a similar enabling role in the early days of the Scottish Minorities Group (later the Scottish Homosexual Rights Group).

HLRS rather than to have them completely out on a limb. But either way, I realised that it would be impossible to control their sayings and doings, even had I wished to – which I did not. They did not affiliate, and relations between the Albany Trust and the NWHLR (later the Campaign for Homosexual Equality) later became strained, though my personal contacts with Horsfall and Harvey remained friendly.

A second local Homosexual Law Reform Committee was set up in the West Midlands in 1966 by Ivan Geffen, a Walsall solicitor whom I had met through our common involvement in the National Council for Civil Liberties. Ivan was an energetic and fearless fighter for individuals' rights, and never refused a challenging case; he was a stalwart legal resource for us in the Black Country. The WMHLRC, however, was a dissimilar body from that in Manchester: there were fewer active committee members, and it was mainly a useful platform for Ivan and a few others to write to the press and address meetings in support of the Bill's parliamentary progress.

XI

American Allies

'If you write a book about us, I bet you'll call it
"I'm Glad They Had a Revolution".'

Zelda Suplee

Our growing contacts were international. Besides keeping in touch
with the Dutch COC we established friendly contact with the French
homophile organisation 'Arcadie', the deputy editor of whose magazine, a scholarly and charming Parisian who used the pen-name 'Marc
Daniel', frequently visited London. Arcadie was presided over by
André Baudry, an earnest, paternalistic Catholic ex-priest. When I
attended Arcadie's twentieth anniversary celebrations in 1973 it was
interesting to compare the differing styles of the various national
organisations with our own by then visible and vocal, but more frag-
mented, British homophile movement.

We were also having much more communication with various
people in the United States. American tourists visiting London found
32 Shaftesbury Avenue a mere two minutes away from Piccadilly
Circus, and frequently dropped in with greetings from the Mattachine
Society, One Inc. of Los Angeles, the Daughters of Bilitis and other
US homophile organisations. They were impressed, and even envious,
at the progress we seemed to be making towards law reform. As I
explained to them, in some ways it was easier for us as we had only
one Parliament (however awkward) to deal with, while they were
confronted with fifty separate State legislatures.

Two out-of-the-ordinary American visitors were a rich, bearded
Southern businessman, Reed Erickson, and his elegant wife, Aileen.
They brought me a copy of a long-playing record, 'Homosexuality in
America', which, while something of a breakthrough I suppose, was
portentously solemn to a laughable degree. Reed (who, I subsequently

138

learned, was a female-to-male transsexual, having been a patient of the pioneer of transsexual therapy, Dr Harry Benjamin)[1] was subsidising One Inc. and a number of other educational and research ventures in the sexuality field through his own charitable foundation, the Erickson Educational Foundation.

Another American link was the Council on Religion and the Homosexual, which had been founded as the result of a ground-breaking residential seminar organised in May 1964 by the Rev. Ted McIlvenna of the US Methodist Church's Board of Education, who was then director of the San Francisco Young Adult Project, and became CRH's first president.[2] Ted, together with Dr John Gagnon of the (Kinsey) Institute for Sex Research at the University of Indiana, and a number of other American clergy and lay people, was in Europe during the summer of 1966, and requested the Albany Trust to organise an Anglo-American Consultation on the Church, Society and the Homosexual. Even though the HLRS was in the thick of the parliamentary battle, I persuaded the Trustees that this was sufficiently important for the Trust to undertake.

The three-day Consultation, held at a London hotel with about sixty participants, was a memorable event. I was invited to be its chairman. We recruited a good cross-section of British clergy and lay people from several denominations – not only those who were already actively helping the Trust, and not all of them necessarily sympathetic to 'liberal' attitudes. The American contingent were an impressive bunch. Six papers were presented, and there were several hours of group discussion, with a concluding session of 'reactions' from a panel of six people.[3] It is indicative of the prevailing climate that, although

[1] Author of *The Transsexual Phenomenon* (Julian Press, New York, 1966).

[2] The report of this event still makes moving reading, 'Forget who you represent. We represent the human race. Let's start there', said Ted McIlvenna in his opening address. This was typical of his inspiringly informal, innovative approach.

[3] The proceedings were not published, though there is a record of the papers and reactions in the Albany Trust's files. The papers read were: 'Demythologising the Homosexual', by Dr Alfred A. Gross, Executive Director of the George W. Henry Foundation, New York; 'The Sociological Perspective on Homosexuality' by Dr John H. Gagnon and William Simon, Institute of Sex Research, University of Indiana; '"Towards a Quaker View of Sex" – Three Years Later', by Keith Wedmore; 'The Churches' Responsibility Towards the Homosexual', by Canon Douglas Rhymes; 'The Homosexual's Experience of the Churches', by Donald Lucas, Director of CRH; 'The Social Worker and the Homosexual', by Douglas Gibson, Secretary of the Central Council of Probation Officers.

the Consultation was entirely private, Ted McIlvenna stressed in opening the proceedings that those who were homosexually orientated
would not be expected to say so, because 'that would be too difficult'.
Even so, the quality of both the prepared papers and the informal
discussions provided welcome relief from the sterilities of Parliament.
The general tone of the papers was refreshingly modern; it is in fact
surprising to realise that these things were said over a quarter of a
century ago.

The problem of the homosexual in modern society, said Gagnon
and Simon, did not stand alone but was part of the general problem
of societies which have shifted not only from country to city, but from
city to megalopolis; it was part of the problem of what is the good
and proper life in a world where the surrounding society is increasingly
man-made. In this kind of world, the role of sexuality and of physical
contact between persons was bound to be an evolving one. Keith
Wedmore, one of the authors of the controversial pamphlet *Towards
a Quaker View of Sex*, and a strong HLRS supporter,[4] commented
that even though Quakers, who abhorred insincerity and hypocrisy,
recognised that these attitudes were at their height in relation to sexual
matters, his group had been astonished at the uproar which their work
had sparked off.[5]

> It is a very odd thing, you know, that if you produce a statement
> on sexual matters which is unintentionally ambiguous and is cap-
> able of being interpreted either in a promiscuous way or in a
> restrained and more chaste way, it is always the first interpretation
> which is placed upon it by the lustful public.

[4] A barrister friend of Andrew Hallidie Smith, he was assistant treasurer of the
HLRS, and later chairman of its successor, the Sexual Law Reform Society.

[5] *Towards a Quaker View of Sex*, ed. Alastair Heron (Friends' Home Service
Committee, 1963, revised edn, 1964), was at once temperate and forthright. One of its
characteristically sensible observations was: 'Surely it is the nature and quality of a
relationship that matters; one must not judge it by its outward appearance but by its inner
worth. Homosexual affection can be as selfless as heterosexual affection, and therefore
we cannot see that it is in some way morally worse.' *Towards a Quaker View of Sex* was
one of the earliest statements of the 'New Morality' which became a focus of fierce
controversy in the 1960s. Another was the Rt Rev. A. T. Robinson, Bishop of Woolwich's
book *Honest to God*, which sought to cut through traditional concepts of God and locate
him in 'the ground of our being'. Despite its contemptuous dismissal by traditionalists as
'the old immorality writ large', the New Morality provided a rallying point for those
who believed that Christianity, and religion generally, required a more up-to-date and
intellectually respectable face.

The group had found themselves unable to say that every homosexual act was sinful; irrespective of whether a relationship was heterosexual or homosexual, the criteria for judging it must have to do with its nature and quality, its unselfishness or otherwise, the real concern and insight, care and tenderness which the parties brought to each other. Such a moral code was more difficult, because less clear, than the existing 'conventional' one, which was no longer widely accepted, believed in or practised.

In his closing reactions Ted McIlvenna said that, despite all the genuine concern manifested at the Consultation, he was troubled by the difficulty which so many well-meaning pastoral advisers evidently experienced in simply *accepting* the homosexual.

> I happen to believe that the only thing Christian faith has to say that is significant and distinctive is an unqualified 'yes' to man. Forgiveness is continuous, and does not depend upon our state of righteousness at the moment.

If the social sciences had taught us anything, it was that people were lonely; 'and I think the number one problem now and in the days ahead is and will be loneliness'.

In my own concluding remarks I echoed this sentiment by pointing out that any adequate counsellor had to face the fact that most human beings, whether homosexual or heterosexual, desired, and would attempt to have, sexual experiences which were satisfying, both physically and emotionally. Most of the problems we encountered at the Albany Trust concerned their inability to do so, rather than overindulgence or promiscuity. I quoted a moving letter which we had received from an eighty-six-year-old homosexual who said:

> It may be that homosexuality has become in general as bad as Viscount Dilhorne declared it to be . . . it was in my glowing time of spring accompanied by an affectionate decency. . . . I would say to any homosexual (if I knew any now), 'Be true to yourself: Why should you be more ashamed of your homosexual inclinations than your sisters? . . . . Be strong; be men. It is not going with women that makes one a man. It is a certain inner integrity.'

And I cited a much younger homosexual's recent expression of 'extreme irritation' at the constant need for evasion and disguise over a personal trait than which, when satisfactorily in love, they cannot conceive of a different or greater happiness. . . . There is a creative urge common to all degrees and kinds of love [this wise young man added], the feeling that out of a relationship *something* good must come.[6]

If the Consultation helped to convince more church people of the respectability, responsibility and cogency of their concern for the homosexual, it would have performed a most valuable service, I concluded. But as with so many of our initiatives there was no immediate or effective follow-through by others.

These transatlantic contacts with Reed Erickson, Ted McIlvenna, John Gagnon and Dorr Legg of One Inc. resulted in an invitation for me to visit the United States for a coast-to-coast visit and lecture tour in the autumn of 1967, sponsored by One Inc. and the Erickson Educational Foundation. The Americans were eager to hear about the recent passage into law of the Sexual Offences Act, and I was of course eager to see America and to meet as many new allies as I could there. So the HLRS executive committee and Albany Trustees kindly agreed to my going, and on a Monday in late October 1967 I set off on what was to prove the most hectic four weeks of my life.

The day after my arrival in New York started with a press conference where I first met someone who was to become another dear friend – Zelda Suplee, who worked for Erickson and was an enthusiast for many causes – not least nudism. Zelda was a short, dumpy white haired grandmother of phenomenal energy who became my publicity agent and general 'fixer' for the trip. She wore that day, I remember, a vivid green dress with a large badge pinned to her bosom proclaiming (or inviting) 'PRESS'. The first question from a radio reporter was almost inevitable: was I a homosexual? Wary of the implications for my entry visa, I half-humourously pleaded the Fifth Amendment.

There followed four crowded New York days of press interviews, radio broadcasts, and formal and informal meetings with editors, lawyers, psychologists (including Kinsey's senior collaborator, Wardell Pomeroy), and clergy. Luckily untypical was the first radio programme the day after my arrival, when I found myself taking part with Zelda and a fanatical Catholic anti-pornography campaigner in the Barry Farber Show. This was live and unscripted; I anticipated

[6] 'Anthony Rowley', *Another Kind of Loving* (Axle Spokes).

the usual British style ten-minute spot, but just before going on the air I blithely asked Farber how long we would be 'live' and was staggered to be told 'three hours'. And indeed we were, getting through somehow by Zelda reminiscing at length about her experiences running a nudist camp, and letting the anti-smut gent talk interminably. (He came up with such gems as 'some pornography is highly dangerous – it even excites *me*'.)

My first encounter with some of America's homophile leaders was at a 'harmony dinner' which proved far from harmonious – they squabbled quite fiercely amongst themselves and there was obviously no love lost between some of the people present. I then went on the air once again – this time with Dr Irving Bieber, a psychoanalyst who had carried out an elaborate research proving to his own satisfaction that all homosexuals were sick. Accordingly, he was the current *bête noir* of the homophiles, who I think were disappointed that I did not weigh into him half as rudely as they tackled one another.[7]

Dorr Legg[8] and I flew from New York to Chicago, via Detroit, where we had a stopover lunch with some One Inc. members. This was my first experience of an American 'banquet' – a kind of glorified rotary lunch, with no better if more plentiful food. In Chicago I encountered the extraordinary Paul Goldman, an elderly Jewish lawyer, influential in the city, who was President of One of Chicago, which he had taken under his wing in extrovertly Jewish patriarchal style. He solemnly informed me that he wished the group would have 'nice meetings where they play bridge, and don't talk sex, so I can take my wife and family'. I also visited *Playboy Magazine*, though I did not meet Hugh Hefner. But I did deliver my lecture on 'Sex, Morality and Happiness' from a pulpit in an impressive episcopalian church, where I was disconcerted to be introduced by a tenor solo rendering of 'God Save Our Gracious Queen'. (Again, I silently pleaded the Fifth Amendment.) Although I met some very nice people there, Chicago struck me as a vulgarly opulent town with some miserable slums on its outskirts, and I was not sorry to get away.

[7] But I am an unrepentant believer in the old North Country wisdom that 'you catch more flies with honey than with vinegar'.

[8] A tall, scholarly, late middle-aged man of deceptively dour appearance who chaperoned me across the States. As I got to know him better I discovered that he had an engagingly dry sense of humour.

We went on to Indiana University at Bloomington – a 'medium-sized' American Campus of about 25,000 students – where the Kinsey Institute for Sex Research was situated, for two days of discussions with the Institute's director, Dr Paul Gebhard, John Gagnon, Bill Simon and other colleagues. I formed the impression that the Institute was languishing, with grant cuts and the impending departure of John and Bill. The library contained a remarkable collection of sexual objects, sculpture and other memorabilia, as well as books, collected from all over the world.

Then back to Chicago airport to catch the Los Angeles flight. I stayed in Hollywood, which oozed wealth but struck me as uninteresting seaside suburbia. I lectured to an audience of over a hundred at One Inc.'s headquarters – which were a considerable surprise, being spacious and very well equipped with a lounge, library and large auditorium; quite a clubhouse, in fact. I had a few glimpses of West Coast eccentricity in LA. One I vividly recall was after a television appearance I made as a panel member sitting on a platform facing a ranged auditorium. After the transmission a formidable matron impressively clad in purple silk and wearing an elaborate hat descended upon me and announced, grim-faced: 'Mr Grey, I am a member of the American Mothers' Temperance Union', at which I blenched, expecting a vitriolic attack. 'Are you going to Washington?' she demanded sternly. I timidly admitted that I was. 'Well,' she said with a triumphant air of inside knowledge, 'you simply *must* go to Leon's, between 17th and 18th streets. It's the best gay bar in Town, and I'm known as Mother of the Flock.' Even the usually unflappable Dorr Legg burst out laughing.

San Francisco was already well on the way to becoming the 'gay capital' of America. I always think of that scenically beautiful and exhilarating city and the kind people I met there with the greatest affection, tinged now with deep sadness because of the suffering and death which AIDS has brought to the city's gay community. I met Ted McIlvenna again, addressed another hundred-strong audience at his Glide Memorial Church, and visited the offices of the Council on Religion and the Homosexual. Another 'character' I met in San Francisco was Captain Elliott Blackstone, a burly senior community cop whose task it was to police the Tenderloin vice district. He came straight out of the Hollywood cast-list of tough, avuncular, warm-

SIR JOHN WOLFENDEN. Proposed reform.
(Courtesy Hulton Picture Company)

A. E. DYSON. Founded the Homosexual Law Reform Society.

C. H. ROLPH. Wise chairman.
(Courtesy John Vickers)

J. B. PRIESTLEY and JACQUETTA
HAWKES. Stalwart executive committee members.
(Courtesy Norman May's Studio)

H.L.R.S. PRESS ADVERTISEMENTS.
Appealed to reason and compassion.

EIGHTH EARL OF ARRAN. *Noblesse Oblige* in the Lords.
(Courtesy Hulton Picture Company)

LEO ABSE MP. Deft tactics in the Commons.

'What I particularly admired about the debate was the way that every speaker managed to give the impression that he personally had never met a homosexual in his life.'

1.vii.60

HOW THE CARTOONISTS SAW IT.
Osbert Lancaster (1.vii.60).
(Courtesy Exors of Sir Osbert Lancaster and John Murray (Publishers) Ltd)

Trog (16.v.65). *(Courtesy Wally Fawkes and the Observer)*

As a great reforming Government, Abse, we'd like to sponsor it but we feel that acts committed in private should be dealt with by a Private Member's Bill.

THE AUTHOR. Amsterdam, 1963.

BOB ANGELO (right) and English friend, Amsterdam, 1963.

LEN SMITH. Bravely gave his address.

DR CHARLOTTE WOLFF. Pioneered research.
(Courtesy Michael Ann Mullen)

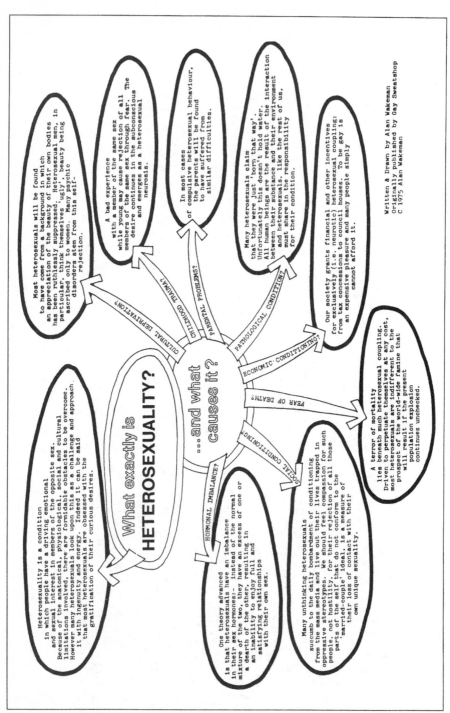

"WHAT EXACTLY . . . ." Gay Liberationist use of satire.
(Courtesy Alan Wakeman)

hearted guardians of the law. He said to me in his deep bass growl: 'If a kid's brought in to me, I say to him "I don't give a damn whether you're a homosexual, a transsexual, a drag queen, or whatever. What I want is that if you're homosexual, you have got to be the best homosexual you can possibly be. Now get out, and mind you don't let me catch you in any trouble."'[9]

In Washington, my next port of call, I did not get to Leon's. I was under the wing of Dr Franklin Kameny, who masterminded the Washington Mattachine Society. So was everyone else, it seemed; Frank was (and still is) a dominant personality, and very knowledgeable. An ex-Government scientist who had been forced to leave the public service when his homosexuality became known, he has devoted his life to campaigning for civil rights for gay people, frequently appearing as advocate at tribunal hearings when servicemen or civilians appeal against their discharge or exclusion from employment because of their sexual orientation. Frank was one of the first to proclaim that 'Gay is Good'.

Back in New York I resumed my busy round, masterminded by the tireless Zelda. I did some more broadcasts, one of them with Lady Gaitskell who was a British delegate at the United Nations and who cooked dinner for me in her apartment before we went to the studio. I talked with the octogenarian Dr Harry Benjamin, and attempted unsuccessfully to converse with his contemporary, Morris Ernst.

This was one of my most bizarre US highlights. Morris Ernst had been a famous liberal lawyer, successfully defending many notable civil rights and censorship cases (Havelock Ellis' *Studies in the Psychology of Sex* and James Joyce's *Ulysses* amongst them). He had written perceptively, in an Introduction to the 1936 edition of Havelock Ellis' *Studies*, that

> when countries go to the Right politically, women go back into the kitchen, books are burned and taboos fence off new frontiers against human adventure.

Naturally I was keen to meet him, and had messages for him from John Calder and others in England. Zelda too was thrilled. 'He was

---

[9] When I got back to London I toyed with the notion of bringing Captain Blackstone over to educate the Metropolitan Police. It was a pity that I never managed it; that would have been a memorable encounter.

one of my father's heroes,' she said. So the appointment was made, and on a rainy afternoon we went to his Fifth Avenue apartment, to be greeted by a wizened, sleepy little old man wearing nothing but a blue bathrobe, protesting that he had not been expecting us until next day.

He and I settled down opposite one another, and Zelda curled up on a settee at the back of the room. I looked forward to a memorable meeting, and indeed it was – but not in the fashion I had anticipated. After a quarter-hour's uninterrupted monologue from our host, I said something. Ernst glared crossly at me and announced: 'I'm not interested in what you've gotta say. Are you going to listen to me, or aren't you?' 'Oh, yes, please do go on,' I stuttered, and fell bemusedly silent for the rest of our visit. I was so traumatised that I do not now recollect anything else he said to me, though I now would like to. When we emerged, still gasping, Zelda said she had almost fallen off the settee. 'If you write a book about us, I bet you'll call it "I'm Glad They Had a Revolution",' she said.

XII

'What More do they Want?'

'A number of [Lord Arran's] supporters . . . felt
that for Our Age matters had ended satisfactorily
and might rest there. But matters never rest.'

Noel Annan, *Our Age*

'You're working yourself out of a job, Mr Grey,' Boofy Arran said to
me in the spring of 1967, some genuine concern mingling with his
satisfaction. I did not agree: three years later I was to write in *Spectrum*
that 'those who have never worked at 32 Shaftesbury Avenue can have
little idea of the pace and pressures continually imposed upon the
staff' (which then consisted of three people besides myself). By achieving law reform we had indeed worked ourselves out of any real prospect of an adequate income to tackle all the demands which would be
made upon the Albany Trust in the immediate future, but we had
certainly not worked ourselves out of a job: indeed at times we felt as
if the roof was falling in.

The office I returned to after my American trip was just as fraught
as it had been when the parliamentary campaign was reaching its
climax. It became even more so; now homosexual people felt there
was a freer climate in which to seek help for their social and emotional
difficulties, their first chosen port of call was the Albany Trust. The
demand was nationwide and in the first twelve months after law
reform the annual number of people approaching the Trust more than
doubled and continued to climb. The chronic lack of competent help
outside London and the large provincial cities brought an incessant
flow of visitors and correspondence from all over Britain.[1] We made
no attempt to advertise our central role – indeed we did not envisage

---

[1] I remember frequent hour-long phone calls over a period of some months from a
totally isolated teenage lesbian in Scotland.

the Trust providing a national counselling service; we saw our job primarily as a catalyst of, and a referral point for, a range of such services which we wished to see established on a regional and local basis. But our hopes that it would be much easier after law reform to stimulate others to take this important social health task on board proved over-sanguine.

During 1968 and 1969 Doreen Cordell and I had a series of meetings with social service departments, church and civic leaders, and voluntary groups such as marriage guidance councils and the Samaritans. Hosted by local Councils of Social Service, we held encouraging discussions in Bristol, Salisbury, Bournemouth, Birmingham and Coventry; early in 1969 we extended our journeyings to Northern Ireland and Scotland.

These meetings were heartening. We found that the publicity which had been generated by the law reform campaign had prepared the ground for a receptive hearing. Our experience had convinced us that the time was ripe for homosexuality and other minority modes of sexual expression to become the acknowledged concern of responsible social workers and counsellors, whether publicly or privately employed. Most of the professional people we met wished to help; many of them became stalwart active supporters of the Trust as a result of our visits. It was somewhat daunting, however, to embark upon a meeting with anything between a dozen and thirty locally influential strangers any of whom might (unknown to us) harbour a strong personal antipathy to homosexuality. I remember one stern looking senior social worker in a provincial city who struck both Doreen and myself as a potentially 'tough nut'. She sat, grim faced, while we stated our case, and made no comment when several of her colleagues began discussing the issue. Finally she announced: 'The trouble with this subject is *the bias*'. We heaved a sigh of relief; she was on our side.

Our three-day stay in Belfast in January 1969, at the invitation of the Northern Irish Mental Health Association and the Samaritans, was ground-breaking both for us and for them. It was my first visit to Ulster. Even in those days, before communal violence had broken out, Belfast was a divided city in somewhat uneasy truce – the BBC and other public buildings were heavily sandbagged. The atmosphere of strong religious sectarianism did not encourage any easy revision of attitudes to 'sins' seen by most Irish Protestants and Catholics alike in terms of biblical condemnation. Nonetheless, our trip seemed highly successful. Besides addressing about eighty doctors, clergy, social and mental welfare workers and a one-hundred-strong students' meeting at The Queen's University we held a number of private discussions and returned to London with the impression that we had created a high level of interest, not only in regard to the need for more adequate social help but also concerning law reform. (The Arran/Abse Act did not apply to Northern Ireland.)

Following our visit the Elmwood Association (Northern Ireland Association for the Better Understanding of Sexuality) was set up with a wide-ranging committee (including the Rev. Robin Eames, now the Anglican Archbishop of Armagh) to encourage the provision of counselling and other help. A year later it reported that its early work had underlined the urgent need for a greater degree of public education in Northern Ireland about sex in all its aspects. It was endeavouring to influence the authorities and the public towards a more enlightened approach. Although relatively short-lived, the Elmwood Association performed a useful pioneering function, as did other local initiatives of a similar kind which grew out of an original stimulus from the Albany Trust.

The Trust's staff were now even more stressed than before. Joy Blanchard had been calamitously stricken in the last months of 1968 with increasing symptoms of an illness which was diagnosed in December as a massive brain tumour. Mercifully, this proved not to be malignant when she was operated upon for its removal; even so the suspension of an early death sentence was the only bright spot for poor Joy. Her convalescence was prolonged and she never recovered fully. Although the Trustees kept her on the staff for as long as they could, she was never able to work again and had to eke out the remaining decade of her life with the tiny pension which was all that had accrued during the seven years she had served the Trust so loyally. She died in July 1979, sincerely mourned by her many friends.

Joy's abrupt disappearance from the office marked a watershed for me as well. She and I had worked together harmoniously and with mutual confidence. She was practical and devotedly loyal; even when we had our differences over priorities and overwork made her lugubrious, I never had a moment's doubt about her staunch support. As long as she was around the ground had been solid under my feet. Unhappily this was never so again although Doreen Cordell and I worked together amicably enough in the months following Joy's illness, coping with the rising tide of work and developing a programme which would, I hoped, attract the funds essential for the Trust's survival.

The workload escalated, with ceaseless requests for individual help, professional consultations, our participation in conferences and research projects, and for talks and articles. Yet many of our previous supporters considered (like Lord Arran) that we had 'worked ourselves out of a job' by achieving law reform, and were unenthusiastic about supporting what they now quite wrongly saw as a 'soup kitchen'. So although we obtained about seventy new deeds of covenant in the year following the reform, successive national appeals with the objective of setting the Trust more firmly on its financial feet brought in only a few hundred pounds, and the Trust's survival continued to be underpinned by the generosity of about a dozen wealthy people. Professional fund-raisers either turned us down flat or else produced unrealistic and vastly expensive proposals. Ultimately one did seem sufficiently convincing for us to invite him to join our new development committee and devise a scheme to build up our new charitable limited company, the Albany Society Ltd, but this initiative too proved abortive. At the end of 1968 only three out of over 450 applications we had made that year for grant support had been successful, while thirty-five were still 'being considered'. Warned by yet more fund-raising advisers that the Trust's association with homosexuality militated against successful appeals, the Trustees felt that the need to overcome such prejudice made it all the more essential for us to make more people aware that the distasteful topic was the source of much human distress which called for the skilled services of reputable organisations such as the Trust. But we knew it was an uphill battle; our most ambitious appeal, for £100,000 to set up a British Sex Research Institute, brought us a good deal of sympathetic publicity but scarcely any money.

The piano recital which Peter Katin most generously gave for the Trust at a West End theatre in September 1968 raised less than we had hoped, and was organisationally taxing – especially for Joy Blanchard, who was already quite ill. Because of these strains, Peter may have felt that his professional courage in publicly championing our cause was not appreciated as it should have been; in fact, I still remember his warm-hearted gesture most gratefully. Another heartening offer from Dame Sybil Thorndike to make a broadcast appeal on the Trust's behalf in the BBC's 'Week's Good Cause' series was not felt by the programme's organiser to be a suitable theme.

In addition to the soaring casework and our series of regional visits, the Trust continued its involvement in a variety of university and other research projects, besides discussing our own ideas for research with the Social Science Research Council and the Department of Education and Science. Eva Bene's research into the results of treatment for homosexuality was unfortunately never completed to publication standards because there were an insufficient number of volunteers to make the results fully comparable.

Around the time that Eva left London to live in Canada, a new and highly original researcher, Dr Charlotte Wolff, appeared who formed valuable enduring links with us. Charlotte, who belonged to my parents' generation, had led an adventurous life. Born into a prosperous Jewish family, she had a happy and secure childhood in Danzig when it was still part of the Kaiser's Germany, and after studying medicine – although her real loves were philosophy and literature – she became a physician in a pioneer antenatal and family planning clinic in one of the poorer districts of Berlin soon after the 1914–1918 war ended. Under the Weimar republic the city was in its too-brief 'Sally Bowles' era. In her autobiography, *Hindsight*, Charlotte recalled it as 'the old story of the dance of death at the edge of an abyss. . . . Culture flourished while the country seemed at death's door. It was the heyday of erotic pleasures, sophistication and wit . . . one's sensuous and emotional needs, whatever they were, could be satisfied.' She flung herself into that bohemian club life with zest. But Berlin's illusory freedom did not last, and with Hitler in power the atmosphere became menacing for Jews, however well qualified and socially useful, and for homosexuals too. Charlotte was briefly arrested, and early in 1933 she succeeded in escaping to Paris, where she practised as a psychologist, specialising in the study of the human hand. In 1936 she came to London, where she spent the rest of her life, always, despite her wide circle of friends, feeling within herself the alienation of the refugee: she was, she said, 'an international Jew

151

with a British passport'.[2] And it is not surprising, in view of her life story, that she had sensitive antennae to the shifting social nuances in Britain. I remember her saying to me in the early 1980s, 'Antony, this country is beginning to smell of Weimar'.[3]

When I first met Charlotte, in November 1967, it was because she wanted the Albany Trust's help in finding subjects for a study of lesbianism.[4] She, Doreen and I soon became friendly, and enjoyed many absorbing discussions about our plans and hopes for the future of sexual research and social enlightenment. Later, Charlotte became a Trustee of the Albany Trust, which was again a recruiting post for her pioneering work on bisexuality.[5] Research, she said, was 'the life blood of my mind', and her original contributions to psychology and sexology are of considerable stature.[6]

Another new ground-breaking area which absorbed increasing (and, in my view, too much) time and energy from 1968 onward was the provision of support for transsexuals and transvestites. The impetus for this came from our links with the Erickson Educational Foundation in the United States. Himself a transsexual, Reed Erickson was primarily concerned to use his Foundation's resources to advance the medical and social awareness of gender reorientation (as sex-change procedures came to be known). He asked the Albany Trust to join with his Foundation in organising and co-hosting the First International Symposium on Gender Identity which took place in London in July 1969. This brought together an imposing array of

[2] She died in the autumn of 1986, aged almost eighty-nine. For her own accounts of her life see her two autobiographical volumes, *On the Way to Myself* (Methuen, 1969) and *Hindsight* (Quartet, 1980).

[3] Soon after her death, the smell grew into a homophobic stench, with the introduction of 'Clause 28'. (See below, chapter XIX.)

[4] Published as *Love Between Women* (Duckworth, 1971).

[5] *Bisexuality: A Study* (Quartet, 1977). She saw bisexuality as 'the root of human sexuality', and came to believe that 'only a *bisexual society* can free us from sexism and the whole gamut of psychosexual and social suppression. The equation of heterosexuality with maturity, and the male with physical and mental superiority, is leading to the destruction of the human race.' (*Hindsight*, p. 225.)

[6] She crowned her life work in this sphere by spending the last six years of her life writing the first fully researched biography of Dr Magnus Hirschfeld, the apostle of sexual research and legal justice for sexual minorities in pre-Hitler Germany. It was a mammoth task for a woman in her mid-eighties, involving, as it did, researching archives in various parts of Europe and translating many documents into English. (*Magnus Hirschfeld* (Quartet, 1986)).

medical, psychiatric and social expertise (including the ever-dynamic Zelda Suplee) from both sides of the Atlantic to study the 'aims, functions and clinical problems of a Gender Identity Unit'.

Gender confusion – disassociation between anatomical gender and subjective psychological perception of one's sex – was roughly estimated to occur in one in every 100,000 children. Some 1000 sex-change operations[7] had taken place in various parts of the world since 1953, and there were already six specialist gender identity units in the United States. There was as yet no such permanent unit in Britain, although individual specialists at a few hospitals – notably London's Charing Cross – were working in the field. In addition to the medical and research aspects of the problem there was an urgent need for greater academic and professional understanding, and for education of the public at large. A wholehearted effort to initiate, encourage and co-ordinate an intensive programme of study and help was required, using every medium of communication to make the public aware of the scope of the problem and to reduce the social waste and misery associated with it.

The Symposium was a success, and proved to be the first of a series organised in subsequent years by the Erickson Foundation in different parts of Europe and the United States. Although the Albany Trust never again played such a high-profile role, the London symposium was not simply a 'one-off' for us in this field; Doreen Cordell was so enthused by the subject and the potential benefits and influence which she foresaw accruing from developing our work around it that she threw herself obsessively into the business of making the Trust into the nationally acknowledged British specialist agency on TS (transsexualism) and TV (transvestism). This was not a goal which I endorsed, since it was clear to me that, however deserving in human terms, TS/TV must, through lack of resources, remain a sideline of the Albany Trust's work for the foreseeable future. As the pleas for help rolled in, I became convinced that Doreen was far too absorbed by the topic. This generated growing tensions in the office, where the caseload became unmanageably heavy. Doreen's stock retort to my instruction to limit the number of people she was attempting to deal

---

[7] Strictly speaking a misnomer, because it is impossible to alter anyone's genetic or biological sex through surgical or chemical intervention. The operations are essentially cosmetic surgery, and are technically described as 'gender reassignment'.

with was: 'but, AG, the first one we turn away may commit suicide.'
So the tension between us grew into a tug of wills which veered over
into her outright rebellion.

Additional pressures were now coming from the homophile movement which was spreading its wings in the new post-1967 freedom.
While our relations with some groups – notably the lesbian Minorities
Research Group and the Scottish Minorities Group[8] – were congenial
and sometimes close, the same could not be said, unfortunately, of
the Committee (later, Campaign) for Homosexual Equality which had
grown out of the North-Western Homosexual Law Reform Committee. While those who were involved in the early days of CHE may see
it otherwise, I can only record my own point of view, which is that
the problems between the Albany Trust and CHE arose out of differences of perception concerning strategy and timing that gradually
ballooned into mutual mistrust.

While there was no disagreement over the shortcomings of the
Arran/Abse Bill, and a common desire to secure further law reform
as quickly as possible, there was an early divergence of views over
campaigning tactics. On the social front I had from the outset emphasised the need for responsible self-help, and had urged the Newalls to
advocate the merits of a Dutch COC-style social organisation as a
feature of the post-reform British scenario. But my close encounter
with the irrational homophobia emanating from the opponents of law
reform had convinced me that careful preparation, and not least a
possibly protracted period of lobbying for broadly based religious,
political and social work support, was essential before such a scheme
could be successfully established in this country. The Manchester
group, however, were determined not to let the grass grow under
their feet, and within a few weeks of the Arran/Abse Act reaching the
Statute Book they were deep in plans to set up a chain of gay social
clubs across the North of England and the Midlands and were
approaching breweries for backing. I endeavoured to slow down this
premature initiative, knowing only too well that it was likely to provoke loud disapproval from Lord Arran and Leo Abse; I suggested

[8] Formed in 1969 under the canny leadership of Ian Dunn and others who made
the group (which became the Scottish Homosexual Rights Group in 1978) an effective
force, at once radical and level-headed, with constructive links to many facets of the
Scottish establishment.

that before launching anything there should be a thorough study of the history and operation of the COC, and also of the Danish and other overseas homophile groups.

But in vain. Blithely ignoring the anti-reformers' recent clamour about 'buggers' clubs', CHE proudly announced in the autumn of 1967 the formation of 'Esquire Clubs Ltd' and naïvely invited leading law reformers, including Lord Arran and Leo Abse, to become patrons. Both recoiled in horror. Boofy telephoned me to expostulate that he 'wouldn't touch Esquire with a bargepole'. And there was a predictable Absean outburst: he demanded a joint meeting of the HLRS executive and the Albany Trust trustees and development committee, and proceeded to pour scorn not only on 'Esquire', but also on the Albany Trust's 'social needs' programme. It was a tense meeting. The setting up of social organisations for homosexuals would, Abse said, give those who were hostile to the recent law reform ample grounds for saying that their worst fears were being realised. Certainly the admission of those aged under twenty-one to licensed premises, combined with the provision of dancing, could be interpreted as a defiance of the law. Other committee members, including Professor Ayer, Lord Byers and Christopher Chataway MP, supported his view that it would be most unwise for the Trust to give its support to any clubs or social organisations before having a full discussion with the Home Office. Tommy Frankland, who was advising the Trust's new development committee on its fund-raising programme, felt that while reasonable, liberal middle-of-the-road opinion would be prepared to support the counselling, research and educational work of the Trust, such support would be lost if the Trust became involved in the setting up of homosexual clubs; these were likely, in any event, to prove dangerous and uncontrollable, and association with them on any level except the provision of counselling help for individuals could gravely prejudice the Trust's charitable status, therapeutic endeavours and public support. He himself would feel obliged to resign should such a policy be followed.

Angus Wilson, on the other hand, thought that the Trust *should* give its support to such a project – but not to the 'Esquire Clubs', because any appearance of flouting the newly-reformed law in the matter of age limits or public behaviour would be damaging. While a suitably structured organisation could be a valuable force for good, he was strongly of the view that the ultimate aim must be the integration of homosexual people into the total community. If a club or social organisation were established the agreement of the Home Office and the police should first be obtained, and there should be minimal publicity. I endeavoured to counteract what I felt to be the excessive timidity of the committee members by pointing out that the issue was not whether clubs where homosexuals could meet should be created – they already existed – but whether they should openly declare a social purpose, and whether the Albany Trust should be associated with any that did so. There was a real need for social integration through a self-help structure, and if a responsible organisation came into being for this purpose the Trust ought to have links with it. Michael Schofield supported me, pointing out that the Albany Trust was the only reputable social work body directly concerned with homosexuality. Any group or club wanting to operate along more socially responsible lines than the existing commercial clubs would desire and need the Trust's support. The Home Office and the police would also most probably prefer to know that there were more reliable centres of social contact and supportive help for homosexuals than at present, and the best guarantee they could have would be the active concern and interest of the Albany Trust in any organisation of this kind that was set up. The Trust was in a position to lay down certain standards, and it should not brush aside its responsibility by limiting itself to giving secret advice. It was part of the Trust's job to see that such clubs were properly run.

Invited to give her views, Doreen Cordell said she envisaged not just a club, but a social organisation which might take various forms. There was a tremendous need for a more coherent social framework of adjustment for people with homosexual problems, and the paramount need for the Trust was to have implicit confidence in any group of people to whom supportive referrals were made; for this to be the case, we needed 'a voice on the inside'. A more socially conscious organisation linked to the Trust could help to create more responsible attitudes among its members and would also help in educating parents, who frequently had a completely wrong picture of the situation facing their homosexual son or daughter. It could also co-operate with the youth services in helping to create a more supportive attitude in place of the hostility and rejection which was all too often experienced by the young homosexual seeking to come to terms with himself.

The Bishop of Woolwich, John Robinson, supported the idea of the Trust associating itself with the foundation of an organisation along similar lines to the Dutch COC geared towards positive contacts with local authorities, police and social welfare workers. So did I. But Leo Abse remained unmoved; we were, he said, being 'ridiculous' in aspiring to organise all the homosexuals of Britain. Whatever evolved socially would have to originate and grow organically; it could not be planned from the centre. He thought that national organisations of homosexuals were highly undesirable; heterosexuals did not go around looking for exclusive clubs before they felt they 'belonged'. The whole idea of separation was wrong, and contrary to what the sponsors of the recent Act had set out to do. They did not wish to see the creation of homosexual ghettos. And, regardless of the way in which such clubs or organisations came into being, it would be impossible to control them; they must accept their own responsibilities. It might be that the Trust or the HLRS might want to protest to the authorities if a well-run club was unreasonably interfered with; but in his view, it would be most unwise to identify the Trust with any of them.

This cold douche effectively swayed the meeting. The most they would agree to was that the Trust should ask the Home Office and the police what their attitude would be to the establishment of clubs whose purpose was openly stated to be for the social recreation of homosexuals; and that the Trust should seek funds to embark upon a major research project to ascertain the most desirable and healthy way of providing for the social needs of homosexuals, meanwhile refraining from giving specific advice to anyone wanting to form clubs.

I was accordingly instructed to disassociate not only the Trust, but also myself personally, from the 'Esquire' project forthwith; and although I pointed out that this was bound to be interpreted by both Esquire and CHE as the Albany Trust's disapproval and rejection of them, and that I would rather defer resigning as one of their vice-presidents until after the meeting which the Esquire board had requested with the Trustees had taken place,[9] the committee were adamant. I was therefore compelled to disassociate myself from CHE

[9] It never did.

157

and Esquire, telling them – sincerely, but unconvincingly as it must have seemed to them – that this did not imply any lack of my personal support for the concept of a responsible social organisation, but simply reflected the Albany Trustees' wish not to identity themselves with any individual project until they had studied the whole question of social adjustment more thoroughly.

It is scarcely surprising that after this rebuff relations between AT/HLRS and CHE slipped from the tepid to the frigid and afterwards remained at arm's length, with unfortunate consequences, I believe, for the subsequent history of the British homophile movement. That, of course, did not bother Leo Abse in the slightest: he disapproved of homosexual organisations anyway. But we at the Trust's office had to work with them in as friendly a way as we could if we were going to achieve the educational and social goals we had in view. Fortunately, not all our committee members were as blinkered about this as Abse. There were valuable allies amongst social workers, and in other, sometimes quite unexpected, quarters. Despite the snub to Esquire, Colin Harvey remained a good friend of the Trust's in Manchester and later in Glasgow.

Another good friend who appeared around this time, and played a powerful supporting role for the Trust for many years, was Raymond Clarke, who was at that time Secretary of the Yorkshire Council of Social Service. Raymond, who came from a Methodist background and was a magistrate, had a very distinguished career in social service. When he left Yorkshire he became for some years head of the national organisations division of the National Council of Social Service in London, where I continued to work closely with him. Later, Sir Keith Joseph asked him to become Director of the Personal Social Services Council and he finished his career as chief executive of the National Council of Voluntary Child Care Organisations. When we first came into contact with Raymond in Leeds he was already well aware of the mental loneliness and physical isolation experienced by homosexuals, especially those living away from large towns. We referred some of our Northern cases to him, and instead of going home to his wife and family after a long day's work he would sometimes spend his evenings travelling out into the country by bus to counsel some desperately lonely person who had contacted the Albany Trust; a generous and selfless gesture which typifies his attitude to social service. We soon realised that in Raymond Clarke we had a sympathetic and highly professional ear for our plans, and he set up and jointly sponsored with the Albany Trust one of the first provincial social work conferences we took part in at York University in 1969. This was so successful that it led to the important residential 'Social Needs' conference at York in 1970, chaired by Raymond.[10]

A welcome breakthrough came in 1969 when the Anglican Community of the Resurrection (the 'Mirfield Fathers') offered the Albany Trust hospitality for a private weekly social group to meet at their new premises, the Royal Foundation of St Katharine, near St Katharine's Dock in East London. This became the venue of what is now the oldest continuous social group for homosexual men in Britain. 'St K's', which celebrated its twenty-first birthday in 1990, has been holding weekly meetings ever since it started, under the auspices of the Albany Trust, as a discreet, well-conducted meeting place for the Trust's clients and friends. Warmest thanks are due to all those who undertook the organisation and management of the group – notably Andrew Henderson and Christopher Spence, who were later to be the co-founders of the London Lighthouse AIDS hospice. The Royal Foundation is under the patronage of Queen Elizabeth the Queen Mother, so (whether consciously or not) the Albany Trust's social endeavours have enjoyed at least indirect Royal patronage for the past two decades – if not as conspicuously as the Dutch COC with its Royal Charter.

Other early stirrings of the homophile movement were not as effective or as sophisticated as the Minorities Research Group, CHE or SMG. In the first year or two after law reform a rash of short-lived projects came into being or were mooted. As a temperamental radical I have always believed that self-government is the only road to good government, and I recognised that we probably could not dissuade, and certainly could not prevent, others from attempting to do whatever they wished, however ill-advised it might seem from our perspective. But we were sometimes quite amazed at the naïvety with which some folk seemed to imagine that now the law had been changed there were no further serious legal, social or practical obstacles to open homosexual groupings.

[10] See below, p. 171–4.

One pleasant but distinctly damp-behind-the-ears nineteen-year-old young man came from the Midlands to see Joy and myself and earnestly lectured us about the 'Male and Female Association of Great Britain' (MANDFHAB) which he was in the process of setting up. Wolverhampton, he solemnly told us, already possessed 'the best gay club in Europe'. He was quite convinced that everyone would rush to join MANDFHAB, and that there were no potential snags he needed to know about or to be bothered with. When we endeavoured to explain that things were really not quite so simple as that, he gazed at us with pitying condescension and departed. We looked at each other open-mouthed. Unluckily, he said much the same to the press, with the predictable result that, following a 'We Exclusively Reveal All' type of article, the police raided the club, charged its owners with permitting 'obscene and indecent acts' (i.e. allowing men to dance together), and began investigating alleged teenage homosexual relationships among its members. MANDFHAB sank without trace.

XIII

No New Deal

'It is surely undesirable to maintain any group in
the status of barely tolerated sub-citizens.'

Antony Grey & D. J. West,
New Society, 27 March 1969

In 1969 D. J. West[1] and I wrote a joint article for *New Society* looking
at the post-reform situation of homosexual men. They would, we
said, seem morally justified in leading active sex lives if the personal
happiness they thereby achieved enabled them to live less anxiously in
society and to make a fuller contribution to the common good. But
in practice, considerable legal and social obstacles still stood in the
way of their doing so. Public ambivalence towards them persisted,
despite the educative effects of the ten-year-long law reform campaign,
and little had as yet been done to translate any greater social tolerance
into practical terms. 'Integration' was sometimes spoken of; but to be
meaningful this had to involve acceptance of minority attitudes and
life-styles as part of the total social fabric; it was a worthless and
hypocritical slogan if it merely envisaged conformity to majority attitudes in all respects, or even the sort of acceptance that amounted to
sexual apartheid. Current social attitudes projected on to homosexual
scapegoats too great a proportion of the sexual crime and guilt that
existed throughout society as a whole. Prophetically, we called our
piece 'New Law but No New Deal'.

There was no shortage of Jeremiahs forecasting the most dire
outcome of the reform – even if not all were as lurid as the elderly
gentlemen who used to parade Trafalgar Square bearing a placard
with the inscription: 'BAN THE SODOMY BILL BEFORE GOD

---

[1] Author of a carefully researched study of homosexuality, and Professor of
Criminology at Cambridge.

161

DESTROYS BRITAIN'. Within a month of the Royal Assent a columnist in the weekly *Time and Tide* was declaring:

> Homosexual badges being sold to young boys instantly disprove (did we need the proof?) the ludicrous hypocrisy of those eminent Lords and MPs who pressured through the homosexual law reform bill. One being sold in Sloane Square last week read 'Boy For Sale' and we hope Parliament thinks this an unimportant development – the only thing we lack now is an Arab slavemarket in Parliament Square.

In a Manchester suburb an application by Esquire Clubs for a licence was predictably rejected, a local version of Alderman Foodbotham saying, 'They might be very nice people for all I know, but we don't want them here – our young people might be perverted.' The 'Green Door' fantasy of the Buggers' Club was alive and well; the Albany Trust's modest and entirely reasonable aim of doing something to lessen the isolation of out-of-town homosexuals was disapprovingly perceived, even by some of our supporters, as a desire to set up 'a huge, purple-coloured series of raging "min" clubs all through the Midlands right up to Bradford where all kinds of dancing will take place.'[2]

In actual fact there was slim prospect of any same-sex dancing, however demure, escaping the menacing attentions of the authorities. Purple-coloured or not, the Flamingo Club in Wolverhampton was fined £500 in July 1968 for permitting what the Court was assured to be 'an orgy of disgusting revelries which perhaps existed in the days of Sodom and Gomorrah' but were not to be tolerated in twentieth-century Wolverhampton. Men, it was said in shocked tones, had danced together and 'behaved familiarly with each other'. Evidence from club members that they had observed nothing disgusting, and that the kind of dancing which went on was mostly in the modern style where the partners did not touch one another, was disregarded, the Judge maintaining that what was going on was 'intolerable by any standards, heterosexual or homosexual'.

It was indeed becoming clear in the months immediately following law reform that its achievement was not going to result in more lenient application of other aspects of the laws affecting homosexual

---

[2] Irma Kurtz, 'The Unlocking of a Law', *Nova*, February 1967.

behaviour; indeed, quite the contrary. Increasing numbers of public indecency and importuning offences were reported to the HLRS, and it looked as if our failure to insert a clause to prevent conspiracy charges relating to activities which were themselves no longer illegal would have unpleasant results. For this reason I felt unable to offer encouragement to a most respectable lady who approached us shortly after the law had been changed for advice about her proposal to set up a Gay Introduction Bureau. I was obliged to warn her that, however desirable such a 'lonely hearts' agency might be, she was quite likely to find herself facing charges of 'conspiring to corrupt public morals', or even of procuring, under the as yet untested terms of the Arran/ Abse Act.

My worst fears were amply confirmed when, in the spring of 1969, the police raided the offices of *International Times* with an Obscene Publications Act search warrant, removed the paper's files, and proceeded to question a considerable number of men who had used the 'Males' personal advertisements column to contact other consenting adults. It became obvious to us and to the National Council for Civil Liberties, with whom we were working closely on this and other cases and who were also being inundated with requests for legal advice from worried *IT* advertisers and their correspondents, that evidence was being collected for a conspiracy 'show trial'; also that the homosexual aspect was being used primarily as a prejudicial smear against *IT* which, as a leading mouthpiece of the anti-establishment pot-smoking and free-love 'underground', was a thorn in the flesh of the authorities. When the case finally came to trial, in November 1970, the paper and its directors were charged with, and found guilty of, conspiring to corrupt public morals and conspiring to outrage public decency; the prosecution's evidence hinged on the 'gay' advertisements. In the event, none of the advertisers and those whose letters to them had been seized and scrutinised by the police was charged with any offence, but the mental anguish which the couple of dozen people involved underwent was severe, and to my mind totally unjustified. The directors of *IT* were not so fortunate: their conviction was upheld on appeal and, although the prison sentences passed upon them remained suspended, their paper went out of business – no doubt to the satisfaction of those who instigated the prosecution. Despite the obvious distaste of several of the Law Lords, common law conspiracy charges were now solidly in business as a telling weapon in the battle for State control of private morals; they were soon to be used even more effectively against *OZ* and in other cases with which we became concerned.

It was impossible to separate effective public discussion of sexual morality and behaviour from the crucial issue of free speech and the impact of the obscenity laws, and I found myself increasingly involved in championing freedom of expression. Early in 1966 the American author Hubert Selby Jr's novel *Last Exit to Brooklyn* had been published in this country as an expensive hardback by the *avant garde* publishers Calder & Boyars, who as a consequence found themselves embroiled in an Obscene Publications Act prosecution which became a landmark in British literary history. As some of the passages objected to contained explicit descriptions of homosexual acts, John Calder and Marion Boyars were quickly in touch with the HLRS, requesting help in mustering as formidable an array of defence witnesses as could be found.

The history of the trial belongs elsewhere;[3] its consequences for me were lasting and quite profound. John and Marion (with both of whom I formed a long friendship) decided that attack was the best form of defence. Finding themselves pilloried by what they considered to be a ridiculous law, they took the initiative in setting up the Defence of Literature and the Arts Society, on which they were joined by several distinguished fellow-publishers, lawyers, and others with a specialist interest, of whom I was one. I remained an executive committee member of the DLAS for more than a decade and its meetings were among the most interesting I have ever attended, not only because of the subject matter and the celebrated cases the Society helped to defend, but also because of the people I met through its activities.

Notable among these was Will Hamling MP, who became the Society's most effective chairman and was both an invaluable political ally (he had been a Labour Whip and was Parliamentary Private Secretary to the Prime Minister, Harold Wilson, so his Commons contacts were wide and influential) and a dear friend until his sudden death early in 1975. Will was a down-to-earth, jovial Lancastrian who had

[3] See, e.g., John Sutherland, *Offensive Literature* (Junction Books, 1982) for an account of this and other obscenity battles.

devoted his life to adult education and was steeped in the longstanding North Country radical tradition. Like his successor as DLAS Chairman, Ben Whitaker, Will was profoundly convinced that freedom of expression was the bedrock of human rights, because without it truth could not be ascertained. He maintained that 'a piece of low-grade rubbish must be as important to us as *Ulysses*, even though that principle may lose us both sympathy and battles'.

The problem was that the boundaries of tolerance were always being stretched further and further by the conscienceless money-grubbers whose activities undeniably degraded good taste whether or not they corrupted good morals. Consequently, the 'literature and art' which the DLAS set out to defend was constantly being elbowed out of the way by the 'low-grade rubbish', which took up far too much of everyone's time in the free speech debate. In fact, such stuff strengthens the case for censorship, however much one opposes this in principle.[4] I know where Will Hamling would have stood over Salman Rushdie; a voice as robust as his has been sadly missed in that affair.

The escalating attacks upon the homosexual minority's freedom of speech and freedom of association brought me into more active membership of the National Council for Civil Liberties as well as the DLAS. I had already formed a good working relationship with NCCL's formidably energetic General Secretary, Martin Ennals,[5] in the pre-reform period, when he had helped me to get the earliest pro-Wolfenden motion through the Council's AGM and to win the NCCL executive committee's support for the HLRS' efforts to liberalise the Arran/Abse Bill. This was by no means automatic; the NCCL was in those days run by an amalgam of progressively minded radicals and old-style trade unionists, some of the latter having distinctly reactionary views on social issues such as homosexuality. But having carried the day with the AGM, and having been elected myself (in a personal capacity) to the NCCL executive, I found that support for the issues of personal liberty which I cared most about grew stronger on the Council, while I became more aware of the concerns of other

---

[4] See my paper 'Pornography and Free Speech' at p. 47 in M. Yaffe and E. C. Nelson (eds): *The Influence of Pornography on Behaviour* (Academic Press, 1982).

[5] Martin Ennals died, aged sixty-four, in October 1991 after a distinguished career with several human rights organisations, notably as Secretary General of Amnesty International.

NCCL members. I also got on well with Martin's successor, Tony Smythe, another dedicated civil libertarian.[6]

In August 1966 a note in the NCCL's bulletin on the progress of the Arran/Abse Bill enquired:

> Is it really necessary . . . to combine an age of consent as high as twenty-one with draconian penalties for any relationship between an older man and one who has not yet reached twenty-one – or, indeed, to continue punishing relationships between youths? Adolescents need sympathy and understanding in coming to terms with their problems and one wonders if there is any sense at all in continuing to apply criminal procedures if they become involved in homosexual practices. . . . We hope that common-sense will prevail.

A motion calling for revision of the Bill along the lines advocated by the HLRS was carried overwhelmingly at the NCCL's 1967 annual general meeting. However, as we have seen, commonsense did not prevail; the NCCL soon found itself being confronted, as was the HLRS, with the hamfisted administration of the post-reform law. Less than a year after the reform, borstal sentences were passed on four teenage boys in Staffordshire because of their mutually consenting homosexual behaviour, and the Court of Criminal Appeal bizarrely released two of them (aged sixteen and seventeen) because 'they had developed some strength of character with prospects of establishing normal relationships with young women' while detaining a third (aged seventeen) who, the Court said, 'required the influence and guidance afforded by Borstal' to consolidate his heterosexuality![7]

So at the NCCL's 1968 annual general meeting I proposed the following resolution, which was carried unanimously:

> This AGM, believing that the individual's freely chosen sexual behaviour is his or her private and personal concern and not the province of the criminal law, welcomes the Government's intention that there should be a review of the laws relating to sexual offences, urges that this should be based upon the principle that the State has no cause to interfere with or punish sexual behaviour or expression which does not involve assault, inter-

[6] He later became Director of MIND and a Trustee of the Albany Trust.
[7] *Sunday Times*, 17 March 1968; *Observer*, 31 March 1968; *Guardian*, 10 April 1968.

ference with children below the age of puberty, or an affront to
decency causing annoyance or nuisance to the public, and calls
for continuing vigilance and protest by the NCCL against laws,
prosecutions and sentences which infringe upon the citizen's right
to pursue sexual happiness as he sees fit.

The Council also carried an emergency motion deploring prosecutions
brought by the State or private individuals with the intention of curb-
ing freedom of artistic expression which is essentially a matter of taste,
and urging the Government to introduce legislation abolishing the
offences of indecency, obscenity and blasphemy – all long overdue
reforms which are still awaited.

Later the same year the NCCL published an excellent pamphlet,
Privacy Under Attack, which contained a section on the private rights
of homosexuals. Three other cases reported to the HLRS around this
time arose out of private letters written to one another by members
of a 'pen pals' club, through whose mailing list the police had system-
atically trawled. One man, who had pleaded guilty before he
approached the Society, had been fined £40 for uttering an obscene
communication, the 'obscenities' apparently being references to homosexual behaviour. The Bench expressed its disgust at this kind of thing,
but evidently felt none at the invasions of personal privacy involved in
these police inquisitions into the private correspondence of consenting
adults.

Commenting on these and other recent prosecutions (including
the Flamingo Club 'Sodom and Gomorrah in Wolverhampton' case),
I wrote in *Spectrum* 24:

> It is noteworthy that in none of them was any evidence produced
> for the prosecution apart from that of the police: no member of
> the public appears to have been annoyed, disgusted, or even aware
> of the various activities alleged. Yet the 'public conscience' is
> apparently so outraged by such behaviour on the part of people
> who wish to pursue it that we employ our undermanned police
> force to ferret it out at considerable expense of their time and
> public money. It would seem that there is something wrong not
> only with our sense of social priorities, but also with the state of
> the law relating to offences against public decency. The Homo-
> sexual Law Reform Society is currently discussing with the
> Josephine Butler Society and the National Council for Civil Lib-
> erties possible reforms to the law dealing with street offences, and

there appears to be a consensus of opinion that the essence of such offences should be the causing of actual *annoyance* or *nuisance* to specific members of the public – not some vague concept of 'public decency' which is allegedly 'outraged' even when no member of the public is in the vicinity. While we are fully aware of the difficulties involved in drafting legislation which will satisfy all concerned in striking a balance between protecting the public, preserving the right of the individual citizen to go about his legitimate business freely without being either molested or arrested, and dealing effectively with the nuisance of soliciting and kerb-crawling, it is hoped that an agreed Bill can be presented to Parliament next Session. . . . In addition, the Society is addressing itself to the wider and important task of preparing evidence for submission to the Criminal Law Revision Committee which is reviewing the entire law relating to sexual offences.[8]

On 17 July 1969 I was one of the speakers at a Parliamentary Civil Liberties Group Meeting at the House of Commons on the theme of 'Privacy and the Outsider'. The 1967 Act, I said, was a far from satisfactory piece of legislation; it had merely placed the male homosexual in a somewhat similar legal and social position to that of the common prostitute. And the operation of the unreformed parts of the law had become tougher – indeed, we were getting the clear impression of a deliberate official campaign to tighten things up. During the past four or five months the Albany Trust's counselling service had had a much higher rate of legal cases than at any time previously since the 1967 Act was passed, and some of these cases were as unpleasant as those in the early 1950s when police methods of arrest, investigation and questioning had aroused such public distaste. Anyone who had the notion that in the current climate of law enforcement as it affected unorthodox minorities we were living in an over-permissive society was, I thought, leading a pretty sheltered life.

With regard to homosexuals society was no longer saying, as the pre-1967 law used to, 'It's all right to *be* one as long as you don't *do* it.' But society seemed to have substituted the scarcely less fatuous attitude of 'Well, do it if you must – but not if we can help it.' The basic problems of homosexuals were social; but lack of acceptance by

[8] A review which did not in fact begin until some years later. (See Chapter XX below.)

families, non-homosexual friends and employers was still bolstered formidably by the law. It was still far from easy, legally or socially, for homosexuals to meet one another. Clubs catering for homosexuals were still regarded by the police as 'disorderly' if those frequenting them behaved in a non-heterosexual manner. The legal status of single-sex dancing between men remained dubious. Was it 'disorderly' or 'indecent' *per se*, or only if there was conduct which would constitute a disorderly offence if committed by a man and a woman? Recent cases had upheld the former, prohibitive interpretation.

So an evening out at a gay club might not prove either safe or pleasurable. What, then, should the lonely homosexual do? Advertise for friends? In view of the then current *International Times* police investigations, this would seem to be most inadvisable. It was very curious that, if the police particularly objected to the advertising columns of *IT*, they should concentrate exclusively upon the homosexual advertisements, since *IT* of course also carried similar heterosexual advertisements. Section 4 of the 1967 Sexual Offences Act specifically provided that it was no longer an offence for a man to procure a homosexual act *with himself*, if that act was not itself an offence; so I failed to see why the 'Males' column of *IT* was so interesting to the police. The possibility that people who imprudently sought partners for private sexual gratification through personal column advertisements were liable to receive an official tap on the door months afterwards, and that a list of them was being built up, was extremely repulsive and reminiscent of Big Brother. I held no particular brief for *International Times*, but its point of view had a right to be heard. That it should be intimidated – or that its printers should be intimidated – was utterly wrong; and that the homosexuals who advertised in it should also be intimidated (whether incidentally or not) was intolerable. And this was by no means the only instance we had heard of adults who had made contacts through pen-pal clubs being visited by the police and questioned about their private correspondence and sexual lives – sometimes years after they had written the letters in question.

Nor did our case files show any fall in the numbers of public indecency cases where the sole prosecuting evidence was that of plain-clothes vice squad men whose evidence, although almost invariably accepted by the Courts, was frequently completely at odds with the defendant's version of events. Plain-clothes police still seemed to be deployed in considerable numbers in public lavatories, parks and open spaces. No one would wish to complain at necessary police activities designed to preserve the decency and salubriousness of municipal parks for the public at large; but it was hard to believe, in most of the numerous cases of this sort we had heard of recently, that the behaviour of the accused was sufficiently offensive to the public at large to require arrests. The law, in this context, should be primarily concerned with preserving public order and decency; and as the HLRS had said many times before, such public order would be much more effectively maintained, and at a lesser cost in police manpower and court time, by the presence of uniformed police patrols as a preventive measure at known trouble-spots.

Arrests on charges of this kind still carried with them social consequences often far more severe than the penalties imposed by the courts: loss of jobs, evictions from lodgings, expulsion from study courses, and other such calamities were by no means unknown when a man had been in court on an importuning charge, and sometimes followed even when he had been acquitted. Such arrests ought not to be made unless the culprits were behaving to the annoyance of identifiable members of the public who were prepared to give evidence. These issues affected not only gay people, but every citizen; for if the standards of British justice declined so that members of minorities were no longer given equal protection with everybody else, and could not live without unreasonable harassment, every man and woman in this country would suffer in the end.

All this will have a familiar ring to present-day campaigners against the iniquities of Clause 28, Clause 25 and other persisting legal injustices. Possibly they will be surprised to realise that the HLRS and the NCCL were campaigning vigorously on these very issues within months of the 1967 Act becoming law.

In the summer of 1968 a weekend study conference of about thirty people, mostly from the caring professions, met to review the social situation following law reform. They concentrated on three topics: the homosexual 'image', as seen by homosexuals themselves and by other people; the need for more supportive social frameworks to reduce the extreme isolation still suffered by so many; and the urgent need to provide better education and information for non-homosexual people, including those in responsible positions. On the first, it was perceived that in their still very negative situation homosexual men and women all too often had a self-centred and socially disorientated picture of themselves, which helped neither them nor society at large. The need for more realistic public education concerning teenage sexuality and the often extensive sexual experience of young people, both heterosexual and homosexual, and the social folly of treating them as criminals on the pretext of 'protecting' them, was stressed. The group requested the Albany Trust to institute a research and practical help project for those aged under twenty-one – the beginning of the Trust's special concern for this very vulnerable age group. Appropriate training for social workers and for Trust supporters wishing to act as befrienders, and the importance of using the most effective groupwork training techniques, was also given high priority, and the Trust was asked to set up a group training advisory panel. While it was not possible to implement all these aims immediately, the weekend served a valuable purpose in itself and also as a significant precursor to the 1970 York Social Needs Conference and the Albany Trust's subsequent development programme.

The continuing social and legal problems evidenced by our casework and the information provided by the growing homophile groups, and the clear need to focus this information as effectively as possible towards the provision of more adequate help, prompted us to plan and carry out in 1969 and 1970 what was probably the largest research survey on homosexuality so far undertaken in Britain. With help from Michael Schofield and other sociologists a questionnaire on social needs of homosexual men and women was compiled and over 5000 copies of this were widely distributed between December 1969 and February 1970. 2672 anonymously completed replies were received – from 2082 men, 588 women and two people who did not specify their sex. Analysis of these replies was largely completed during the spring and summer of 1970, and a weekend residential conference, sponsored by the Albany Trust and the Yorkshire Council of Social Service, took place at York University in July to discuss the results of the survey and their implications for future work.

Although a considerable amount of analytical work was done on the Social Survey results, these were unfortunately never published[9] because of the chronic crisis in the Albany Trust's fortunes. Following an introductory section identifying the sex, age, marital, educational, working and geographical status of the respondents, the questionnaire concentrated on people's attitudes to their homosexuality; their early sexual experiences and later relationships; the degree of helpfulness they had encountered from people whose advice they had sought; their social lives; the degree of secrecy they maintained; details of any trouble they had been in because of their homosexuality; and their views on what was most important for the future: further legal reforms, more tolerance and understanding from the general public, more opportunities to socialise or join campaigning organisations with other homosexuals, and research. More than half (58 per cent) of the respondents fell into the 21–40 age group. A very high proportion of the men had experienced their first homosexual feelings when they were very young, and the survey results highlighted the need for much more adequate supportive provision for adolescents grappling with their homosexual feelings. There were marked differences in the degree of social isolation and self-imposed secrecy endured by those in large cities and smaller towns and rural areas. Many reported themselves as feeling lonely, and while only a minority of the sample had sought any form of help, more than half of those who had done so found it beneficial. While most of the results were unsurprising to those of us who had been at the receiving end of hundreds of homosexual and bisexual people's confidences during the previous twelve years, the Social Needs Survey was an extremely useful source of evidence with which to acquaint Government, social workers and the general public of some of the realities, as opposed to the myths, of the characteristic situations in which many homosexual and bisexual people were living their lives. Yet again, however, the Trust's straitened circumstances prevented us from deploying this tool as effectively as we would have wished to do.

The York Conference brought together men and women rep-

[9] Except in a highly selective and garbled, though amusing, form in a Gay Liberationist pamphlet produced by a disgruntled employee of the business systems firm we had asked to computerise the results. His basic, characteristically GLF, attitude was 'fuck you Albany Trust, you've shown your true colours. We don't need you – we don't want you – that's the message from this report'. (*The Joke's Over*. Gay Prints/Rat Studies, 1973.) See Appendix 2.

resenting most of the then existing homophile groups in Britain, as well as some delegates from the churches, education, social work and counselling with an interest in the topic. The conference ran smoothly, thanks largely to the urbanity and diplomatic chairmanship of Raymond Clarke. Plenary sessions were supplemented by small group discussions on a variety of topics including national organisation, regional frameworks, law reform, problems of the elderly and the under-twenty-ones, community development and public education, counselling, and fund raising.

The York Conference produced two major decisions. The first was that a constitution should be drafted for a national federative body of homophile groups which would co-ordinate decision-making and representation of homophile interests on other national bodies such as the National Council of Social Service. This was duly done, and NFHO – the National Federation of Homophile Organisations – came into being in 1971, with the objects of providing a forum for the discussion of the problems of homophile men and women in Great Britain and Northern Ireland, acting as a central clearing house for information, co-operating and liaising with others in the initiation and provision of social meeting places, and educating the public with a view to improving the legal and social status of homophiles.

The second decision was to convene a working party to produce a report on the particular problems involved and skills required in counselling homosexuals. The resulting document, *Counselling homosexuals: a study of personal needs and public attitudes*, compiled by Peter Righton and published by the NCSS Bedford Square Press in 1973, still merits attention. In his Introduction, Raymond Clarke referred to the growing openness of society, with less stigma than formerly attaching to certain areas of social need, but commented that 'when one member of the conference referred to the "hell of alienation felt by many homosexuals" there was a general agreement that this was all too common'. The aim of the report, he added, was not to promote a separately structured specialisation in homosexual counselling, but rather to make a claim upon the skills and time of all who provided counselling services in the hope that they would respond to the invitation to learn about the particular stresses in personal and community relationships that accompanied homosexuality. This invitation was echoed by the report, which saw a need for consultation and co-

173

operation at a national level between the many interests – the professions, government departments, local authorities, voluntary bodies – whose practical support was needed in developing the required services.

By the time the York Conference had borne these substantial fruits, I had left the Albany Trust. I had been intensively involved in the running of the HLRS and the Trust for more than twelve years, and had sat in the 'hot seat' for eight. I was physically and mentally jaded, emotionally drained by the burdens imposed by the work and by staffing problems at the office. So, soon after the York meeting, I told the Trustees of my decision to go at the end of September 1970. They appointed a new Director, Michael De-la-Noy, who had previously worked as a journalist for the Trust's current chairman, Lord Beaumont of Whitley, before becoming press secretary to the Archbishop of Canterbury, Dr Ramsey. Shortly before becoming Director of the Albany Trust De-la-Noy had been precipitately sacked from Church House for having written, in a personal capacity, two magazine articles on sexual topics,[10] and was consequently feeling quite militant about the subject.[11] He was to find that he needed all the militancy he could muster when he took over my desk at 32 Shaftesbury Avenue.

[10] In one of them, for *Forum*, he had maintained that 'the question of freedom (was) really at the heart of controversy over the Permissive Society', and that sexual behaviour in Britain had been so damaged by fear, secrecy and guilt that only a handful of people were now finding it possible to take the first tentative steps towards a sufficiently relaxed state of mind in which to enjoy themselves – adding that 'the hallmark of the reactionary is his desire to punish and to be punished'.

[11] He gives a vivid account of his experiences at Lambeth, and some trenchant views on the contemporary Church of England, in his book *A Day in the Life of God* (Citadel Press, 1971).

XIV

Out of the Closets

> 'Every person has the right to develop and extend their character and explore their sexuality through relationships with any other human being, without moral, social or political pressure ... We DEMAND honour, identity and liberation.'
>
> Gay Liberation Front

A fortnight after I left the Albany Trust the London Gay Liberation Front[1] held their first meeting at the London School of Economics. They introduced totally new concepts into gay and sexual politics in Britain, inspired by the US gay liberation movement which had erupted from nowhere in July 1969 when the patrons of a New York gay bar, the Stonewall, in Christopher Street, Greenwich Village, fought back for two days and nights against what had begun as a routine police raid for alleged infringement of the liquor licensing laws, but which turned into an historic riot that permanently transformed gay consciousness. Gay Pride and Gay Power were born that weekend. 'The guys there were so beautiful', said the poet Allen Ginsburg; 'they've lost that wounded look that fags all had ten years ago'.[2]

Two young gay English students, Bob Mellors and Aubrey Walter, who met through GLF in the States in the summer of 1970, determined to launch its concepts in Britain, and were the moving spirits behind the coming together of London GLF in October 1970. In his

---

[1] There are various versions of the etymology of 'gay'. Since the eighteenth century it was a slang term for a woman of easy virtue. Its adoption by homosexuals as a self-chosen description, as opposed to all the pejorative and insulting terms thrust upon them by others, contained a tinge of irony. Its use in this sense remains a bone of contention amongst homosexual as well as heterosexual people.

[2] For a contemporary history of the early American gay liberation movement, see Donn Teal, *The Gay Militants* (Stein and Day, New York, 1971).

account of the Gay Lib years,[3] Aubrey says that the twenty or so people who came to that first meeting did not really understand their transatlantic rhetoric and jargon, such as 'We gotta get out of the ghetto' and 'Out of the closets and into the streets'. But the notion of gay liberation caught on, and soon there were two or three hundred regular attenders at the LSE weekly meetings.

As I was now no longer constrained by my former Albany Trust role I went along to several of the early GLF meetings. They were extremely interesting, most enjoyable and generally heartening. The interest arose from the fact that here, for the first time in my experience, was a large gathering of gay men and women of widely differing ages, lifestyles and attitudes who came together to discuss what to do about their disadvantaged situation in society, and not merely for social relaxation or sexual interest. The enjoyment came from the very varied mix of people and the atmosphere of the meetings, which were often entertaining and light-hearted to the point of exuberance, and mildly chaotic as well as having a serious purpose. It was as if someone had said, 'Let a thousand pansies bloom in the basements of LSE'. GLF politics were left-wing in a light-hearted rather than a dourly doctrinaire way. Refreshingly, ideology was for once being put to the service of people, and not the other way round. I came as a matter of course to preface my remarks with 'Well, I'm *glad* to be bourgeois, and what I want to say is . . .' It was amusing to find myself striking up a political rapport with, and a strong personal liking for, a flamboyantly dressed Canadian with a striking 'Afro' hairstyle, Warren Hague; I think that, because we looked so unalike, the fact that we often agreed with each other quite spontaneously from opposite sides of the room lent added weight to our views.

GLF's new-found mood of infectious self-confidence was most heartening in its potential for serving redundancy notices to the gloomy peddlers of sickness, sin and punishment. Slogans such as 'Gay is Proud – Gay is Angry' struck a new note of self-assertion which was basically healthy, even if they did on occasion make an impact on the hostile world outside which resembled that of a butterfly stamping its foot. As a well-informed, shrewd, sympathetic, but by no means radical, commentator on homosexual issues has pointed out, the Gay

[3] *Come Together: the years of gay liberation 1970–73* edited and introduced by Aubrey Walter (Gay Men's Press, 1980).

Liberationists had cottoned on to one really crucial issue: they saw the need for a genuine sexual revolution:

> Well-meaning liberal ideas sometimes aggravate the situation. The notion that everyone is potentially bisexual contributes nothing towards the recognition of the differing needs of the average homosexual or heterosexual. The condemnation of gay clubs as ghetto situations carries the unwarranted assumption that ordinary clubs will allow gay people to seek each other out, to talk in endearments, to dance together and to kiss each other, as freely as heterosexuals can. The absence of crude legal discrimination is cold comfort to homosexuals who find themselves in an alien society where every institution, from housing estates to dance halls, caters only to the needs of heterosexuals. True homosexual equality means the homosexual millions making their presence felt, and this would mean a radical change in every walk of heterosexual life.[4]

But how were the 'homosexual millions' to make their presence felt when all but a handful of them stayed firmly in the closet?[5] GLF made a brave and pioneering effort to galvanise many more people into greater openness, and succeeded in creating a new image of 'gay consciousness' as well as in transforming a great many people's ways of thinking about themselves. As evangelical conversion therapy Gay Liberation was great. But remoulding the world inside one's head is difficult enough; it is far harder to revolutionise the world outside. GLF had some built-in weaknesses as an effective political movement, so that in the long term their lasting influence – paradoxically, in view of their socialist philosophy – has been stronger upon individuals than on society. As Aubrey Walter chronicles it in *Come Together*, GLF's trajectory resembled a collective orgasm: initial high excitement, a great upsurge of energy, a proliferation of groups, activities and projects, and then a sudden implosion into comparative quiescence; though with subsequent spin-offs into other areas of gay action, including *Gay News* and even CHE, which was to some extent radicalised by GLF's influence.

With hindsight this dispersal of GLF's energies was probably inevitable, given the conscious choices they made from the outset not

---

[4] D. J. West, *Homosexuality Re-Examined* (Duckworth, 1977), p. 149.
[5] Still a major problem. See Chapter XXI.

to become just another stodgy organisation with leaders, committee structures, formal 'democratic' procedures and all the endless bureaucratic kerfuffle already too obviously bogging down CHE – which GLF regarded as hilariously over-respectable and prissy. For their part, some members of CHE viewed this disturbing new phenomenon on their far left with dismay. All this boat-rocking would, they feared, turn the clock back and isolate gay people in a ghetto of their own making, denied by their own stridency the social acceptance they sought.[6]

Although evanescent, GLF made a lasting impact – some of it beneficial, some unhelpful in the long run. The neo-Marxist, Marcusian stance of some of its key spirits resulted in pronouncements which, however exhilarating at the time, provided millstones for other campaigners' necks. Thus the *GLF Manifesto*, published in 1971, began with the ringing assertion that

> The oppression of gay people starts with the most basic unit of society, the family, consisting of the man in charge, a slave as his wife, and their children on whom they force themselves as the ideal models. The very form of the family works against homosexuality.

The manifesto then dealt in similarly abrasive terms with school, church, the media, employers, the law, and psychiatry. But the ultimate form of oppression, it said, was *self*-oppression, when the gay person adopted and internalised straight people's definitions of what was good and bad. And the ultimate form of self-oppression was saying 'I am not oppressed', and believing it.

For many, such viewpoints had all the charismatic power of a religious conversion process. As the late Laurence Collinson (who later taught me most of what I know about Transactional Analysis and other aspects of counselling) put it in CHE's magazine *Lunch*,

---

[6] E.g. Martin Stafford, *Gay Lib/Homosexual Equality. A Reactionary Appraisal or a Realistic one?* (1973). Stafford, a young gay man of 'small-c' conservative views, wrote disgustedly of 'the blatant indecency of [GLF's] publications, their untoward appearance and unseemly deportment' and declared: 'What is now required is a new responsible organisation formed by homosexuals to oppose the fatuous excesses committed . . . and by forthright denunciation of those who perpetrate them, to redress the balance of bad publicity. . . .' He also lamented that 'even CHE is now committed . . . to an alliance with the screaming sisterhood of women's liberation'.

'CHE is an organisation; GLF is a way of life'.[7] Another GLF-er, living in a commune with 'twelve beautiful brothers', wrote that 'GLF is a key and only a key through which gay people can begin to understand their oppression right the way through back to the beginning'.[8] There was no scope here for compromise with sexist society, or for seeking to win friends and influence people in a gently persuasive way as the HLRS and Albany Trust had sought to do over the previous decade. Indeed, the Trust was seen by GLF (which bragged that it was the first pro-gay campaign without bishops[9]) as the epitome of archetypal Uncle Tom-ism, and I was consequently – according to the historian of gay liberation, Jeffrey Weeks – 'widely distrusted' by GLF and soon withdrew from their meetings.[10]

There is, of course, no sharp dividing line between 'revolutionaries', 'radicals' and 'reformists' when all are working in their various ways to improve existing conditions. Some of their goals conflict while others coincide; some tactics which seem right to one group appear crazily reckless or absurdly timid to others. But in my view their activities can often be successfully complementary; and it seems sad and wasteful when newcomers to the fray indulge in disparagement of those who have been hacking away longest at the coal face and who have created the freer climate in which their critics function.

Positive images of homosexuality were not, in fact, the invention of GLF. In an American symposium published in 1969,[11] Dr Franklin Kameny, whose skilled opposition to the US Federal Government's

---

[7] *Lunch* no. 5, January 1972.

[8] *Come Together* no. 15 (Notting Hill), Spring 1973.

[9] They did not realise, or care, how crucial the support of the bishops they scorned had been to the HLRS during the Lords' debates.

[10] Jeffrey Weeks, *Coming Out*, revised edition, 1990, p. 190. I was unaware of being 'widely distrusted' at GLF. In fact I greatly enjoyed the meetings, made some good friends there, and suggested GLF's first public demonstration, at Highbury Fields, with which they were immensely pleased. I withdrew because, when I returned to the Albany Trust in October 1971, I no longer felt able to attend GLF in a private capacity. Maybe they did not appreciate that I was there simply as myself; and there must have been some mild paranoia around my presence, because I was considerably surprised to read Aubrey Walter's melodramatic account of their success in roundly defeating my 'machinations' to 'capture the energy of GLF for the cause of respectable pressure-group politics'. (Op. cit., p. 16.) These machinations were mythical; it is fascinating what one sometimes learns about oneself from other people's writings, as I have discovered more than once.

[11] *The Same Sex: An Appraisal of Homosexuality,* ed. R. W. Weltge (United Church Press, Philadelphia, 1969), p. 145. Reprinted with permission.

discriminatory practices against homosexuals in the public services and the military I had so much admired when I met him in Washington, had written:

> It is time to open the closet door and to let in the sunshine; it is time to doff and to discard the secrecy, the disguise, and the camouflage; it is time to hold up your heads and to look the world squarely in the eye as the homosexuals that you are, confident of your equality, confident in the knowledge that as objects of prejudice and victims of discrimination you are right and they are wrong, and confident of the rightness of what you are and of the goodness of what you do; it is time to live your homosexuality fully, joyously, openly, and proudly, assured that morally, socially, physically, psychologically, emotionally, and in every other way: *Gay is good.* It is.

With all its brashness, GLF brought a welcome breath of fresh air and optimism to gay politics. Its energetic, largely young members[12] really believed, as had the Paris students of 1968, that it was going to be possible for them to transform the world; and one could only savour their enthusiasm and wish them well, while feeling circumspect about the outcome. Others – including the apparatchiks of CHE, and Michael De-la-Noy at the Albany Trust – were far more dismayed than I was at what they saw as GLF's irresponsibility and 'lunatic antics'.[13]

One useful product from the GLF stable was a critical analysis by its 'anti-psychiatry group' of the largely oppressive role of psychiatry in relation to homosexuality.[14] Like the Speijer Committee's report,[15] they attacked the very concept of homosexuality as a 'problem', pointing out that 'when a homosexual arrives to consult his GP (about his homosexuality), he endorses the illness theory by his mere presence'; and tartly observing:

---

[12] A misnomer, as there was no membership and no formal organisation.

[13] One entertaining 'antic' occurred when I was speaking with Lord Longford at a students' meeting in Cambridge. Some obviously nervous young men sitting in the front row, who had been fortifying themselves throughout the evening with liquid refreshment, suddenly stood up and took off all their clothes; whereupon Lord Longford became even more nervous than they were and marched out, remarking 'I think it's time to go'. I stayed.

[14] *Psychiatry and the Homosexual. A brief analysis of oppression.* Gay Liberation pamphlet no. 1.

[15] See Chapter XVI.

why then should a medical qualification be allowed to give weight to the ill-informed rubbish psychiatrists speak about homosexuality, or indeed any other aspect of the personality. A diploma in accountancy would be just as relevant.

Criticising the 'humane and liberal' trend of seeing deviants (sexual, political or criminal) as sick, the authors retorted:

> as one such 'deviant' group, we become increasingly resentful of this notion of tolerance for the unfortunate, which results in less savage punishment but also in a denial of our integrity and responsibility.

They perceived a sinister progression from sick through degenerate and disgusting to expendable:

> Only a generation and a stretch of water separates us from Hitler's gas-chambers, where thousands of homosexuals were murdered for no other reason than that of their homosexuality. . . . Today in Franco's Spain there exists in Huelva a concentration camp specifically for homosexuals, where they are subjected to intensive 'treatment' for long periods. . . . Throughout the world a blanket of silence and indifference covers the treatment of gay people. Freedom to love as one pleases is a human right to which the UN pays scant attention!

Psychiatrists, they noted, had not made the slightest effort to assess the potential of a homosexual way of life; they were only interested in its negative aspects.[16]

An offshoot of the GLF anti-psychiatry group was Icebreakers, an informal team of befrienders who, denying the need for any acquired skills or formal training, offered an initial contact with the gay world to lonely, shy and young gays. As they declined to observe any boundaries concerning age or status, their activities did cause some of us who were involved in the development of acceptable counselling services some worry. But luckily they did not become embroiled with the law.

At the opposite extreme of the respectability curve, the National Federation of Homophile Organisations, born out of the York Social Needs Conference, had finally been instituted. Quite unexpectedly I

---

[16] Around the same time the Albany Trust also published a critical pamphlet on the notion of homosexuality as illness: *Homosexuality and the Sickness Theory* by Louis Crompton Ph.D.

was invited to become its first (and, as it proved, its last) chairman; and, somewhat rashly, I accepted. NFHO had a long and elaborate constitution, drafted by a working group chaired by H. E. ('Ike') Cowen of CHE, an academic lawyer who worked extremely hard to produce a draft which satisfied all the reservations and hesitations voiced, mostly by CHE and SMG. So it seemed rather perverse that when these two groups walked out of NFHO a couple of years later, effectively busting it, they did so making the complaint that they could meet together when they wanted to 'without a 20-page constitution, a sliding-scale set of fees, joint group or individual membership, another executive committee and another round of annual general meetings and elections'.[17] This elaborate set-up was precisely what they themselves had insisted on having.

While the smaller groups – of whom there were several, both for men and for women, some with a membership almost as big as CHE's – saw NFHO as a safety-belt, and a useful structure for co-ordinating ideas, CHE and SMG saw NFHO as imposing tiresome constraints upon them. So I felt like a whipless ringmaster in a circus where the heavyweight animals did not want to jump through the hoops of joint National Council of Social Service membership, common policy framing, co-ordinated press relations, and so forth, which the smaller ones perceived as benefits. The NFHO executive committee meetings became increasingly frustrating, and when the end came I regretted NFHO's effective demise, but did not strive officiously to keep it alive.

GLF's frontal attack on the ignorant popular stereotypes of gay people was overdue. In reality gay people have only two things in common: their emotional/sexual interest in other members of their own sex, and their legal/social oppression. And even these common factors are experienced in a uniquely different personal way by each individual. All the stereotypes which lump 'homosexuals' into categories which only exist in the minds of those inventing them are false; some, such as Richard Hauser's forty-odd types, are meaningless.

The Wolfenden Committee had also dismissed stereotyping with its customary succinctness:

> Homosexuality is not, in spite of widely held belief to the contrary, peculiar to members of particular professions or social

[17] *Gay News* 31.

classes; nor, as is sometimes supposed, is it peculiar to the intelligentsia. Our evidence shows that it exists among all callings and at all levels of society; and that among homosexuals will be found not only those possessing a high degree of intelligence, but also the dullest oafs. (para. 36)

Homosexuals knew the old, negative stereotypes were false. Their experience taught them that homosexual inclinations and behaviour occurred amongst many who did not fit into any such moulds. Nevertheless, as homosexuals became increasingly visible some of them adopted distinctive dress styles and other overt characteristics which gave them a common feeling of positive identity. Gay Liberation accentuated this process, extending it beyond the wearing of pink triangle badges[18] to fresh ways of thinking and new personal/political attitudes. For some, 'breaking the mould' involved overturning conventional concepts of dress and behaviour – deliberate 'gender-fucking' activities such as appearing publicly in beards, beads and frocks.[19]

The snag with this GLF stance, though, was that, whether it wished to do so or not, it implanted a new stereotype of 'gayness' in the public mind, and also in the minds of a new generation of homosexuals: the image of the blatant, flaunting, determinedly iconoclastic, far-out, far-Left sexual rebel, despising and challenging all society's accepted values and scornful of those homosexuals – the majority – who still kept their heads down. For some young gay people this new phenomenon was inspiring and liberating; for others it was distasteful and dismaying. And it was a gift to the unscrupulous polemicists of the 'New Right' who sought to entrench old-fashioned, traditional, conventional sexual values as a pillar of their brand of conservatism by ridiculing anyone seeking changes in sexual laws and *mores* as belonging to the 'Loony Left'. The high profile of such militancy in the early 1970s, and the success as the decade wore on of

[18] The pink triangle was the identification mark which homosexual prisoners were forced to wear in the Nazi concentration camps, where tens of thousands of homosexuals were exterminated for no other offence than their sexual nature. Gay Liberationists wear the pink triangle as a badge of honour. For the harrowing details of the Nazi pogrom against homosexuals, see Heinz Heger: *The Men with the Pink Triangle* (GMP Publishers, 1986) and Richard Plant: *The Pink Triangle* (Mainstream Publishing, 1987).

[19] This too might result in legal penalties for such vague offences as 'insulting behaviour likely to cause a breach of the peace'.

more conventional campaigns such as that waged by the Labour Campaign for Gay Rights to get homosexual equality accepted as a plank of the Labour Party's platform, made the slur that gay rights was a 'Loony Left' issue more plausible in the 1980s than it was previously.

Over the past decade it has, in fact, become much harder to approach the subject on an even-handed, non-party basis as the HLRS was able to do during the law reform campaign of the 1960s – when the consistent support of some sixty Conservative MPs was a crucial factor in changing the law. Although the Liberals and (more hesitantly) the Social Democrats both supported further reforms towards legal equality (the Liberals, indeed, more strongly and consistently than the Labour Party), most Conservatives held aloof; and in the Thatcher years the party machine became increasingly hostile. The alleged misdeeds of 'Loony Left' local councils in supposedly 'promoting' homosexuality – in fact what they were doing was to include sexual orientation in equal opportunities programmes aimed at combating discrimination – became a live issue in the 1987 general election, and ultimately spawned the illiterate and contemptible section 28 of the 1988 Local Government Act which prohibited the 'promotion' by local authorities of homosexuality as 'a pretended family relationship'.[20]

Margaret Thatcher herself – apparently unmindful of her libertarian principles which had impelled her to vote in support of the 1967 Sexual Offences Act as a young backbench MP – proclaimed sarcastically in her post-election party conference victory speech in October 1987 that 'children who need to be taught to respect traditional moral values are being taught that they have an inalienable right to be gay': and so – whether intentionally or not – she gave the green light to assorted queer-bashers in her party and its sycophantic tabloid press supporters. There was a small and determined Conservative Group for Homosexual Equality, but most Tory MPs (including some widely known to be gay) shunned it, and it carried no weight within the party. This state of affairs was paradoxical, since the Conservatives presented themselves as the party of the individual's freedom of choice against the interfering Nanny State. Yet on this issue, in particular, they seemed determined to go on playing the heavy father.

[20] See below chapter XIX.

XV

Testing Times at the Trust

'It is a time of very exciting moves. . . . There can
be few organisations which attract such a fund of
goodwill and support as the Albany Trust. . . . The
Trust is now, in staff terms, able to forge ahead.'

Harold Haywood
AT Work No. 1

In the autumn of 1971 I returned to the Albany Trust in totally
unforeseen circumstances. The staff crisis which had contributed to
my leaving had swiftly engulfed Michael De-la-Noy and put paid, for
the time being, to the forward thrust of the Trust's work and influence.
Within a few weeks of his arrival De-la-Noy had felt obliged to rid
himself of the remaining staff, including Doreen Cordell. This
unleashed considerable resentment amongst some of the Trust's supporters who, after my departure, had seen Doreen as the ongoing
embodiment of the Trust – which she herself had mistakenly come to
believe she was.[1]

The avalanche of casework continued to cascade in as Michael
De-la-Noy endeavoured to concentrate on building up the Trust's
public relations and social work contacts, which he felt to be more
than ever necessary because of the emergence of GLF. With only
enough resources to employ one secretary, and having himself to
undertake many speaking engagements involving much long-distance
travel (he was then living at Brighton), he soon became exhausted to
the point of near-breakdown. Even when the Rev. Michael Butler,
who was then Deputy Director at the London Samaritans, temporarily

---

[1] After leaving the Trust Doreen Cordell started her own counselling agency,
'Access'. She died of a throat complaint in May 1976. It was a great pity that her exceptional
energy and enthusiasm were marred by her refusal to accept the inevitable constraints
imposed upon an impoverished and overstretched agency such as the Albany Trust was.

took over all the Trust's casework, the problems facing the Trust remained formidable. By the summer of 1971 De-la-Noy concluded that he was not getting enough active support from the Trustees to put the Trust back on its feet, and so he resigned.[2]

Meanwhile, I had been vainly endeavouring to build up a freelance consultancy for small charities and other social service groups. I found that many of those I approached were extremely interested in my knowledge and experience, but few had any spare money to pay me with, and I had no intention of getting involved with the treadmill of fund-raising on a percentage commission for any of them. So when Michael De-la-Noy threw in the towel the Albany Trustees asked me to return to Shaftesbury Avenue on a temporary, fort-holding basis. With very mixed feelings, I agreed; and (not, as it proved, for the last time) I found myself unexpectedly once more the custodian of the Albany Trust's papers and affairs after I had thought that I had left them behind me for ever.

Going back into that familiar, now empty, office was an eerie experience. When I had left, almost exactly a year before, there had been a staff of four and several thousand pounds in hand. Now there was no staff, and a sizeable deficit to be cleared off somehow. For me that office was peopled with ghosts – some of living people, some of the dead: memories (nice and horrid) not only of Joy, Doreen and other staff, but of many outside the Trust with whom I had worked over the years on the business of law reform and the exciting phase of developing social work which had followed. Now what? I quickly decided that it was not realistic to remain in Shaftesbury Avenue; the offices were too large and expensive for the time of retrenchment ahead. So I moved out to the suburbs – first to Kilburn, and then (more satisfactorily) to Highbury. There I singlehandedly dealt as best I could with the Trust's still large correspondence, while Michael Butler continued to look after the counselling work, an aspect with which he has been continuously associated ever since.

---

[2] 'Each day has become a demoralising grind revolving around financial worry and administration', De-la-Noy wrote in a memorandum to the Trustees preceding his resignation. 'I see no prospect of this burden being lifted (on my return from holiday I have been faced with 250 letters to answer in the first week), to think, to plan, to write, to act creatively . . . my sitting room has simply been turned into an office. . . . I only returned home at 1.30 a.m. this morning from an Albany Trust speaking engagement.' I knew the syndrome, and sympathised.

It soon became clear that the Trust must be placed on a firmer footing, or else wind up. Once again Raymond Clarke came to the rescue. Now head of the national organisations division of the National Council for Social Service, he approached Miss (later Dame) Geraldine M. Aves CBE who had recently retired as Chief Welfare Officer of the Ministry of Health, and she agreed to chair a small working party to examine the Trust's future. Miss Aves was a formidable personage who was widely held in considerable awe – though she was never anything but extremely charming to me. She quickly perceived that the Trust was a pioneer in an increasingly visible field of unmet need. Largely thanks to her guiding hand and influence a three-year development grant, initially of £10,000 a year, was obtained from the Voluntary Services Unit of the Home Office late in 1973, conditional upon the Trust giving an undertaking 'that these public funds will not be used to exert pressure on the Government for any change in the law on homosexuality'.

I was sitting alone in the small house in Highbury which was the Trust's temporary home when I received the anxiously awaited phone call telling me that our application had been successful. My feeling of relief was profound. But not for long: two or three weeks later – ten days before Christmas – I went into central London to do my Christmas shopping. I remember walking about the festively decorated streets and eating lunch in a familiar Soho restaurant feeling strangely detached from everything going on around me as if it was all rather unreal. During the night I awoke with intense stomach pains. The usual home remedies were of no avail; I became much worse. On the next (Saturday) morning I was taken by ambulance, semi-conscious, to hospital; then, after several hours' agonising wait, to an isolation hospital because it was thought I might have some mysterious tropical disease. What I in fact had was a burst appendix which, fortunately for me, was at last accurately diagnosed. So I was transferred to yet another hospital, where I was operated on immediately for peritonitis and spent Christmas day propped up in bed on a post-operative drip-feed. I did not return to the office until the following April.

The Voluntary Services Unit grant offered the Albany Trust a new window of opportunity. It also brought a new set of mounting pressures and strains to be struggled with for the next six years – years of considerable, though transient, achievement.

Our grant application, after explaining how the Trust's inability to provide adequate counselling and other help for the rising tide of applicants (over 2000 in 1970) had led it to decide to concentrate its limited resources on providing advice, training and information to other agencies, instead of seeking to run a nationwide counselling service itself, commented that there was even less help available in most towns and cities outside London than in the capital, so that many calls were still reaching the Trust from all parts of Britain. The Trust therefore wished to appoint a Field Officer whose basic task would be to establish and build up links with a nationwide network of agencies and individuals competent to counsel and otherwise assist members of sexual minorities and others with psychosexual problems. This would involve creating a national information index showing where and what type of help was available; such an index would also make it possible to bring helpers together and improve standards.

The setting up of adequate training programmes would be another important aspect; at present, there were no such courses dealing primarily with those areas of need with which the Trust was mainly concerned. 'Courses in all aspects of psychosexual development and their implications for individuals and society are an urgent need.' So was further research – 'so far, there has been very little responsible research (and no large-scale research) in the psychosexual field in the United Kingdom'. And a far more extensive programme of education was called for, both about sex itself and social responses towards its various aspects; since lack of such education, at school and later, was exacerbating the prevailing attitudes which gave rise to many of the problems.

The Trust's traditional threefold aims of research, education and social action thus remained guiding principles; and the VSU grant enabled the Trust to regroup and look forward – for the first time in its fifteen-year life – to a modest assurance of survival for at least three years, so that a start could be made on a more coherent programme than the hand-to-mouth damage limitation measures of the early 1970s. The Trustees regrouped, bringing in some new blood – notably Charlotte Wolff, and the Hon. Lucilla (Lil) Butler, former Home Secretary 'RAB' Butler's daughter-in-law, who was heavily involved in youth work both at the National Association of Youth Clubs and with the Soho Project, where I had first met her. Other new Trustees who joined us in 1975 were Sue Barnet of the Family Planning Association's 'Grapevine' sex education project; Harold Haywood, ex-director of the National Association of Youth Clubs; and Tony Smythe, formerly of NCCL and now Director of the National Association for Mental Health – MIND. Before my illness we had recruited an administrative officer, David Barnard, who had previously worked for the NCCL, and who brought a welcome touch of administrative competence to our affairs. During my four months' absence from the office David did a great deal of hard work and forward planning, as his comprehensive agenda papers prepared for the Trustees' meetings testify. He became Secretary of the Trust at the end of 1974 until he left a year later.

Another stroke of luck for the Trust was to be offered, at the end of 1974, rent-free offices for two years in Clapham on the premises of a perfumier's company. These had been newly decorated, carpeted and rewired by our generous landlords, and were centrally heated – a palatial home compared to those we had previously occupied. There was also an adjoining derelict warehouse on several floors, and this immediately caught our imagination for possible conversion into a social centre or a youth club (not necessarily associated with the Trust).[3]

Partly thanks to the new Trustees, applications to two livery companies for grants to cover the salary of the Field Officer were successful. And an application to the Department of Education and Science for a grant to appoint a Youth Officer was also successful. So by the end of 1975, when the Field Officer, Jan McHugh, took up her post, the Trust's situation had been transformed and we were more optimistic about the future. Small-scale training courses were being undertaken, including one for the National Association of Youth Clubs and another for teachers, youth workers and educational welfare workers employed by the Inner London Education Authority, who were interested in the possibility of the Trust undertaking further counselling and training work on their behalf. Our publicity material was being overhauled by another new Trustee, Rodney Bennett-England, a pro-

---

[3] Through Lil Butler's youth service contacts we explored this idea for a considerable time, but without any practical outcome.

fessional journalist,[4] who proposed replacing *Man and Society* with a new Trust broadsheet paper, *AT Work*, which would appear quarterly.

Public relations were, as always, a matter of balance. Too low a profile meant that the Trust was insufficiently known; yet prominent involvement in every controversy surrounding the inevitably contentious topics we were concerned with might be counterproductive, by getting us sensational publicity of the kind we would rather be without which might jeopardise our relations with the Government and 'establishment' agencies whose goodwill depended upon our proceeding quietly and unobtrusively. Awareness of these dangers did not, in the event, help us to avoid them entirely, although we sought to pursue a middle-of-the-road course. A lunch which we gave for Fleet Street 'agony aunties' in March 1976 was a success, and one of them, Angela Willans ('Mary Grant' of *Woman's Own*), later became a Trustee.

Relationships with the homophile movement and the new-fledged gay press[5] were another problematic area. Earlier differences of emphasis, and consequent misunderstandings of the Trust's basic stance, had been compounded by the passage of time when so little had been achieved because of our dire financial and practical straits. So a newly emergent Trust, apparently opulent (to judge from its new offices) and partly Government-funded, was regarded with considerable suspicion and some envy. References to the Trust in *Gay News* and other homophile publications tended to be ill-informed. This was a continuing problem; a good deal of our new Field and Youth Officers' time was taken up in endeavouring to dispel the hostile atmosphere, which initially surprised and puzzled them, and which they in their turn tended to blame on to me and earlier workers at the Trust.

We were by no means out of the financial wood. The salaries and overheads for the new appointments were not fully covered by the VSU, DES and livery company grants, so that we were back to 'square minus one' so far as fund-raising was concerned. This remained a major and time-consuming worry throughout the expansionist early 1970s. Professional fund-raisers proved as unhelpful as ever. Even the

---

[4] He was President of the Institute of Journalists in 1985, and its Honorary Treasurer for many years.

[5] *Gay News*, the first national newspaper for homosexual men and women, was launched in the summer of 1972.

occasional large single donations which had been life-savers during the law reform campaign of the 1960s were much rarer now; the Trust was only saved by the totally unexpected arrival of two or three residuary legacies during the 1970s, bequeathed by old-time supporters who appreciated what we had previously achieved. These, though an enormous relief, were only 'windfalls'. With expenditure already running at some £1850 per month by the end of 1975, the Trust's financial situation remained precarious and extremely worrying. By the middle of 1976 annual income was running at just under £24,000, £19,000 of which came from Government grants.[6] This support was of limited duration, and would almost certainly be rapidly withdrawn if we put a foot wrong in the eyes of the civil servants or the politicians.

A carefully planned and sustained fund-raising drive seemed essential, and in order to mount this the Trustees agreed in the Spring of 1976 that Rodney Bennett-England should be retained as publicity and fund-raising consultant for two days a week. He proposed launching a major appeal which would ensure the Trust's survival for the next decade. This proved to be the beginning of a much greater involvement for him in the Trust's chequered fortunes than either Rodney or I envisaged at the time.

It is remarkable that with such an uncertain future the Trust managed to achieve so much in these years. Even before the new staff officers were appointed the Trustees were taking initiatives in the training field, and involving the Trust in inter-agency discussions on teenagers at risk in central London – a topic which was currently causing considerable public concern following a television programme, *Johnny Go Home*, about male prostitution in the West End.[7] They were also involved in talks with the National Association for Care and Resettlement of Offenders (NACRO) and the Home Office about a NACRO project to study and improve the way sex offenders were dealt with within the prison system. The Churches were another

[6] Which had risen to an annual £27,000 by the end of 1979, when the grants were terminated.

[7] This interest eventually led to a meeting with senior officers of the Metropolitan Police division which covered Soho, from which Harold Haywood and I came away with the clear message that the police regarded social workers and voluntary groups as ineffective and unimportant in the West End scene. What they said to us, in effect, was: 'We know how to do our job, and we don't need you to tell us anything.'

area of continuing contact and discussion, the Trust sponsoring meetings on 'Christian Response to Sexual Variation' and attending a Catholic Renewal Movement day conference on homosexuality.

1975 had been a busy year. 1976 was much busier, with both the Field Officer and (from July) the Youth Officer in post, and their work opening out new leads to be followed through by the Trustees and other staff. Direct counselling was resumed by the Trust, with a team of part-time counsellors being recruited and trained under Michael Butler, who had urged that a higher proportion of the Trust's income should be allotted to this work in view of the extent to which the Trust's reputation and credibility was founded on its counselling expertise.

The new influx of people and energies caused me to consider what structure would best enable the Trust to function effectively. The old, informal relationship which had existed between the previous Trustees and myself since my return in 1971, when Michael Butler and I had been the only functioning members of the Trust, could obviously not continue. With so many important policy decisions to be made, and their implementation requiring the active attention of other Trustees, it seemed sensible to reorganise ourselves into several sub-committees which could co-opt appropriate 'outsiders' who were not Trustees, and for the full body of Trustees to meet once a quarter to transact necessary legal, financial and administrative business. In addition an advisory panel of suitably qualified people would be recruited. This was agreed between myself and the new Chairman of Trustees, Harold Haywood, who took a more active role than his predecessors. I welcomed his involvement, though as time went on demarcation problems arose between us.

During the first half of 1976 the Field Officer embarked upon the challenging task of mapping out her sphere of activity. With hindsight the Trustees perhaps expected too much from this post, whose nationwide scope and potential for new initiatives was virtually limitless.[8] I had first met Jan McHugh through the Standing Conference for the

[8] The Field Officer's job specification stated that 'the primary task of the Field Officer is to establish and build up links between the Trust and counsellors and welfare agencies in all part of the United Kingdom, with the aim of improving the standards and amount of psychosexual counselling and other help available, with especial reference to the needs of sexual minorities. This will entail involvement in training programmes and being cognisant with the Trust's own counselling work.'

Advancement of Counselling, which was now in the process of transforming itself into the British Association for Counselling (BAC),
on whose executive committee I sat. Jan was American, bright and
enthusiastic, with a refreshingly direct approach. We liked each other,
and I admired the determined way she tackled her daunting assign-
ment. Her early months were spent in getting to know both the Trust
itself and its network of outside contacts, especially the homophile
movement. Both aspects proved unexpectedly difficult; the Trust, she
thought, was surprisingly disorganised, not only in its record-keeping
but also in its internal communications. It seemed to lack a clear
identity: she had expected more interest and involvement from the
Trustees, and was disheartened that 'the establishment of a new post
was greeted with little or no interest or support for some time'. She
was surprised that there seemed to be no clear remit for her job. This
was to some extent true, in the sense that the Field Officer's role
inevitably depended on the personality and perceptions of the
appointee – it was not possible to lay down hard priorities until the
new Field Officer had first explored the field; we simply did not know
what the most pressing needs of other workers out in 'the sticks' might
be until they had been visited and talked with at some length.

Confusion about the Trust's purpose and role was, she discovered,
almost universal outside it. In the

> newer and more popular homophile organisations . . . no one
> knew what the Trust was doing, what its present activities and
> future plans entailed, and there existed an extremely unhelpful
> history of the more recent dearth of communication. . . . The
> relieving of unnecessary antagonism between ourselves and the
> homophile movement became one of my greatest concerns. . . .

What was the nature of the Trust's vaunted 'expertise'? she asked. If
we claimed to know better about counselling than many other agencies
we must be clear about our own standards, and what we had to offer
in terms of training and back-up support. We must have 'gifts, parcels,
packages to give or to sell in order to obtain anything at all in return'.[9]
We needed a higher media profile, more and better publications,

[9] 'At the moment', she wrote in one of her reports, 'we do not offer anything
particularly saleable, apart from the renown and expertise of one man – and it is unrealistic
to base *all* our future worth on little else.' I was gratified by the compliment, although
it exaggerated my contribution and downplayed that of others, including Jan herself.

including a history of the Trust, and visual aids, including, if possible, films.[10] While I understood, and sympathised with, Jan's feelings of frustration, the situation was, from my longer-term perspective, more of a 'chicken-and-egg' one than she realised.

By the late summer the Youth Officer funded by the Department of Education and Science, Ric Rogers, had been appointed, as well as an Organising Secretary, Arlo Tatum, to relieve me from the burden of routine administration, and the Trust had moved from Clapham to its last office home in Strutton Ground, Westminster. Steering groups had been convened for both the Field Officer and the Youth Officer (the latter's including a representative from the DES). There was an air of optimism around, and the stage seemed set for a new surge forward.

But this did not occur easily. Although both appointments had been made with a three-year work programme in view, both the Field Officer and the Youth Officer decided to leave the Trust after they had only been in post for twelve months. This inevitably caused disruption, as their successors had to familiarise themselves with what had already been done and pick up the threads. And welding so many new Trustees and staff into a smoothly running team was complicated, not least because both the Field Officer and the Youth Officer spent the bulk of their time out of the office.

The Youth Officer began his out-of-London work mainly in two pilot areas – the North East, and the East Midlands – contacting local education authorities and counselling services and offering Trust input into their training courses. Some responded enthusiastically; others ignored his approaches. His job remit was clear, but his title was misleading – because he was working with the youth *services* and with educators, not directly with young people – and there proved to be ample scope for misunderstanding and misrepresentation of his role. While we knew only too well the very real situations of fear and isolation, and sometimes of actual scapegoating, endured by all too many teenagers because of their homosexual orientation, and their urgent need for better understanding and practical support, those of us who had been longest at the Trust were also very aware of the strength of the 'corruption theory', and the virulent prejudices and

---

[10] The making of an Albany Trust-sponsored film was an aspiration whose fulfilment eluded us down the years.

antipathies likely to be unleashed against anyone perceived as recruiting officers for homosexuality.[11]

These hostile perceptions of the Trust were of course quite illogical, but we were soon to discover their strength. The Trust's frank interest in two such emotionally-charged areas as the sexual orientation of teenagers and the problems of paedophiles were to be churned together by our enemies into a lethal cocktail.

[11] 'Whereas the predominant concern about heterosexual molestation of girls is that they may find the experience off-putting, and thereby become anxious, frigid or even lesbian, the concern for boys involved homosexually with older men is that they may find the experience attractive and be seduced into homosexuality'. (Howard League, *Unlawful Sex*, 1985, para. 4.16.)

XVI

Young Gays: A Burning Issue

'Why should boys and young men continue to have
the door of law-abiding society slammed in their
faces? It does not matter whether it is slammed by
a policeman, a doctor, a teacher or anyone else –
the result is a tragedy for the individual and one
more criminal for society.'

HLRS correspondence files

The Trust's endeavours to alleviate the plight of adolescent boys and
girls growing up into awareness of their homosexuality stemmed from
our conviction that much of the mistreatment meted out to homosexual
people originated in social ignorance and fear rather than from deliberate cruelty. A great many people were still, as Harold Haywood put it,
pig-ignorant not only about homosexuality but about practically everything to do with sex and sexuality generally. The provision of sound sex
education remained woefully inadequate, as the postbags of newspaper
'agony aunties' abundantly testified. We believed that the Trust's unique
experience as a receptacle of social misery qualified us to make a valuable
contribution in the sex education and training fields.

Our growing concentration during the mid-1970s on the need
to provide more adequate training and accurate information about
sexuality for youth workers and teachers was bound to incur the hostility of those who vehemently denied that there was such a thing as a
genuinely gay teenager because, they maintained – flying in the face
of our twenty years' experience of counselling hundreds such young
people – homosexuals were seductively manufactured and did not
simply grow into unforced awareness of their erotic preferences. Harsh
sentences passed in pre-law reform days on teenagers convicted of
homosexual misbehaviour were still sometimes copied with little

modification after 1967 as the new law continued to be applied with severity against those who broke it. A middle-aged housewife supporter of the Trust, Mrs Rose Robertson, had bravely started a counselling service, 'Parents' Enquiry', run from her South London home, for gay teenagers and their parents; she has done invaluable work over the years in a low-key way, combating ignorance and prejudice and alleviating much adolescent fear and unhappiness. In the later 1960s Doreen Cordell and Michael Butler were also specifically concerned to help young people in trouble. It was therefore a natural progression for the Trust to obtain a Department of Education and Science special project grant in 1975 to appoint a Youth Project Officer for three years to explore the training in sexuality currently being carried out in the youth service field, and to develop and increase the scope of that training.

One aspect of which we were very aware was the difference between official and educational attitudes towards sexuality and homosexuality in this country and in most others. One of our reasons for appointing a Youth Officer was to begin remedying this state of affairs.

We had the Netherlands particularly in mind. I had discovered in the early 1960s how that small country impressively combined pragmatic social conservatism with enlightened commonsense attitudes to aspects of sex which usually produced only punitive or titillating responses of the 'shock, horror, nudge nudge, wink wink' variety in Britain. As long ago as 1970 the Sexual Law Reform Society had commissioned and paid for the translation of a Dutch government-sponsored report which had made some eminently sensible observations about teenage sexual development.[1] Although no-one who had read it attentively could have recognised it from her description, it was this report which Mrs Whitehouse luridly called 'a campaigning document which seeks to justify the gratification of adult lust for children';[2] while a body calling itself the 'Responsible Society' mislabelled it 'a document which seeks to justify adult sexual gratification with minors'. That the Sexual Law Reform Society had presumed to sully the English language by having such a dreadful document translated, and that the Albany Trust dared to distribute it, gave these indignant worthies major cause for offence.

---

[1] As the translation was obscure in places, a few explanatory 'Albany Trust footnotes' were added – with most unfortunate future consequences.

[2] *The Guardian*, 10 January 1979.

What did the Speijer Report actually say?

In December 1967 a Dutch woman MP proposed repeal of the law passed in 1911 which had raised the age of consent for male homosexual behaviour to twenty-one. A Catholic psychiatrist, she said, had recently expressed the opinion that an individual's sexual orientation was decided before the age of six, so that it was 'out of the question that a person in his sixteenth year of life could be made into a homosexual by seduction'. The Minister of Justice replied that, at his request, the Minister for Social Affairs and Health had asked the Health Council to report on what consequences were likely to arise from repeal, with special emphasis on the dangers of homosexual seduction and of otherwise heterosexual adolescents being permanently deflected into a homosexual way of life.

A committee was accordingly set up in 1968 under the chairmanship of Professor Dr N. Speijer, professor of social psychiatry at the State University of Leyden, with five other members all but one of whom were eminent psychiatrists or neurologists. (The sixth was an Inspector for Public Moral Welfare.) The questions which they examined, with their answers, were:

1 Q: What are the current medical and scientific views about homosexuality? A: A homosexual orientation is fixed in most people long before they reach puberty, and is perfectly compatible with mental and moral health.

2 Q: Is there any danger of the seduction of minors above the age of sixteen by homosexual adults? A: No, generally speaking.

3 Q: Does a homosexual experience turn minors aged over sixteen permanently homosexual? A: No.

4 Q: Could a young person's heterosexual development be adversely affected by homosexual experiences between the ages of sixteen and twenty-one? A: No.

5 Q: Are there any other harmful consequences for young people's psychological development of a change in the law which need to be taken into account? A: No.

The committee unanimously agreed that a youngster's homosexual disposition was usually determined long before puberty. They found that most researchers believed there was usually a congenital factor in the causation of homosexuality, but that environment – especially relationships with parents in early childhood – sometimes played an important part. They examined the concept of 'normality' in sexuality, and noted that this was determined according to the context in which it was being discussed – statistical, biological, ethical, sociological, or medical – pointing out that

> the very act of making a certain category of people (e.g. homo-
> sexuals, women) into an 'object of study' is of itself judgemental,
> and leads to alienation and to generalisations which are not always
> valid and which may create discrimination.

If, for example, someone conceived the idea that we should no longer divide people according to the colour of their skin but according to their height, the entire world would be different, the committee said. (And giants and dwarves do indeed experience discrimination.)

It was the committee's considered opinion that homosexuality should not merely be tolerated as a 'deviation', but ought to be recognised as a distinct form of human love. In this way the common attributes of homosexuals and heterosexuals would be acknowledged. Many researchers had clearly stated that it was incorrect to discrimi-nate between the quality of love that can be found in heterosexual and in homosexual relationships. In each, the mutual giving of love could have a positive influence on personal development and moral health. In the current state of knowledge it was only possible to give subjective answers to the question of whether homosexuals were both morally and emotionally healthy and mentally fit; but if the World Federation of Mental Health's 1948 definition of mental health as a condition permitting the optimum physical, intellectual and emotional develop-ment of the individual was applied, homosexuals who were fully self-accepting and socially well-adjusted could not be regarded as 'sick' – although this did not exclude the desirability of a supportive thera-peutic, psychological and pastoral environment. To a great extent the emotional conflicts and disturbances of homosexuals could be attributed to the prejudice and discrimination which society exercised against them. Even so, many homosexuals lived in harmony with themselves and their environments, and could be considered as healthy persons who were not legitimate subjects for therapy.

The Speijer Committee then examined the concept of 'seduction' – a term which, they commented, with its connotation of 'leading astray to do wrong', implied a morally disapproving judgement. They preferred to use the more neutral term 'initiation' in discussing the establishment of sexual contact (whether heterosexual or homosexual) between adults and younger people. Such situations, they emphasised, could be initiated by either the older or the younger person; and frequently they were mutually constructed. A large proportion of human behaviour – and, especially with young people, their appearance, mode of dress and form of transport – involved the creation of 'seductive' situations and was comparable with the decoy, 'showing off' and sexually motivated behaviour observed in the animal world:

> A society which seeks to eliminate all seductive situations as much as possible will not encourage public moral welfare. On the contrary, it is desirable for young people of both sexes that they are able to meet and cope with such situations. A normal development requires broad possibilities of introduction, experiment, contact and initiation. Only the existence of such possibilities will enable the young person to choose independence and responsibility, to accept and to reject, to recognise and acknowledge himself and by so doing to realise himself. The risks and dangers of sexual maturing and self-realisation are part of life, and like other fields of exploration they belong to the growing-up process.

Fears of 'seduction' into permanent homosexuality through adolescent experience were, the Speijer Committee said, greatly exaggerated:

> Permanent homosexuality only occurs in those who are already predisposed towards it, and it has not been proved that homosexual initiation has a damaging effect upon such young people. On the contrary, far from being damaging to a young person who was homosexual, initiatory contacts could often be of positive help to them by reducing or eliminating the stress and frustration caused by isolation; the young homosexual, unsure of her- or himself in the formative stage of personality, urgently requires sympathetic and understanding support, for lack of which he might remain in an emotional vacuum for a long period. Not only will a greater amount of honesty about their situation, and appropriate possibilities of contact, assist young homosexuals in their maturing process; it may also have a positive aspect for heterosexual young people, who are often extremely ignorant of, and prejudiced against, homosexuality.

No doubt it was this robustly unequivocal rejection of the notion that all initiation into homosexual lovemaking was evil and harmful which earned the Speijer Committee the ire of Mary Whitehouse and her friends.

The disadvantages of the existing law for moral welfare were real and important, the Speijer Committee concluded. They discerned many positive advantages in reducing the age of consent so as to eliminate discrimination between heterosexuals and homosexuals. Beneficial effects of repeal included greater possibilities of providing adequate and realistic help to young homosexuals; reduction of the corrupting potentialities of blackmail and teenage prostitution; and removal of disadvantages and dangers created by the law for homosexual adults, whose relationships with over sixteens were treated as criminal in circumstances which would be innocent for heterosexuals.

> These people, who do not experience their unasked-for propensity as criminal, are now additionally subjected to the humiliating effect of police prosecution and legal punishment. This may cause a loss of self-esteem and of valuable relationships, resulting in serious consequences for psychological health.

The Committee asked whether, bearing in mind that homosexuals experienced the same need for contacts and relationships that heterosexuals did, homosexual initiation was likely to cause greater damage to an adolescent than heterosexual initiation? They concluded that a youngster of sixteen and over was quite capable of forming his or her own opinion, not least concerning sexual activity. By sixteen, sexual orientation was well established in most cases, and they saw little possibility of a heterosexual youngster being diverted by 'seduction' into permanent homosexuality. If, after such an approach, the young person responded positively, 'it must be assumed that he or she was emotionally ready for this approach, and in a sense had been waiting for it'. The dangers of sexual activity, whether heterosexual or homosexual, for children and young people were commonly overestimated. However, youngsters needed, and should be given, protection against abuse of authority by parents, teachers and others, and the laws prohibiting sexual activity between those over and under sixteen should be retained.

Legal or social discrimination against young homosexuals created an obstacle to the provision of support and help for them, the Committee said:

The minor who realises his propensity to homosexuality is nearly always deprived in his own surroundings of possibilities to learn to accept this form of sexuality in a heterosexual society which is usually anti-homosexual. For the most constructive way of adapting to his sexuality, it is necessary that the homosexual minor is admitted to environments with equals, where he or she will be able to meet persons of their own age-group as well as older people. Youth societies, student clubs and other forms of institutionalised opportunity to meet other homosexuals are important from a mental health point of view.

'Sexual dangers and the risks of seduction are greatly exaggerated amongst the other dangers to which a young person is exposed in life', the Speijer Committee sensibly concluded. The findings of the Committee, as well as its general tone and temper, were indeed remarkable, coming from a Government-appointed committee of mental health experts. But they were of course anathema to that vociferous school of moral and sexual stoneagers who want society to treat adults as children and teenagers as toddlers, and who view homosexuality as an 'unnatural perversion'. As the Speijer Committee said, such homophobic people were too easily inclined to advise the prohibition of homosexual behaviour: but such a prohibition could only rightfully be founded on the dangers which such conduct might cause to other people.

It is heartening that within a few months of the publication of the Committee's eminently sensible report the Dutch Government asked Parliament to repeal the age of consent law of 1911 (article 248 bis), and that this was approved by a large majority in April 1971. But the Dutch, as I had discovered in the early 1960s, were light-years ahead of us in their social and legal attitudes to sexual questions. And this despite the fact that they were probably far more generally religious than the British.

In an article on the plight of homosexual teenagers published in *Social Work Today* in 1976,[3] a British supporter of the Albany Trust, who was himself living in the Netherlands, attributed the difference in national attitudes to the persistence in Britain of what he called the 'corruption theory'. Late adolescence, he said, is the age when, for heterosexuals and homosexuals alike, acceptance and approval by the

[3] Bill George: 'Young Homosexuals and the Corruption Theory'. *Social Work Today*, 16 November 1976.

peer group are more than at any other age needed for healthy and happy personal development. 'Yet for this very reason the heterosexual majority are at this age least tolerant of the homosexuals among them.' The outcome for those so ostracised was often unhappiness, nervous trouble and even mental breakdown. Acceptance was most likely to come from those peer-group heterosexuals who were most confident of their own sexual orientation; the 'queer-basher', whether actual or verbal, was usually a person in conflict with his own strong homosexual impulses.

Dutch and British legal and social attitudes were in strong contrast. Dutch law drew a realistic distinction between what was public and what was private, and there was no discriminatory definition of homosexual privacy, as in England. Dutch homosexuals now enjoyed equality before the criminal law. In readily accepting the change, the Dutch public had demonstrated a widespread belief that it is not necessary to discriminate legally against homosexuals to prevent the corruption of young people. The remaining legal provisions designed to protect the young from sexual exploitation applied equally to homosexuals and heterosexuals. Homosexual indecency in public places was much less of a problem for the Dutch authorities than for the British, because 'the Dutch police are not interested in homosexuals. The policy of the authorities is generally to facilitate opportunities for homosexuals to contact one another rather than drive their activities underground'. Local COC groups were regularly listed in the town newspaper's information column alongside the chemist's duty rota; there was a file on the group prominently displayed in public libraries, and posters for it in doctors' waiting rooms. The COC received a grant from the Ministry of Cultural Affairs to pay for the salaries of a couple of group counsellors, while some local branches also received local government grants.

One reason for this difference in attitude, George thought, was that a higher proportion of British people believed in the 'corruption theory' of the origins of homosexuality which equated it with an addiction like alcoholism or hard drug abuse. Consequently, many still feared that homosexuality was 'catching'. This belief was reinforced by the tendency of some homosexuals when interrogated by the police to say that they were introduced to their practices by someone else, in the hope of being treated more leniently by the courts. Young people, especially, tended to say they were initiated by older men, rather than admit that they sought such relationships:

> their parents in most cases have brought them up to be too ashamed to admit freely to homosexual desires, particularly when faced with authority figures such as policemen, judges, barristers, or even social workers, who may be ignorant of the facts about homosexuality. In this situation the youth defends himself by minimising his own willingness to enter into the homosexual relationship, and by placating the authorities with statements which conform to their prejudices.

Encouraging the reconsideration of such prejudices and unconscious biases was an underlying aim of the Albany Trust/DES Youth and Sexuality project, which ran from the summer of 1976 when the first Youth officer, Ric Rogers, was appointed, until October 1979 when his successor, Alan Smith, presented his final report. Whereas Rogers had concentrated his out-of-London activities in two main areas – the East Midlands and the North East – Alan Smith followed a more general itinerary, going wherever he found that a local authority or youth organisation training programme wanted him to offer a training event. As the Trust could not afford to offer prolonged training, a major objective was to motivate those who attended these sessions to carry the work forward in their own agencies and locations. The emphasis was on self-awareness, as well as increased understanding of others' experience.

> The areas I wished to open up [Smith wrote in his final report] were sensitivity to, and respect for the reality of, the sexuality of others, and awareness of the role of [the trainees'] own sexuality in their dealing with the sexuality of others.

Smith held that a meaningful personal morality was something for the individual to attain through his or her own thinking and feeling processes, as opposed to its stemming from any 'moral authority'. While he found a surface consensus amongst those who invited him to work with them[4] that this was a valid contemporary approach to training and counselling work on sexuality, and that examination of one's own feelings and attitudes was a prerequisite if any sort of meaningful learning was to take place, Smith encountered frequent resistance to this in prac-

---

[4] His discussion of the attitudes of those who declined his offer to do so is interesting, but has been omitted here for reasons of space.

tice. There was also a good deal of covert censoring of information on the basis of 'acceptable' attitudes – for example, as to what was to be regarded as 'normal' and therefore unembarrassing.

Discussion of sexuality involving the frank revelation of one's own attitudes and preferences, and acknowledgment of ignorance in some respects, is a challenging and sometimes threatening prospect, even for professional people. Yet being put in touch with and given permission to acknowledge their own sexuality and the dilemmas it posed could itself be a liberating experience. Indeed, 'permission to be sexual' proved to be

> the major factor which enabled individuals to respond dynamically to the training sessions. . . . Implicit in being allowed to be sexual is, of course, being allowed to be oneself.

A broadening of sympathy and comprehension often followed on:

> It struck me on a number of occasions that a brief summary of the sort of difficulties that young homosexuals often go through – persecution at school, pressure or rejection from parents, self-rejection, loneliness and other such really very obvious and predictable problems – seemed to come as a complete surprise to people who were, without doubt, generally perceptive and intelligent individuals. The reason for this surprise was apparently that they had simply never thought about it; and the reason for that is, I would think, simply that the conditioning to react aggressively and negatively to the subject of homosexuality is so immensely strong as to be able to pre-empt a rational response even in an individual who prides himself on rationality. This phenomenon can be observed in numerous writers who in general display a clearly humanitarian and liberal outlook, but who make pejorative statements about homosexuals without it apparently occurring to them that five per cent of their readership is likely to be deeply hurt by such statements. This is partially attributable to the psychological mechanism whereby we assume that anybody who poses a threat to us is incapable of being hurt by us. Thus the reaction of surprise in some people at being told the sort of pain that young homosexuals may experience is perhaps analogous to the surprised dismay of a soldier who shoots one of the enemy and then sees that he has killed someone not very different from himself.[5]

---

[5] A perception which the soldier's training goes to great lengths to blot out.

205

Once the rules of how one 'ought' to respond to homosexuality had been questioned, a great many course participants

> seemed to achieve a sudden realisation of the sort of suffering that non-acceptance of homosexuality causes. . . . A number . . . actually stated their own awareness of a sudden change of attitude in themselves and it is this, I think, that has proved one of the major justifications for the project. I do not believe that attitude change stopped at homosexuality. Because attitudes towards homosexuals generally epitomise attitudes towards anybody who is 'different' whether that difference be sexual, religious, racial or whatever, any change in those attitudes can . . . pave the way for change in a range of other areas. In the specific area of sexual attitudes I would gauge that in the West, at least, homosexuality is the most anxiety-provoking of all sexual topics; hence, once a person, whether heterosexual or homosexual, has honestly confronted and come to terms with his feelings towards that topic then other topics are automatically dealt with.

In conclusion Alan Smith commented that the provision of training to equip youth workers to deal realistically with the sexuality of young people varied greatly and was covered by no acknowledged guidelines. Policy making in this field was hindered by inertia, a major component of which appeared to be the worry of many in a position to influence the situation that if they were seen as being too 'progressive' they would be judged as being somehow sexually deviant themselves, or simply amoral. He saw sexual insecurity in educationalists and politicians being exploited and manipulated to substantial effect by those who wished private morality to be dictated by public authority. Such sexual insecurity sprang from poor sex education, and this vicious circle acted as a major hindrance to improved sex education.

The Albany Trust's existence during its final years of activity is amply justified by this impressive report. Doubtless it is now mouldering forgotten in some dusty pigeonhole at the Department of Education. It should be resurrected, studied afresh, and acted upon.

XVII

Assault and Battery

'Accuracy is a duty and not a virtue.'

A. E. Housman

The social reforms of the 1960s, modest though they were, incurred the resentment and in some cases the outright hostility of those who perceived them as undermining the nation's moral fibre.

During the 1970s pressure groups which, though numerically small, claimed to represent the 'moral majority' gained increasing media attention and political clout in both the United States and Britain. Many (though not all) of these people were religious fundamentalists and 'born again' Christians who were highly affronted by what they labelled as the 'permissive sixties'.[1] Far from perceiving the modestly liberalising reforms of that decade as an overdue acknowledgment of the valid role of personal choice and individual responsibility, they regarded the updating of laws concerning capital punishment, abortion, homosexuality, and divorce as retrograde steps. Some of them repudiated the key Wolfenden distinction between sin and crime and wished the State to resume its historic task of punishing vice and immorality through the agency of the criminal law.

Leading anti-permissive campaigners appeared to be convinced that a worldwide conspiracy existed, linking everything they most hated and feared with 'subversion' (atheism and communism) deliberately fuelling 'perversion' (sexual immorality and deviation – especially homosexuality) through pornography.

In a 1980 magazine article on sex education,[2] one of those inter-

---

[1] 'Permissiveness' is a silly and misleading term because it wrongly implies that there are some people in society who are entitled to permit, or to withhold permission from, the moral choices of others. Its sloppy use in debate is a potent source of confusion.

[2] *Now*, June 1980.

viewed, Mrs Valerie Riches, Secretary of the Responsible Society (later renamed Family and Youth Concern), described a 'devilish' plot involving a 'tremendously powerful' network involving some 35 agencies including government departments, the Health Education Council, family planning agencies, the Communist Party, humanist organisations, and the Sexual Law Reform Society, all of whom were (she said) engaged in deliberately promoting teenage promiscuity and sexual irresponsibility. 'I don't really know what it is,' said Mrs Riches: 'Communism, humanism, world domination. I don't know. But I do know it's happening. And it's terribly clever.' In similar vein, members of the National Viewers' and Listeners' Association were reported by a sociologist in 1979 as claiming that the Albany Trust came 'under the Communist umbrella', together with the National Council for Civil Liberties, the Campaign for Homosexual Equality and the Humanist Society (*sic*).[3]

The anti-permissive parliamentary Family and Child Protection Group notched up several legislative scalps in the 1970s and 1980s, including the Protection of Children Act 1978, the Indecent Displays (Control) Act 1981, and the Video Recordings Act 1984. Clause 28 of the Local Government Act 1988, forbidding councils to 'promote' homosexuality as 'a pretended family relationship', was originated by people close to their network, and they conducted successful campaigns to force the Department of Health to revise its guidelines to doctors for the provision of contraceptive advice for under-sixteens and to oblige the Department of Education to allow parents to withdraw their children from school sex education lessons if they so wished.

In September 1975 I attended, together with the Albany Trust's incoming Chairman, Harold Haywood, a seminar on sexual minorities and their problems which had been organised by MIND. One of the speakers was a young man in his early twenties who described in a very courageous and moving way his experiences, thoughts and feelings as a paedophile.[4] Afterwards, Mr Haywood said to me that, of all sexual

---

[3] Dallas Cliff in Roger King and Neill Nugent (eds.): *Respectable Rebels. Middle Class Campaigns in Britain in the 1970s* (Hodder & Stoughton, 1979, p.136).

[4] Paedophilia is a much misused word. Its accurate meaning is emotional and physical attraction towards, and feelings of love for, pre-pubertal children. Emotional paedophilia does not always result in sexual activity between a paedophile and a child-object of his or her affections. However, popular usage of 'paedophile' as meaning a sexual molester or abuser of children has made realistic discussion of paedophilia extremely difficult.

minorities paedophiles were the most misunderstood, execrated and doom-laden; and that the Albany Trust had a moral duty to see whether anything could be done to help those who carried this heavy burden to live more at peace with themselves within the law.

I agreed with him; and, although I was already worried at the increasing diversification of the Trust's interests, and the growing workload bearing upon the few of us working full time for it, I arranged for a few private discussions to be held at the Trust's office between psychiatrists, psychologists and social workers whom I knew to be concerned with paedophiles in their professional work, to explore with them the nature and availability of support needed. I also invited some paedophiles to join in these talks, including the young man who had spoken at the MIND conference and other members of the newly-formed (and ill-fated) Paedophile Information Exchange (PIE) and another group, PAL (Paedophile Action for Liberation).[5]

These meetings were in accord with the philosophy and policy of the Trust as an educating and helping agency. One of the possibilities discussed was the provision by the professionals of a support group for lonely, isolated and frightened paedophiles; another was the joint production by the group (including its professional members) of a 'Questions and Answers' booklet on paedophilia, to be published by the Albany Trust. A drafting committee[6] produced a text, but the Trustees could not agree on it, so the project was dropped. The Trustees decided that, apart from public educational work, any Albany Trust supportive help for paedophiles, including counselling, should be linked to the NACRO sex offenders' project. I never thought, and did not intend, that paedophilia should become a major focus of the Trust's work; but it seemed to me – and still does – a legitimate area of potential counselling support and social concern to explore.

I did not foresee what a minefield we were walking into. Years previously, Tony Dyson had said to me that paedophilia was an issue which would not be sensibly confronted by society in the foreseeable future: how right he was.

PIE and PAL were radical in style, fashioned in the mould of the Gay Liberation Front. As one of PIE's leading lights, Tom O'Carroll (who was subsequently imprisoned for 'conspiracy to corrupt public

[5] Pilloried by the *Sunday People* as 'the Vilest Men in Britain'.
[6] Of which I was *not* a member.

morals') later said, the Albany Trust's respectable, sober-suited persuasive lobbying tactics of 'doing good by stealth' did not appeal to PIE:

> There was no way in which we in PIE were going to go through all that palaver. . . . We were just not prepared to wait for decades or centuries before declaring ourselves. It just wasn't in our nature. Instead, we naïvely supposed we could be both open *and* play the lobbying, PR game to some extent; we thought we could manipulate the Establishment and find allies within it, simultaneously with being the ogres of the popular press and the Church-based reactionaries like the Festival of Light.[7]

PIE's mistake, O'Carroll admitted, was to believe that having identified their visible enemies they would still find elsewhere 'if not friends, then at least rational, liberally-minded people'. They did not expect *The Guardian* to react to the notion of paedophilia in the same way as *The News of the World*.

The Albany Trust's mistake was to be willing to behave as rational, liberally-minded people towards PIE and PAL, and so to expose ourselves to violent attacks from the 'moral majority' upon the Trust's hard-won credibility.

In the first (autumn 1976) issue of its broadsheet, *AT Work* the Trust mentioned the meetings we had convened 'to discuss possible ways of providing supportive help for paedophiles who feel themselves to be in need of it'. In the context of the Trust's counselling activities, fully detailed elsewhere in *AT Work*, the meaning of this phrase was perfectly clear. In the same issue I reviewed a new book on paedophilia, *The Forbidden Love*.[8] Although the authors (one of them, a Jungian psychiatrist, was a friend of mine) took no exception to what I wrote, it greatly incensed the Responsible Society, who described it as 'aggressive' – presumably because I had said that the Victorian assumption that childhood and sexuality were mutually exclusive could no longer be sustained without question: a commonplace enough notion in the 1970s, I should have thought.

In the summer of 1976 I had spoken (in my capacity as Honorary Secretary of the Sexual Law Reform Society) about the age of consent

[7] Tom O'Carroll, *Paedophilia: The Radical Case* (Peter Owen Publishers, London, 1980), pp. 219–20.
[8] W. Kraemer, R. Gordon, M. Williams, K. Lambert, *The Forbidden Love. The Normal and Abnormal Love of Children* (Sheldon Press, 1976)

at a National Council of Social Service Women's Forum; and in October I addressed a meeting arranged by the National Council of Voluntary Youth Organisations on the same topic. Present at the latter meeting was Mrs Riches of the Responsible Society, who voiced her strong disapproval of the SLRS' proposals. [9] Over lunch I vainly tried to convince her that we were as anxious as she was to protect and guide young people during their formative years of growing up, but without making them or their consenting partners into criminals.

A few weeks later, on 24 November 1976, a violent storm burst around the Albany Trust. Mrs Mary Whitehouse, honorary General Secretary of The National Viewers' and Listeners' Association, got shockwaves of national publicity for her claim (in a speech to a 'Christian Lunch and Dinner Clubs' meeting at Central Hall, Westminster) that the Albany Trust – which she described as 'the homosexual lobby front runner' – was using its public funds to

> 'support paedophile groups' so that 'we are all subsidising and supporting, at least indirectly, a cause which seeks to normalise sexual attraction and activity between adult males and little girls'.

And she began her reference to the Albany Trust's public funding by pointedly remarking, 'One constantly has to ask oneself – does the right hand of the Government know what the left hand is doing? And I MEAN the left hand!'

Her allegations were groundless. All that the Trust had actually done was to invite half a dozen paedophiles to contribute their points of view at some private meetings held under our auspices with medical and social work professionals. The 'public funding' which they had received from the Albany Trust amounted to a few cups of tea. However, PIE had bought from the SLRS a single copy of the Speijer Report, which they proceeded – without our knowledge or permission – to photocopy and sell for £1.

My immediate reaction to Mrs Whitehouse's speech was that it must have been made on the basis of misinformation; and I believed that she would naturally wish to make a public correction when she realised that what she had said was false. The Trustees were legally advised that her words were defamatory, but did not wish to resort

[9] See chapter XX, below.

to a court action. A carefully drafted letter[10] was therefore sent to Mrs Whitehouse, listing the numerous errors of fact in her speech and requesting her to make a public withdrawal of what she had said. Despite several requests for an answer, the Trust never received one. And though we did not publish the contents of our letter until the summer of 1977, extracts from it had by then been printed in Mrs Whitehouse's book, *Whatever Happened to Sex*[11].

In the House of Commons a number of parliamentary questions concerning the Albany Trust were tabled. Sir Bernard Braine MP alleged that the Trust was using public funds to 'support' PIE. His 'reasons' were that PIE had sold photocopies of the Albany Trust-annotated translation of the Speijer Report for £1 each; and that under my Directorship the Trust had 'openly campaigned' for reduction of the age of consent.

I wrote to Sir Bernard Braine telling him that what he had said under the cover of Parliamentary privilege was totally without foundation, and asking him to withdraw it. He sent me a forceful letter repeating his assertions and full of underlined questions such as 'May I ask if you are the Mr Grey who spoke at these meetings?' I replied pointing out the errors in his attack, and stated:

> I do not approve of paedophile practices. I do not favour the social acceptance of paedophilia. I do not belong to or support PIE. I disagree with PIE's aims, pronouncements and activities. I would not advocate or support any changes in the law other than those proposed in the enclosed Sexual Law Reform Society's report. [I added] Just as I suppose you have done, I have participated in many hundreds of meetings during my working life where numerous bodies with whom I quite violently disagreed were represented – but nobody has ever before accused me of holding views which I in fact reprobate because I have sat round a table and engaged in dialogue.

I heard nothing more from Sir Bernard Braine.

In its autumn 1977 Broadsheet the Festival of Light castigated PIE, and referred to the Albany Trust as 'a sympathetic and related body' – a description which they later withdrew following a strong protest from the Trust's new Chairman, Rodney Bennett-England

[10] See Appendix 3.
[11] Wayland, 1977.

(practically all of whose time was by now occupied in dealing with anxious enquiries from ministers and Government funding bodies about the Trust's allegedly nefarious activities).

Others, however, were unwilling to retract their twisted versions of the Trust's views and conduct, so Bennett-England eventually wrote a letter to *The Times* in January 1978 complaining that for some time the Albany Trust had been the victim of 'a particularly vicious campaign' and was 'completely powerless' to defend itself against a barrage of MPs' questions. He was promptly answered by the Responsible Society's chairman, who reiterated that the Trust had given PIE 'encouragement and assistance', and that it was 'clearly linked' with the English translation of the Speijer Report ('a document which seeks to justify adult sexual gratification with minors'). Bennett-England sent a reply which did not get published, pointing out that the Speijer Report's proposal was to reduce the Dutch age of consent for homosexual behaviour to sixteen; *not* to legalise paedophile relationships.[12] Further private correspondence between the two chairmen failed to shake the Responsible Society's conviction that the Albany Trust condoned child-molesting.

Mrs Whitehouse took up the cudgels again in the correspondence columns of *The Guardian*, declaring that 'for Rodney Bennett-England to deny an association between the Albany Trust and PIE is to move the debate into such a realm of unreality as to make rational argument impossible', to which he retorted 'it is she who makes rational argument impossible by refusing to accept the truth if it doesn't suit her purpose'.

Echoes of the conflict continued to reverberate around the country for several months, surfacing in a variety of parish magazines and local newspapers and causing the Albany Trust an enormous amount of extra work and worry. One such article, called *Gay is Sad – and Bad* which appeared in a West Country parish magazine early in 1978, claimed that:

> 'the Government has made available large sums of public money
> to organisations which exist to promote homosexuality and are
> sympathetic to paedophilia (sexual interference with children)',

---

[12] The Responsible Society's dim view of the Speijer Report was not shared by the Criminal Law Revision Committee and its Policy Advisory Committee, who referred to the Report several times, in appreciative terms, in their review of the law on sexual offences (see chapter XX). Presumably they too used the SLRS translation.

and accused the Albany Trust of being 'aggressively sympathetic to paedophilia,' of 'spreading the message that homosexual activity is normal and natural and the equivalent of sexual intercourse', and of labelling adolescents as 'teenage gay people', 'long before they have the opportunity to develop fully, thereby possibly inhibiting the maturing process to heterosexuality.'

This sensational piece was prominently featured in the local press. Fortunately the Bishop of Malmesbury, who (as he wrote to Bennett-England) had always had a considerable regard for the Albany Trust's work, and was puzzled and concerned at the sudden spate of adverse publicity which it was attracting, sent a copy of the newspaper to the Trust. Bennett-England had a letter published setting the record straight, and received a handsome apology from the clergyman who wrote the parish item. In a letter also published in the local press, he said:

> These allegations [against the Albany Trust] were not manufactured here at my desk. I took them word for word, from a source which one would naturally have supposed to be entirely reliable and trustworthy. Nevertheless, I now contrast the fact that Rodney Bennett-England has set out the Albany Trust's position clearly and openly with the insistence of my own source that on no account must it be revealed. I must, therefore, prefer the former; and I do so readily and completely.

One can see his point. After all, God made no bones about telling Moses who had inscribed the Tablets of Stone on the mountain.

Looking back upon this sorry episode more than a decade later I am still distastefully perturbed by the way in which such fierce attacks were launched upon the Albany Trust upon such flimsy grounds, and were persisted in even when the Trust repeatedly exposed the falseness of the allegations against it. The chorus of misrepresentations inside and outside Parliament undoubtedly influenced the newly elected Thatcher government to cut off the Albany Trust's public funding at the end of 1979. Repeated requests for face-to-face meetings at which our real views and actions could be explained to our accusers in a friendly manner were stonily ignored. An appeal by me to Lord Longford to see fair play met only with the plaintive reply that he liked both me and Mary Whitehouse very much, and that she was 'a Good Christian Woman'.

The protection of children concerns everyone of good will in our society. Children most certainly do need protecting – not only from physical abuse and emotional cruelty, but also from simplistic beliefs which ignore the complexities of living and loving and which see human sexuality through a glass, darkly. The young are not benefited by assiduous efforts to discredit those of us who work for a society with a compassionately balanced and mature approach to sex, a facet of life so crucial to human happiness.

XVIII

Decline and Fall

'Those who will believe nonsense must expect awkward consequences.'

A. L. Rowse[1]

I finally left the Albany Trust at the end of April 1977, but the Trust
still did not leave me; I remained involved in the unseemly argy-
bargy around the Mary Whitehouse accusations, and in 1980 found
myself yet again the unpremeditated custodian of the Trust's
archives.

Until the Whitehouse bombshell in November 1976 we had
no idea that such a ferocious assault upon the Trust was brewing.
Her speech was made, as it happened, on the day of a Trustees'
meeting, and I was telephoned about it by the Press Association
just as the meeting began. Her remarks sounded too grotesque to
be taken seriously. Even when her allies added their salvoes,
the affair remained, for most of the Trustees, a cloud no bigger
than a man's hand and irrelevant to the serious business of the
Trust.

It was at this point that I began to get seriously alarmed at the
unrealistic notions that were around. Those Trustees and staff who
had only recently come on board, and who had not been associated
with the Trust in its lean, pre-grant days, seemed to be under the
complacent impression that its future was now secure and that the
path ahead climbed rosily upwards. They were unable or unwilling to
grasp that sexuality – and especially homosexuality – remained an
explosive topic, and that the Trust was liable at any time to be attacked
for almost anything it said and did. Our grant income was only of

[1] Letter to *The Times*, 11 July 1978.

limited duration, while income from non-grant sources had not increased despite the efforts of Rodney Bennett-England and myself. Indeed, by the end of 1976 the Trust was back in an overdraft situation which was set to persist beyond the receipt of the next quarter's grant income.

Inevitably the homophile movement had siphoned off most of the financial and other support which the Trust used to receive in the 1960s. This could not be helped, and I did not grudge it, even when misunderstandings – such as a bitter row with Icebreakers, who took umbrage at some comments in *AT Work* about their negative attitude to training in helping skills – soured and complicated our task.[2] We now had more 'parcels' to sell, but we urgently needed some buyers. Convincing public authorities and other agencies that we had expertise within the Trust which would be of benefit to them was going to be neither quick nor easy.

A great deal of my own work was necessarily 'low-profile' and largely consisted of maintaining in good repair and building upon the wide range of personal contacts which I had accumulated over the previous fifteen years. I continued my 'outreach' activities, visiting Scotland in October on behalf of both the Trust and the British Association for Counselling. A meeting with the General Secretary of the British Council of Churches raised hopes of a high-level BCC conference on the theology of sexuality, and I was invited by the Church of England Board for Social Responsibility to be one of the speakers at a consultation on 'Police in the Community' in February 1977.[3] I also took part in National Council for Voluntary Youth Services and British Federation Against the Venereal Diseases working parties on homosexuality. Richard Hauser invited me to discuss some possible joint work on bisexuality. There was certainly no lack of

---

[2] In her final report before leaving at the end of the year, Jan McHugh outlined the tensions and wariness she had encountered from the homophile groups she had met: 'The Trust had been put "on trial", questioned about its motives, aims, backing; and some of the groups demanded that we justify our position to them. Despite all our attempts to answer their queries as fully as possible, it seemed to me that our answers were not really wanted or listened to, and that the meetings had become only a platform for some individuals to voice their own frustrations and anger against a symbol of establishment and authority.' I called this the 'Kick Mummy' syndrome.

[3] Where I was fascinated to meet Manchester's outspoken chief constable, James Anderton. God's mouthpiece was quite demure on this occasion.

potential initiatives: the limiting factors, as always, were time, energy, and money.

Because of Michael Butler's removal from London to Brighton a long-time helper of the Trust, Margaret Branch, a former senior psychiatric social worker at Guy's Hospital, offered to co-ordinate the Trust's counselling appointments for three months. She was an asset, especially as she had extensive professional experience in counselling transsexuals and transvestites.

A training working party had been convened with a broadly based professional membership drawn from within and outside the Trust, and this reported in July 1977 (after I had left the Trust). The need for greater counselling provision on a national scale, which the Trust had perceived in its 1974 application to the VSU, was now even greater, and was described by the training working party in terms which give a clear picture of what the Trust was then facing:

> During the decade since the passing of the 1967 Sexual Offences Act, there was been a growing awareness in the community of the frequency and extent of the individual and social problems experienced by sexual minorities and an increasing acceptance of the fact that such people are not necessarily either mentally or physically sick, but that their most common problems, including stress, result primarily from social pressures. In turn, many more members of those minorities, and many more professional workers in the health, education and social work fields, have been seeking information, advice and help in dealing with their problems. . . .
>
> Too many people are asking for help from too few workers: and qualitatively, the range of problems being presented is frequently beyond the competence of voluntary befrienders, many of whom have no professional training or support. . . .
>
> It is clear that professional workers . . . are referring psychosexual cases to, and seeking advice from, organisations and individuals whose qualifications they would not consider sufficient to deal with cases of similar complexity in a more conventional field. This must indicate that many such workers feel themselves inadequate to deal with psychosexual problems without further training and 'back-up' support.

The working party drew up a model training programme for psychosexual counsellors involving a six-month intensive course consisting of three residential weekends and twenty three-hour evening sessions. The content would be a balanced mixture of information; experiential groups to enable trainees to learn about their own emotional responses, attitudes, behaviour and communication skills, and to explore their own strengths and weaknesses; and supervised counselling practice. The initial six months of intensive training would be followed by eighteen months of work with the Trust, at least once a week, under supervision. The report was a thorough piece of work – indeed, almost a counsel of perfection.

The Field Officer and the Youth Officer were busily occupied – the former mainly in Sussex and the West Country, the latter in London, the Midlands and the North East. Notwithstanding her difficulties with the gay groups, Jan McHugh had found a broad recognition amongst other educational, counselling and research agencies of the 'great need' for further information, training, education, and counselling services for sexual minorities, and growing concern for their problems. She had also continued in her efforts to catalogue the Trust's archive – 'a major resource for anyone wishing to study the development of changes in law and social attitudes relating to sexual minorities in this country'. In her final report before leaving the Trust at the end of January 1977, Jan concluded:

> Looking back over the year, I am impressed by what seems to be only the tip of an iceberg: the massive weight of work before the Trust was only just touched upon by my efforts. What remains, for me, is the conviction that the Trust's role in the field of sexual education and counselling is both unique and of tremendous potential value.

Alas, such hopes that the Trust's value would be properly used were never fulfilled. Despite all the upbeat activity of 1976 fresh sources of funding remained elusive and internal relations were strained. Matters reached such a pitch that following a residential weekend for the trustees, staff and voluntary helpers in the spring of 1977, I decided to resign and leave those who believed they knew better than I did to work out the Trust's destiny. This time, I believed that I had finally severed my links with it; but I reckoned without the 'boomerang' or 'yo-yo' effect which was yet again to involve me in some aspects of its affairs.

After my departure, fund raising continued to produce negligible results, though the gravity of the situation was partially masked by legacies whose proceeds were swiftly eaten up. The Trust continued to be heavily dependent upon its VSU and DES grants, and even with these was overspending its income. A new Field Officer (Mike Wilson) and a new Youth Project Officer (Alan Smith) were appointed and had started work by the autumn of 1977. Both did lastingly valuable work under increasingly difficult circumstances.

In June 1979 the Trust celebrated the twenty-first anniversary of its foundation with a service of thanksgiving at which Bishop John Robinson preached a sermon recalling the early days, and his own long association with the cause. He pointed to all the work remaining to be done on law reform, education, and counselling. It was the time of the Jeremy Thorpe trial, of which the Bishop said:

> The compounding of charges and counter-charges is an appalling commentary on the fears and unfreedoms of our society, in which *people* are destroyed, whether they are innocent or guilty.

He believed that the work of the Trust, as of the Church, was about true Liberation through the power of the one Spirit.

The three-year limit for VSU funding was approaching, and negotiations were begun for responsibility for the Trust's funding to be transferred to the Department of Health and Social Security. For a time these appeared to be going quite well, but a final decision kept on being postponed. It was obvious that the government funding sources were increasingly uneasy over the Trust's activities, and were bothered by the political ripples arising from the Whitehouse/Responsible Society/Festival of Light attacks. A few weeks after the change of government in October 1979 when the Conservatives won the general election and Mrs Thatcher became Prime Minister the Trust was brusquely informed by letter that no further government funding would be forthcoming.

By this time Harold Haywood had departed to run the Prince of Wales' and other Royal charities. The new Chairman, Rodney Bennett-England, believed it was essential to keep the Trust going if at all possible. The Youth Project Officer, Alan Smith, was made redundant at the end of the year, and the Field Officer, Mike Wilson, also left in the spring of 1980, after a few weeks as Director in what he quickly came to realise was a no-win situation.

In June 1980 I was invited back by Rodney Bennett-England to the Strutton Ground office, which was then as deserted and staffless as Shaftesbury Avenue had been after Michael De-la-Noy had left. The occasion of my return was a 'three-line whip' emergency summons to discuss the crisis after the withdrawal of the government grants. Rodney Bennett-England, by now Chairman of a rapidly dwindling group of Trustees (and soon to be the sole survivor), had SOSed his remaining colleagues and management committee to decide how best to liquidate the office, arrange for the continuation of counselling and such other work as was practicable, and deal with the Trust's debts. Apart from myself and Rodney, only the Trust's solicitor turned up.

It was transformation scene again. This time, I was neither able nor willing to wave any magic wand over the Trust. I did not resume any executive function, but I did once again take charge of the bulk of the Trust's archives and arrange for their temporary storage until they were eventually loaned to the Hall-Carpenter Archives and finally deposited permanently in the British Library of Political & Economic Science at the London School of Economics.

Apart from its counselling group, who have maintained a semi-autonomous existence up to the present day, the Albany Trust went effectively into limbo in 1980. What lessons can be drawn from its chequered history? First, that it was by sheer good luck that the Trust survived not only its earliest years but so many subsequent vicissitudes. Secondly, that the mistakes made at various times by everyone involved, including myself, originated in over-enthusiasm generated by an intense awareness of the urgency of the needs the Trust sought to meet and the unique contribution it had to make.

Even the best-run small voluntary agency is in a very weak position, both structurally and financially, to deal on equal terms with government departments and other large well-funded institutions. Throughout its precarious career the Albany Trust was dealing with people and organisations of widely differing natures and perceptions. Perhaps inevitably, it fell between a variety of stools. It was seen by the homophile movement as stuffy, timid and conformist, and by the paedophiles as a high-powered life-raft. Mary Whitehouse and her allies perceived it as a highly dangerous morally and socially corrupting influence. Civil servants and most politicians, even when personally well-disposed, increasingly came to see it as an embarrassing boat-rocker of which they would be well rid. Some other agencies in the sex education and training field disliked the Trust's challenge to their own adequacy. Given such an environmental can of worms it is really quite surprising that the Albany Trust managed to do so much for so long, and generally to do it so well.

XIX

Culture Clash

'And we are here as on a darkling plain
Swept with confused alarms of struggle and flight,
Where ignorant armies clash by night.'

Matthew Arnold
'Dover Beach'

After leaving the Albany Trust in 1977 I gave a good deal of my time and attention to the counselling movement, playing an active part in the development of the British Association for Counselling and the Standing Conference for the Advancement of Training and Supervision. I took a diploma course in counselling skills, and also did some training in Transactional Analysis with the late Laurence Collinson – one of the first generation GLF activists, and an inspiring trainer and therapist for whom I had a warm regard.

All of this work, together with my long-standing links with sex education and counselling bodies such as the National Marriage Guidance Council, the Family Planning Association, Brook Advisory Centres, and so forth, strengthened my conviction that it is impossible to split off a sound, balanced and well-informed approach to homosexuality and the personal and social issues it poses from a healthy approach to sexuality as a whole. This view, while still novel in the early 1970s, has in the past twenty years become the accepted perspective of most sex educators and counsellors. It is a welcome advance from the almost universal ignorance and frequent prejudice displayed by a majority of the medical profession in the pre-Wolfenden days.

Such an attitude, however, calls for more than lip-service; and there is still much strenuous work to be done to create an adequate, generally recognised standard of training and competence amongst

223

sex therapists and counsellors. While I have much *emotional* sympathy with the view of many gay activists that not being gay disqualifies an 'outsider' from fully understanding, and therefore from giving effective help, I have not found this to be true professionally. Non-gay people with the requisite empathy *can* provide valuable insights for those who are homosexual or bisexual, just as I can use my homosexuality creatively in working as a counsellor with heterosexuals. Surely there needs to be a broad spectrum of skilled and concerned help available; and such help is still so sparse that it is foolish to limit its source by arbitrarily excluding entire categories of people.[1]

I am convinced by my experience at the Albany Trust and afterwards that sexuality requires an across-the-board approach. An effective way to combat discrimination is through a comprehensive revision of the entire body of existing law relating to sexual offences. This has indeed been the logic of official thinking during the past two decades, although gay reformers have concentrated their efforts on single-issue campaigning – primarily defensive in recent years. Another important route to future advance lies through the broader path of the European Community's institutions, which have already been instrumental in securing progress which the national parliaments in Westminster and Dublin were reluctant to grant.

The history of the post-1967 years has been well chronicled elsewhere,[2] and I shall summarise the main events here only briefly. So far as further law reform was concerned the reference by Home Secretary Roy Jenkins of the whole area of sexual offences to the Criminal Law Revision Committee effectively precluded efforts to secure fresh legislation in advance of the CLRC recommendations,[3] and channelled reformers' energies into supplying evidence to the Committee (as described in the next chapter).

---

[1] I call this the 'green-eyed, wooden-legged dwarf' syndrome. It declares that only green-eyed, wooden-legged dwarves can be of effective help to other green-eyed, wooden-legged dwarves. Apart from its falsity, it has cripplingly divisive consequences for the spread of human understanding and mutual sympathy.

[2] By Jeffrey Weeks in *Coming Out* (Quartet, 1977, 1990) and Stephen Jeffery-Poulter in *Peers, Queers, and Commons* (Routledge, 1991).

[3] The Home Secretary's reference was originally made in 1967, and again in 1975: the review did not get under way until 1976, and the CLRC's final report was issued in 1984.

By the time the CLRC's final report appeared in 1984 the political atmosphere was far less favourable to the early adoption by parliament of even the modest reforms it proposed; the immediate reality was of a gathering 'moral majority' backlash, stirred up by our old adversaries and their political associates in the parliamentary 'Family and Child Protection Group', and orchestrated through sections of the press who had by the mid-1980s completely forgotten – if they ever knew – C. P. Scott's dictum that 'comment is free, facts are sacred' to an extent that made one wonder if they would recognise a fact if they accidentally bumped into one.

These allies pursued an increasingly hysterical witch-hunt not only against 'paedophiles' (as they persisted in calling child-molesters) but also against non-heterosexual people in general. This escalating torrent of vituperation was fuelled by the onset of AIDS and its persistent misidentification as the 'gay plague', though the same newspapers' endless titillating stories about heterosexuals' extramarital 'bonking' exploits continued to be treated as merely good for a giggle. By the beginning of the 1990s the prospects for a more civilised British attitude to sexual matters by the year 2000 looked considerably dimmer than they had done when the 1970s began.

Soon after I had left the Albany Trust Tony Dyson, alarmed by the rising tide of homophobia, approached the Trustees proposing that they should collaborate with him in launching a public manifesto supported by a wide range of public figures affirming that anti-homosexual prejudice was a social evil which should be eradicated, and urging 'less hate in '78'. The Trustees felt unable to commit themselves to this, so Tony went ahead under his own steam and *Towards a Charter of Homosexual Rights* was published under the auspices of the 'Campaign for Reason' early in 1978. It was a judiciously moderate document, phrased almost too temperately for the climate of the time. Fear or hatred of homosexuality was, it said, a social evil akin to anti-semitism, racism, slavery, and with the same evil consequences – harmful both to the victims and to the society which tolerated it. Yet, unlike racial or religious prejudices which were now widely recognised as being wrong, anti-homosexual feeling was still allowed to masquerade as 'respectable'. Indeed

> we are rapidly approaching a situation in which homosexuals
> are the *only* natural minority who are still regarded, by some, as

225

intrinsically evil, and who are still liable to be mocked or persecuted by people claiming to represent ordinary social opinion,
or the Christian church.

In point of fact,

> homosexuality in no way impairs normal physical, creative or
> spiritual development, and is consistent with the highest attain-
> ment in every human profession. . . . The actual disabilities
> experienced by many homosexuals are the result of enforced sexual
> repression, secrecy, fear of honesty, or socially induced shame –
> all highly destructive forces for *any* human being to bear. . . . We
> believe that the basic need for homosexuals is to be able to accept
> themselves with dignity, and then to follow their own moral and
> spiritual lights.

Those who hated homosexuals should no longer be able to dictate
accepted social attitudes from their own broken state. Such homophobic people were themselves social casualties who required understanding and help, rather than rejection and bitterness matching their own;
it was for civilisation to combat ignorance and fear with reason and love.
The remedy was for as many homosexuals as felt able to do so to come
out – not in a sensational or flaunting manner, but calmly and without
fuss, to their close friends and associates. 'There may be a few rebuffs to
endure, but perhaps fewer than expected.' Heterosexuals of good will
should firmly and calmly confront and reject discrimination wherever
they encountered it, in private circumstances or public debate. If everyone made the minimal effort required, 1978 could see the end of 'one
more long-standing, utterly irrational evil'. Prejudice and phobia would
linger on as the recognised eccentricity of untypical people.

It was a pious hope. A distinguished list of 178 people signed the
manifesto, which on publication received a good deal of favourable
publicity from the 'quality' press and thereafter vanished without trace.
Lacking funds or a permanent organisation, the Campaign for
Reason's first public utterance was its last. It was a great pity: a campaign to make precisely this point about the antisocial nature of homophobia, and to hammer it effectively home, was a prime need of the
1980s when public opinion, goaded onward by a handful of aggressively homophobic pressure groups and journalists, became increasingly intolerant. The need still remains in the 1990s.

During the 1970s, however, the homophile movement maintained an appearance of growing strength. After its walk-out from NFHO the Campaign for Homosexual Equality for a time achieved its ambition to become the major British homophile organisation, with a network of local groups throughout the country[4] and holding annual conferences attended by several hundred people in the mid-1970s. Together with the Scottish Minorities Group and the Union for Sexual Freedom in Ireland, CHE produced a draft homosexual law reform bill in 1975.[5] This proved to be a high water mark; although it received a good deal of press sympathy there was little parliamentary backup. Lord Beaumont of Whitley, the Albany Trust's former chairman, took soundings in the House of Lords as to the prospects of support for a motion advocating an equal age of consent for homosexuals and heterosexuals, but did not table one after discovering that half the peers he consulted considered the existing law to be satisfactory, while very few of those who told him they would vote for a lower age were prepared to speak in its support.

It was therefore less of a surprise to the Sexual Law Reform Society than to Lord Arran that, when he introduced a Bill into the House of Lords in June 1977 to reduce the homosexual age of consent from twenty-one to eighteen, it was resoundingly defeated by 146 votes to 25. The shock for Boofy was all the greater because, only a month previously, the House had given a majority of 125 to 27 for Lord Boothby's Bill to extend the 1967 Sexual Offences Act to Scotland (and Boothby had stipulated a consenting age of eighteen in his draft, in anticipation of the success of Arran's impending Bill). Boofy was in 'utter despair'. And well he might be; the stridently homophobic opposition was led – for the first time, but not the last – by the Earl of Halsbury, descendant of a Victorian Lord Chancellor and stalwart advocate of the 'moral majority' line. He was to become the 'hammer of the homos' a decade later, with his promotion of the earliest version of what became the notorious 'Clause 28' of the 1988 Local Government Act.

Reform of the Scottish law finally came in 1980, when Robin Cook MP successfully introduced it by way of an amendment to the Criminal Justice (Scotland) Bill which was passed by 203 votes to 80

---

[4] Which proved as vitally cathartic for many isolated gay men in the provinces as had the early GLF meetings for Londoners. (See Porter & Weeks (eds), *Between the Acts* (Routledge, 1991).)

[5] This, like later homosexual equality Bills, was poorly drafted.

– all the other Scottish MPs, including the Conservative Malcolm Rifkind, who had previously supported the reform, voting against change.[6] Northern Ireland, too, achieved its belated reform in October 1982 in the teeth of unanimous local opposition; this was spearheaded by the Rev. Ian Paisley's 'Save Ulster from Sodomy' campaign which, he preened himself, supplied the sole issue which united the Province's Protestants and Catholics.

The Northern Ireland reform only came about after several years of sustained pressure through the European Commission and Court of Human Rights. Police raids early in 1976 on the homes of several leading members of the Northern Ireland Gay Rights Association led one of them, Geoffrey Dudgeon, to petition the European Commission on Human Rights claiming that, by refusing to legalise homosexuality between consenting adults in private, the United Kingdom Government was invading his privacy and discriminating against him. In 1978 the Labour Government tabled a draft Order in Council to implement the 1977 recommendation of the Northern Ireland Human Rights Commission that the 1967 Sexual Offences Act should apply to Ulster, but then backed off in the face of strenuous protests in the Province. The European Human Rights Court found in Dudgeon's favour on the privacy point in October 1981, finally forcing a reluctant British Conservative Government to amend the Northern Irish Law.[7]

My good personal relations with the contemporary Campaign for Homosexual Equality executive, and growing friendship with Maureen Colquhoun, the Labour MP for Northampton, North, whose lesbianism had been publicised by a gossip columnist late in 1977, led to my being invited to CHE's 1978 annual conference at Coventry, where Maureen made a fighting anti-discrimination keynote speech accurately forecasting the impending Thatcher government's 'family values' rhetoric and the likely spread of social homophobia in years to come. Maureen and I and some others urged the appointment of a

---

[6] On this occasion *Gay News* scored a fatuous own goal by drawing attention to the welcome fact that the draft law omitted the 'Dilhorne' definition of privacy with the banner headline 'MPs Pass Orgy Law'. The Bill was promptly amended into line with English law.

[7] The European Court did not uphold Dudgeon's case on the discrimination point, and only awarded him two-thirds (some £3300) of his legal costs. The amount of these was meanly disputed by the British Government, which had itself spent an estimated £500,000 of taxpayers' money in fighting the case.

CHE General Secretary of comparable stature to that of the equivalent officers of the NCCL and other major national pressure groups. This would have involved raising in the region of £20,000 a year for the next three years, and after we had carried out a feasibility study for them CHE's executive shrank back from such a prospect. Thereafter they restructured themselves once more so as to separate their campaigning and social wings; this accelerated the Campaign's fragmentation and decline. The majority of the women members had already departed into the women's movement; now the militant enthusiasm of the activist men was also increasingly siphoned off into single-issue organisations and campaigns such as *Gay News*, Gay Switchboard, 'Friend' counselling service, and gay rights groups within political parties. Some of these came to wield more effective influence in their chosen spheres than CHE, as an aspiring umbrella organisation, had ever been able to do. As one historian of gay rights has commented,[8] CHE seemed incapable of reacting with any agility when genuine emergencies cropped up.

Yet there was an obvious and growing need for a campaign of the intensity which Maureen Colquhoun, David Bell and others envisaged. In the summer of 1977 Mary Whitehouse had exhumed the common law of blasphemy, which had been dormant for half a century, against *Gay News* and its editor Denis Lemon for publishing a poem by Professor James Kirkup on the theme of a Roman centurion's reverie over the crucified body of Christ. The paper and its editor were fined a total of £1500 and Lemon was given a nine-month suspended prison sentence. There was an outcry amongst the gay community, who donated a total of £21,000 to *GN*'s fighting fund. This case, and the resounding defeat of Lord Arran's age of consent bill, clearly showed that the knives were out. *Gay News* survived this crisis, but folded ignominiously in April 1983.[9]

The return to office in October 1979 of a Conservative govern-

---

[8] Jeffrey Weeks, *Coming Out* (Routledge, revised edn 1990), p. 212.

[9] For a gripping though partisan account of its end, see G. E. Hanscombe & A. Lumsden, *Title Fight: The Battle for Gay News* (Brilliance Books, 1983). Maureen Colquhoun and I sought to salvage something from the wreckage, and invited some of the former *GN* staff and others to a meeting to discuss the possibility of launching a gay community broadsheet. One of those whom we invited brought along 'a friend' – *GN*'s former owner-editor Denis Lemon (with whom several of the others present were at loggerheads, and we had therefore not invited him). So the meeting turned out to be more memorable for its delicate personal dynamics than for any solid achievements.

ment headed by Mrs Thatcher gave the moralists a fillip. The new prime minister, though not known as being personally homophobic, was a strong advocate (temperamentally, as well as from perceived political advantage) of 'family values' and 'anti-permissiveness'. These both struck a vibrant chord with what I mentally dubbed the 'lace-curtain vote'. The first, at any rate, was unexceptionable as a vacuous statement of intent; though the likely details in which it might be clothed were ominous. 'Permissiveness' was an incoherent concept, but one which appealed powerfully to those who wanted to turn the social and legal clock back.

The 1980s witnessed an upsurge of irrational comment on sexual topics, punctuated by some legislative inanities and an increasingly hysterical tabloid press which did not scruple to run unbridled homo-phobic campaigns. Their excesses were spurred on by the determi-nation of some editors to depict AIDS as the 'gay plague'. In this bleak atmosphere both the Liberal and Labour parties commendably supported the principle of gay rights and opposed discrimination. A number of Labour-controlled local councils were determined to put non-discrimination against gay people and equal opportunities employment policies for members of sexual minorities on to their political agenda. This enlightened endeavour was bravely spearheaded by the Greater London Council whose leader, Ken Livingstone, pub-licly pledged his support for gay rights, thereby intensifying the press pillorying of him as the standard-bearer of the Loony Left and adding fuel to the Thatcher Government's determination to put paid to the GLC.

Livingstone's espousal of justice for gay people in the face of a torrent of derisive abuse was a good deed in a naughty world. As well as proclaiming solidarity, he proceeded to impel the GLC to hand out some £300,000 of ratepayers' money to various gay groups in the capital, and to put up a further £750,000 to purchase the freehold of a building which was to become the London Lesbian and Gay Centre.[10] These were astronomical sums by the standards of the HLRS/Albany

---

[10] Policies inevitably castigated by Tory critics as 'buggery on the rates'. Since the GLC's demise, the Centre has had a chequered history of management disputes and financial troubles. It has not emulated Bob Angelo's Amsterdam COC of the 1950s and 1960s, the prototype of fruitful collaboration between a gay group and municipal government.

Trust penny-pinching days, and not all of the groups who received handouts used their money wisely. The predictable outcome was a howl of rage from the Rabid Right at the alleged excesses of the Loony Left. This was stoked up by the GLC's cheeky publication, when on the brink of demise in the autumn of 1985, of a glossily printed 'London Charter for Gay and Lesbian Rights', *Changing the World*, which forthrightly attacked heterosexism and homophobia and listed 142 recommendations for remedying the existing situation. It is a useful compilation, and there are very few (if any) of the individual recommendations which anyone who is aware of the extent of bias and discrimination which exists could quarrel with. It is doubtful, however, if most of them will be achieved quickly; without a wholesale revolution in social thinking and action, homosexual equality remains a state of affairs that is as unthinkable for most people as a flying elephant.

As the 1980s wore on much of the concerned energy and financial support of middle-of-the-road gay people was diverted to the new agencies and units combating the AIDS crisis such as the Terrence Higgins Trust and London Lighthouse. Apart from the annual Gay Pride marches, which attracted several thousand people but passed largely unnoticed by the media, there was little if any effective campaigning against the rising tide of anti-gay sentiment in the press and on the Government backbenches. Homophobic hysteria reached a new and sordid pitch with the campaign of smear and innuendo against Peter Tatchell, Labour's losing candidate in the February 1983 Bermondsey by-election. For many months after his defeat Tatchell was subjected to personal abuse and insults from total strangers, and received several death threats. Greatly to his credit he was undeterred by such unnerving experiences and went on to become one of the most respected and effective gay activists and anti-AIDS campaigners.[11]

The currents were, as always, contradictory. When Chris Smith, the Labour MP for Islington South & Finsbury, came out with a public declaration that he was gay less than two years after the Bermondsey debacle he suffered no perceptible injury to his political career, substantially increasing his majority against the anti-Labour London swing at the next general election and becoming an Oppo-

---

[11] He tells the by-election story in Peter Tatchell. *The Battle for Bermondsey* (Heretic Books, 1983).

sition front bench spokesman. The moral seemed to be that in politics it was now safer, as well as more creditable, to be out of the closet.

But the closet continued to exercise its malign influence on the quality of gay visibility. While CHE seemed sunk in somnolence, efforts to secure legal improvements and to combat the growing anti-gay bias in press and Government led some more radical spirits to convene a national conference in May 1987 at which several hundred people gathered with the rather utopian aim of drafting *en masse* a Gay Rights Bill to lay before Parliament. It proved to be rather a shambles. Immediately after the opening platform speeches – including one by Ken Livingstone pledging the Labour Party's full support for total homosexual equality with heterosexuals (how had he squared the square Roy Hattersley, I wondered) – the meeting became increasingly rowdy and bad-tempered.

Its final session, which was supposed to receive reports from a series of small groups, was hamstrung by the organisers' inability to provide sufficient copies of the recommendations, and degenerated into a vituperative slanging match between an angry group of black lesbians, a far-Left clique, and various other factions all yelling at one another from different parts of the hall. When the meeting finally voted to allow its decisions to be vetoed by a series of 'self-organising caucuses',[12] the whole thing became pure Alice in Wonderland:

> The caucuses and trotskyites
> Went waltzing hand in hand.
> They each demanded different tunes
> At once from all the band.
> 'If everyone agreed with *us*,'
> They said, 'it would be grand.'

I wearily departed, convinced that I could have spent a more profitable weekend elsewhere, and wondering how on earth gay rights were ever again going to become a viable political issue. What other interest group aspiring to be taken seriously would have presented itself to the world in this grotesque manner?

A feeble phoenix rose from the weekend's ashes – the Organisation for Lesbian and Gay Action (OLGA), which was quite soon eclipsed

---

[12] Claiming to 'represent' lesbians, lesbian mothers, black people, people with disabilities, older people, young people, and young people in care.

by shiny new competitors such as ACT-UP, OutRage and the well-heeled, sober-suited Stonewall Group. The last emerged from the hitherto comparatively unmilitant world of the theatrical and artistic professions in reaction to the most blatant and sustained parliamentary homophobic attack so far in the shape of what ultimately became Section 28 of the Local Government Act 1988. This was originally floated as a Bill in the Lords by the implacable ('they will push us off the pavement if we give them a chance') near-octogenarian Lord Halsbury, spurred on by the wildly false claims of the tabloids that the Inner London Education Authority was distributing homosexual propaganda amongst young schoolchildren. This story had been launched – maybe not entirely coincidentally – a few weeks before the 1986 ILEA elections. Its only basis in fact was that a Danish picture story book, *Jenny Lives With Eric and Martin*, about a small girl living (with her mother's willing agreement) with her father and his male lover, and published in England by Gay Men's Press, had been placed in ILEA's library reserve stock for individual teachers to consult. The book had never been distributed to any schools, or shown to children, and was not at all pornographic or offensive, except in its challenge to prejudice.[13] But this hyped-up stunt gave the homophobes of the Family and Child Protection Group their opportunity in December 1986 to push Lord Halsbury's Bill, which sought to prevent local authorities from 'promoting homosexuality as an acceptable family relationship'. The noble heterosexists had a virtually unanimous field day. Despite the Government's obvious dislike of the Bill's imprecise terminology and its possible adverse effects on balanced sex education – an objective to which at that stage (though not for much longer) ministers still paid lip service – it was given an unopposed Second Reading.

Voluble homophobia in the media and the long grass of Tory politics increased in the run-up to the 1987 general election,

---

[13] *Jenny* is in fact artlessly naïve, in that peculiarly Scandinavian way which humourless British bigots find so infuriating. (As they notoriously did with the *Little Red School Book*.) 'Why is Mrs Jones so grumpy?' the little girl asks, and is told it is because Mrs Jones disapproves of two people of the same sex loving each other. 'There are so many things people think are wrong', says a grown-up; '[it] can never be wrong to live with someone you are fond of'. Jenny wonders if Mrs Jones will stop being so grumpy if someone explains that to her. 'If she doesn't', says her father's lover, 'it will be a pity – more for her than for anyone else.'

prompting the sour editorial comment in *Capital Gay* that 'a gay who votes Conservative is like a turkey voting for Christmas'. At the end of the year, with Mrs Thatcher comfortably back in power, the Halsbury initiative surfaced in the Commons as an amendment to the Local Government Bill forbidding a local authority to 'promote homosexuality or publish material for the promotion of homosexuality' or to 'promote the teaching in any maintained school of the acceptability of homosexuality as a pretended family relationship'. This time it had Government support on the ground that it was 'no part of a local authority's duty to encourage youngsters to believe that homosexuality was on an equal footing with a heterosexual way of life'[14] – 'a piece of red meat' thrown to the backbench 'wolves' with Mrs Thatcher's personal blessing.[15] But placating the Tory wolves roused the already restive gay rights tiger. A great many ordinarily non-political homosexual men and women who usually steered well clear of activism were stung by this gratuitous attack, and at least 20,000 of them took to the streets on more than one occasion during 1987 and 1988, alerting the Government to the simple fact that homosexual people are voters too, some of them in marginal constituencies.

Intensive lobbying, not only by various gay groups but also by an arts lobby alarmed by the censorship implications of the clause – amongst them the actor Ian McKellen[16] – put the Government on the defensive. An advertisement in the *Independent* of 1 February 1988, signed by over 280 well-known people from many different walks of life, stated their 'sense of alarm' at the 'unthinking intolerance' expressed through the clause. Having been approached for help in obtaining these signatures, I was pleased to see that over fifty of those whom I had contacted had signed. Unfortunately no further use was made of the collection; as with Tony Dyson's 'Campaign for Reason',

---

[14] Michael Howard, Local Government Minister.

[15] The Prime Minister did not, Ian McKellen was privately assured (according to a report in *Gay Times*, April 1988), object to homosexuals as individuals, but disliked them in publicly visible groups; she evidently thought that Clause 28 was a neat way of keeping them 'privatised'.

[16] Who, having very publicly come out over the Clause, proceeded with Michael Cashman to form the Stonewall lobbying group. He subsequently discovered that having done so was no bar to being offered a knighthood, a significant marker against discrimination, despite predictable criticism from other gay activists of his acceptance.

a valuable nucleus of support was laboriously assembled and then allowed to drop into limbo.

I also wrote a personal letter about the clause to Nicholas Ridley, who had been such a Tory stalwart of homosexual law reform and champion of a lower age of consent in the 1967 parliament, and who was now, as Secretary of State for the Environment, in charge of the Local Government Bill. I reminded him of his past support for my work, and pointed out that only a few days previously the Government had signed the international 'London Declaration' on AIDS, in which the participating governments pledged themselves to 'forge, through information and education and social leadership, a spirit of social tolerance'. In view of this, I commented, the spectacle of this same Government simultaneously legislating to bar a disadvantaged group from receiving local authority assistance in lawful endeavours to improve its own lot was quite bizarre. Nicholas eventually replied, somewhat lamely, that though the Government were against discrimination in any form, and did not believe that Clause 28 would increase prejudice and intolerance, it was needed because some local authorities had misused ratepayers' money to 'glamourise' homosexuality to youngsters. Remembering his forthrightly libertarian stance over the age of consent in the Committee Stage of Leo Abse's Bill more than twenty years before, I wondered how Nicholas had managed to convince himself of this absurd thesis.

Although the Government had to push Clause 28 through to save face, the 'Stop the Clause' campaign vigorously demonstrated to them that further anti-gay legislation was not likely to be worth the hassle;[17] and this was an undeniably beneficial result, making unlikely any future Government action in response to the maverick calls for repeal of the 1967 Act now emanating from a few far-Right fringe groups.

Another good outcome was a new resurgence of confidence and determination amongst gay people not to be further scapegoated. This led to renewed and successful pressures upon the Labour Party to make gay rights a basic plank of their election programme, and to the

[17] When the Local Government Bill finally passed its Committee Stage in the Lords a posse of lesbians abseiled down from the public gallery upon their astonished Lordships, and when Section 28 was about to come into force some intrepid women invaded the BBC's Six O'Clock News studio and chained themselves to Sue Lawley's legs as she was reading the bulletin. The butterfly had stamped again – this time with picturesque effect.

formation of 1989 of the Stonewall lobbying group with the objective of putting gay rights and homosexual equality firmly back on to the mainstream political agenda.

The advent of AIDS brought a vicious escalation of homophobia. The consequential depths to which some public discussion of homosexuality and other sexual issues sank, reminiscent of the most bigoted utterances of the 1950s, has been well documented by Richard Davenport-Hines in his impressive study *Sex, Death and Punishment*.[18] The urgent need to get some constructive social initiatives going to counteract this new wave of prejudice led me in the mid-1980s to undertake some AIDS-related work with Parliament, in the counselling and training field, and also in assessing the likely longer-term social impact of AIDS.

The first two initiatives were taken through the framework of the Albany Society, the small charity originally set up alongside the Albany Trust with the objective of promoting psychological health, and with which I had remained associated after leaving the Trust in 1977. The Albany Society, of which I was now Chairman, took early steps, with the help of Maureen Colquhoun (who, though no longer an MP, was still working in the House of Commons as a research assistant), to fund and service an embryonic all-party parliamentary group on AIDS. I am glad that the now well-established APPGA was sustained and fostered by the Albany Society's slender purse and Maureen's unstinted free help during the first months of its life, until it became sufficiently consolidated to obtain other funding and to employ its own staff.

My second AIDS-related task was to convene, on behalf of the British Association for Counselling, an AIDS training panel (also initially funded through the Albany Society),[19] to produce a short and simple basic training manual in counselling skills for those working in the AIDS field. This enthusiastic and highly skilled group speedily produced a first draft which we intended should be quickly and cheaply produced and widely circulated by BAC to fill a glaring gap in helpers' resources. Our draft was taken up and developed by the

[18] Collins, 1990.
[19] Which was wound up, because of continuing funding and administrative problems, in 1991.

Government-funded Scottish Health Education Group; while most welcome at the time, this proved to be a mixed blessing in terms of the greatly lengthened production timescale and the much bigger size and cost of the final manual.

I was also invited to join an 'AIDS concern team' set up in the spring of 1986 by the Centre for Explorations in Social Concern (a unit of the Grubb Institute) to consider the long-term implications of AIDS for social policy. Although this was the most 'abstract' of my AIDS tasks, it was also the most thought-provoking. The team, which originally formed around Dr Alec Dickson, the founder of the Community Service Volunteers, was especially interested to consider what contribution individuals and voluntary agencies in the wider community could make to the mounting social crisis which we foresaw AIDS would bring. Besides holding, in addition to our frequent group meetings, day seminars for widely-drawn participants, the CESC team submitted a memorandum to the House of Commons Social Services Committee's 1987 enquiry into problems associated with AIDS, and did much to focus public and parliamentary attention upon the implications of the crisis. I was the principal draftsman of the CESC's evidence, and I also gave oral evidence, mostly concerned with counselling, to the Social Services Committee on behalf of the Albany Society.

The CESC memorandum emphasised the potentially far-reaching implications of AIDS, and urged a multidisciplinary response. We did not believe that the crisis could be effectively dealt with merely by a technological 'quick fix', and urged that besides searching – as scientists were bound to do – for a 'magic bullet' cure and vaccine, society needed to face up to the fact that 'AIDS confronts us all with many salient and permanent aspects of the human condition: our mortality; our sexuality; our interdependence; our existential insecurity; our moral and temperamental frailties; our sometimes conflicting belief-systems; our cultural and religious symbols and rituals; our responsibilities'. The team perceived that AIDS is far more than just a medical crisis: it also has profound emotional, psychological and ethical implications for the quality of human life.

We urged Parliament to grasp the measure of this situation, and to recognise that while the AIDS threat calls for clear heads, 'it is even more vital for us to keep warm hearts'. Ignorance, prejudice and bigotry must be confronted and overcome:

> There are some people, including those in positions of authority who should know better [we commented], who apparently regard AIDS as a God-given opportunity to ride hobby-horses and to thump tubs.

But we believed that

> The challenge of AIDS is essentially one of opportunity, offering a choice between regaining greater social cohesion and unity in the face of an unprecedented threat to the nation's health and wellbeing, or else falling still more deeply into social divisiveness, demoralisation, defeat and perhaps even national despair.

It was a sombre diagnosis, but not an unrelievedly gloomy one; we saw a gleam of hope that

> if greater openness, honesty and kindness towards one another can be sought for and found amongst people who are confronting AIDS – which now means everyone in our society – our cultural environment and social relationships can be transformed for the better, instead of for the worse, because of the AIDS epidemic.

In some respects the developments of the past few years have borne out some of the CESC team's fears; but not all our hopes have proved illusory. While a great deal remains to be done to eradicate the ignorance and prejudice still surrounding not only AIDS, but human sexuality in general, the ground for fruitful and constructive work during the 1990s and into the twenty-first century is now being laid and tilled by many organisations and individuals who were not involved at the time when the CESC report was written.

XX

The Law is Still an Ass

'The function of law in society is not to prohibit but to protect, not to enforce morals but to safeguard persons, their privacies and freedoms.'

Bishop John A. T. Robinson[1]

Even Leo Abse acknowledged, with hindsight, that the terms of the 1967 Sexual Offences Act were too restrictive. Writing in *The British Journal of Criminology*,[2] he pointed out that

> the penalties attached to some public displays of homosexuality are too harsh: but the courts are, it is hoped, unlikely to apply the maximum sentences. The provisions concerning servicemen and seamen aboard merchant navy ships are unrealistic and could, if harshly administered, cause grave anomalies. More important, the interpretation of privacy within the Act, if too narrowly applied, could thwart the legislature's intentions.

Vigilance, he warned – oddly, in view of the restrictive influence he had exerted on the drafting process – would be required amongst reformers in the early years of the Act. But he justified its shortcomings with the characteristically Absean claim that it 'reflected the appeasement required to assuage the irrational fears which otherwise could have overspilled and totally engulfed the Bill', while concluding that 'the ten-year debate, and its conclusion, helped to make our country a little more rational'.

The Homosexual Law Reform Society's repeated efforts to convince Abse and Lord Arran of the desirability and practicality of liberalising the Bill as it passed through Parliament had proved fruitless

---

[1] *The Place of Law in the Field of Sex*. The Beckly Lecture for 1972 (Sexual Law Reform Society, 1972).

[2] January 1968, pp. 86–87. Reprinted by permission of Oxford University Press.

– they had brushed aside all our pleas, and provided us with no opportunity for discussing with the Home Office any of the points which worried us. While it was obviously tactically preferable not to depart too drastically from the wording emerging from the lengthy series of Lords' debates, some improvements could have been made in the Commons without sacrificing the Bill. But the sponsors, jaded by the long battle, wanted an end to the matter with no more fuss.

Our supporters were loudly unhappy. At a meeting in the spring of 1967, when Leo Abse was detained at the House and I had to deputise for him as speaker at short notice, about one hundred of them gave me a severe roasting about their concerns. The 'Dilhorne' definition of 'in private' was heavily criticised as illogical, unworkable, dangerously conducive to blackmail, and in conflict with the clear intention of the Wolfenden Committee. Unease was also felt over the severity of the proposed new higher penalties in the Bill, in conjunction with an age of consent as high as twenty-one; and in particular at the provision making it still an offence for consenting youths both aged between sixteen and twenty-one to have a homosexual relationship – since this would greatly handicap the task of teachers and youth workers attempting to deal openly with their charges' possibly transient homosexual tendencies.

Sometime previously a group of the HLRS' most faithful voluntary workers, including Marian Dutta, had written a letter to the executive committee, urging them to press for a better Bill so that 'future historians would have no opportunity to criticise the HLRS' for a law which would perpetuate police interference with private morality. 'It may take many years for the Society ever to get amendments adequately discussed in Parliament again. The public will feel they have done enough.' An age of consent of twenty-one would, they predicted, bedevil future reform, and might turn out to be more cruel in the long run than the existing set-up. 'Future reformers are not going to thank the HLRS for a bad Bill', they concluded. I agreed with them – except that it was *not* the HLRS's Bill: ultimately it was the Home Office's, however much they clung to their chant of 'look, no hands' and hid behind Arran's and Abse's skirts.

In Parliament the HLRS had privately prompted a series of amendments in both Houses seeking to lower the age of consent and to rule out the possibility of 'Ladies' Directory type' common law charges of 'conspiracy to corrupt public morals' in relation to activities decriminalised by the Bill. These, too, were resisted by the sponsors. Yet in the months immediately following the Royal Assent to the Sexual Offences Act it became crystal clear that there was going to be no let-up of police prosecutions for public indecency offences and other aspects of homosexual behaviour which were not covered by the new law.

The HLRS executive committee (save for Professor Ayer and Leo Abse, who advocated winding up) were therefore acutely conscious of the need for the Society to stay in being, and if possible to bring pressure to bear for further reforms. At their first meeting, (in October 1967) after the Act became law, they agreed that further legal changes were necessary – especially in view of the recently issued report of the (Latey) Committee on the Age of Majority, which had recommended a legal age of majority of eighteen for a variety of purposes, including the capacity to marry without parental consent.[3] Also the Home Secretary (Roy Jenkins) had announced an impending review by the Criminal Law Revision Committee of the entire law relating to sexual offences; so the executive committee decided that as its next task the Society should prepare a memorandum of evidence for the CLRC.

In March 1970, therefore, the HLRS reconstituted itself as the Sexual Law Reform Society, with the Rt Rev. John A. T. Robinson (the former Bishop of Woolwich, who was Dean of Trinity College, Cambridge) as Chairman, and proceeded to convene a working party to draft evidence for the CLRC.[4] The working party was set up in October 1970, and held fifteen meetings before issuing its report in September 1974. Its terms of reference were:

> To review the existing law and its enforcement in relation to
> sexual behaviour; and to make recommendations for its reform
> so as to provide for the maximum degree of personal liberty
> compatible with social wellbeing.

The working party met many times, and exchanged a great deal of internal correspondence, before issuing its report in September 1974.

[3] Implemented by the Family Law Reform Act 1969.
[4] The members were: Lord Beaumont of Whitley, Monica Furlong, Antony Grey, Dr David Kerr, John Lloyd-Ely QC, C. H. Rolph, Keith Wedmore and Dr D. J. West. Mr Rolph was the working party's chairman until October 1972, when Dr Kerr succeeded him. Keith Wedmore was secretary until the end of 1972, when I took over.

More than two years before it did so the SLRS's chairman, Bishop John Robinson, gave a lecture[5] to a Methodist church audience which provided a benchmark for forward thinking. In his preface to the published text Dr Robinson described, with some bemusement, the treatment he had received from the press, with headlines such as '"Sex at 14" Call by Church Leader' – not, he commented reproachfully, 'unwitting distortion by ignorant reporters, but the work of sub-editors who knew perfectly well what they are about'. What he was in fact advocating was an age of *protection*. 'Consent', he thought, was too personal and subjective to be determined by an arbitrary age, but there must be a line below which society has an absolute duty to assume responsibility for protection of the immature. The question was, how to do this most effectively?

What I particularly liked about the lecture was its endeavour to substitute for the current cant of 'permissiveness' an ethic of mutual social responsibility. When people were confronted with something of which they deeply disapproved, especially if they had not thought deeply about it, said Dr Robinson, there was an instinctive reaction to say 'There ought to be a law against it'. The charge against the 'permissive society' was that the controls had slipped; things were being permitted that ought not to be permitted. But this was an essentially negative view of the law's function, and a paternalistic social attitude. The true function of law in a democratic society was 'not to prohibit, but to protect, not to enforce morals but to safeguard persons, their privacies and freedoms'.

In this Dr Robinson followed John Stuart Mill's classic argument in the essay *On Liberty*. Where there was no need for protection, the law should not intervene. It was not there to express 'the anger of morality'; it was there as far as possible to *enable* people to be free, mature, adult human beings, or what the New Testament called 'sons'. It should be a hindrance to hindrances against this process – playing a limited role, because the free processes of influence, education, example and persuasion were so much more productive. Only as a last resort, if a person refused to respect the freedom of another, should there be a provision to compel him to do so.

The Bishop said he would prefer sexual offences to be abolished

[5] See footnote 1.

as a separate category and dealt with as 'offences against the person', because this would be a real step towards eliminating the 'peculiar vindictiveness' which our society visited upon sexual aberrations and deviations. There were only three circumstances where the law had the right and the duty to protect the citizen:

1 where there was not true consent;
2 where there was not adult responsibility;
3 where there was obtrusion on the public.

With regard to the age of consent, Dr Robinson emphasised (only to be totally ignored on this point by the sensational reporting his lecture received) that this concerned 'not the age at which we think young people *morally should* have sex relations, but the age at which they *legally can* consent to what they are doing'. He had no doubt about this age should be the same for homosexual as for heterosexual relations, 'since it is capacity for personal consent which is at issue and not sexual proclivity'. This age should be sixteen at the highest; the only question was whether or not it should be lower, 'because the criminal law is a very blunt instrument for this purpose.' On reflection, he favoured a legal age of consent of fourteen, bolstered by additional protections – notably, increased powers to take young people into care and to safeguard them against exploitation.

As a positive principle, Bishop Robinson went on, one might say that any discrimination between the sexes should itself be made illegal, and that this should involve an equalisation of penalties for equivalent heterosexual and homosexual offences. And 'it should surely be accepted that homosexuals should be harassed and prosecutions initiated only when public decency is palpably outraged or actual annoyance caused to specific persons'. He had a similarly 'hands off' attitude towards pornography, whose main offence was to be *anti-erotic* ('hard-bore rather than hard-core'), and whose addicts were 'depraved because they were deprived, and should be pitied rather than prosecuted – and above all helped'.

It was not the law that altered social attitudes so much as social attitudes which formed the law. If the law was out of tune with social *mores*, it simply made the provision of effective advice and protection more difficult. Yet people had a deep-set fear that if you lifted legal controls anything could happen and probably would – 'a catastrophic expectation of unlimited indulgence'. However, it was precisely the sign of a civilised society that it progressively substituted the free processes of social judgement for the sanctions of penal suppression.

This lecture was an impressive one, and its high quality stands the test of the years. It could be read with benefit today by all would-be reformers. Yet as Dr Robinson himself discovered (not for the first time) what he actually said was wildly garbled by the press. And it produced the usual crop of rancorous epistles, of which the following is typical:

> Dear Sir,
>
> *Honest to God, Lady Chatterley's Lover, Age of Consent, etc.*
>
> If you can look at your activities impartially, may I ask you two questions –
>
> 1 Do you not think that on the whole you have done more harm than good in stirring up controversy, blurring the line between good and evil and getting nowhere?
>
> 2 Do you not think that lending your name to doubtful causes gives much support to those whose aims are immoral?

Although not a member of the SLRS' working party, Dr Robinson, as the Society's chairman, was naturally in close touch with the working party's thinking; and although the Beckly Lecture was entirely his own, his thinking was informed by that of the working party, whose own report was finally published in September 1974. This too remains challenging reading; a challenge still largely unmet nearly twenty years on. The working party began by considering what principles should properly govern the laws relating to sexual behaviour, and after much discussion came up with the following formula:

> 1 There should be a general freedom, upheld by the law, for individuals to engage in such sexual activities as they may freely choose, subject only to restrictions which are clearly socially necessary.
>
> 2 These [restrictions] arise . . . only from the need to (i) protect those who by reason of their age or condition are not fully responsible; (ii) prevent the infliction of involuntarily received pain, anguish or physical damage upon participants; and (iii) punish affronts given to third parties whose complaints are held by the courts to be justified.

3 It follows that only those sexual activities should be illegal (a) which are not willingly consented to, or which are subject to restriction on grounds of age or limited responsibility; or (b) which result in clinically demonstrable mental or physical damage or suffering; or (c) which have given rise to reasonable complaints from a member of the public.

4 It should also be an offence to indulge in any sexual activity or display where this is observed by others and causes them actual annoyance; but it should be a defence that no such observation could be reasonably expected, or that the observer did not object. (This defence should apply regardless of the numbers involved or the nature of the activities in question.)

5 Where an offence contravening one of the above principles is alleged, the burden of proof should in all cases lie on the prosecution.

The working party's objective in framing these principles was to shift the emphasis of the law away from the existing presumption that (as the report put it) 'all sexual activity except that between husband and wife is a bad or negative thing, and that the law should always discourage it and at times positively prevent it'. In contrast to this traditional view, the working party declared that they did not regard it as a proper use of the law to enforce standards of morality in sexual behaviour upon individuals.

> The capacity for sexual enjoyment, whether experienced heterosexually or homosexually, is a natural endowment of human beings. All citizens should possess, as of right, the maximum possible degree of free choice in its exercise – provided always that others are not directly harmed or unwillingly involved.

They expressed no collective view on the moral issues:

> There is much behaviour, sexual and other, which is deplorable but which one would not wish to see punished, because the consequent restriction upon individual liberty is more harmful than the fault.

People should be free to do or see what they wished in the sexual sphere; they should also be free not have what they objected to forced upon or thrust in front of them. Responsible human beings must be allowed – and indeed were surely entitled – to do what they chose with their own bodies and minds, unless medically verified harm was done to others immediately involved. Laws which denied this personal freedom were foredoomed to failure, and would merely create more social damage than they could prevent.

The working party advocated a further break with tradition by urging the elimination of the separate category of 'sexual offences' from our legal system, because (like Bishop Robinson) they believed that this would work towards the reduction of emotional prejudice against the accused and have a beneficial effect on court attitudes. All those acts which properly required legal sanctions could be reclassified as assaults, breaches of protective provisions, or offences against public decency and invasions of privacy. Legal language too should be over-hauled by substituting neutral descriptions of prohibited conduct for pejorative terms such as 'gross indecency', which fostered prejudice.[6]

Turning to the content of the law the working party began by criticising the concept of an 'age of consent' as a legal fiction, out of touch with reality and incomprehensible to most young people:

> the arbitrary determination of an age level below which willing participants in a sexual act are deemed incapable of consenting to that act is inconsistent with contemporary sociological and psychological thought. The consequential sentencing of one or both partners is offensive to common sense. We should prefer, if possible, to abolish this fiction altogether, and to substitute a more realistic justification for appropriate social intervention in the sexual behaviour of adults – namely, that until they have reached a certain age – which we recommend should be the present legal age of majority, eighteen – they may in certain circumstances require to be brought within the care and control provisions of the Children and Young Persons Acts. . . . In this event, a young girl or boy under the age of eighteen could be treated, if necessary, as being in moral danger. Older sexual part-ners (heterosexual or homosexual) of such young people would commit no offence if there was in fact willing consent.

If the working party's recommendation was not accepted, however, and an age of consent was retained, it should be the same for homo-sexual as for heterosexual conduct; and the working party recom-mended, after a full discussion of the pros and cons of various alternatives, that it should be lowered to fourteen, with the 'care and protection' provisions applying until eighteen.

[6] Both highly important matters which have still not been adequately taken into account in either professional or political discussions of legal reform.

In our considered opinion (they concluded), revision of the law along these lines will strengthen the likelihood of those young people who need either moral or medical help seeking and obtaining it, while in no way making easier or encouraging their seduction or exploitation.

So as to ensure this, they proposed that it should be an offence to procure anyone under eighteen to commit an act of prostitution.

With regard to homosexuality, the report listed the remaining legal inequalities and anomalies relating to the age of consent, the definition of 'in private', the armed forces and merchant navy, heavier penalties than for some equivalent heterosexual offences, and the exclusion of Scotland and Northern Ireland from the 1967 Act, and called for further reform to bring the law into accordance with the working party's principles.

Logically, the 1967 Act and those provisions of the 1956 Act which provide for the different treatment of homosexual as opposed to heterosexual behaviour should be repealed and replaced by provisions relating impartially to all sexual conduct, regardless of the sex of those participating. The notion that young men need a higher degree of legal protection from homosexual assaults than young women do from heterosexual assaults strikes us as absurd.

The law dealt in a curious way with prostitution (the working party pointed out), surrounding an activity that was not in itself illegal with an array of peripheral offences. If prostitution itself was not to be made an offence – and there had never been any serious call for this – its surrounding circumstances should no longer be dealt with so harshly. There should be no move towards State regulation. 'Social policy should be neutral towards the fact of prostitution. Prostitutes, in common with everybody else, should pay income tax on their professional earnings.' Living on immoral earnings should no longer be a crime, unless coercion or violence was involved; brothels should be dealt with, where necessary, because they caused a neighbourhood nuisance – not on moral grounds. The 1959 Street Offences Act, which had implemented the first half of the Wolfenden Report, aimed to 'sweep them off the streets', and was heartily disliked by social workers no less than by the prostitutes themselves. It should be replaced by a general measure regulating all public street behaviour.[7] This should also replace the notorious section 32 of the 1956 Act which provided a maximum of two years' imprisonment for men who persistently solicited or importuned in a public place for immoral purposes. Originally introduced at the end of the nineteenth century to catch prostitutes' 'bullies' (touts), this section had in fact been used almost exclusively against male homosexuals, the threat of its severe penalties making it an easy matter for the police to persuade arrested men to plead guilty to lesser charges under other provisions such as local bye-laws. It also led to frequent allegations of *agent provocateur* police activities.[8] The working party asked for a non-discriminatory street offences law, preserving public order and decency by punishing men and women impartially for offensive, annoying or injurious behaviour (whether sexual or non-sexual) towards specific citizens whose evidence in court would be required in order to secure a conviction. We are still waiting for such a law in the 1990s, and it is long overdue.[9]

The working party also urged more liberal obscenity laws and supported the Law Commission's proposals[10] for a tighter definition of conspiracy so as to rule out further prosecutions along the lines of the *International Times* case, whose conclusion that anything which assisted or promoted the commission of homosexual practices – even

[7] I had set out my views and proposals on this score in an address to the Josephine Butler Society in 1969 (published as an Albany Trust 'Talking Point' pamphlet, *The Citizen in the Street*, 1969).

[8] The files of the HLRS contained numerous instances of the abuse of this law in circumstances where no public annoyance was caused; those accused who consulted us alleged provocative behaviour by the police so frequently that it was impossible for us to doubt that this was a widespread practice. To judge from recent reports in the gay press, and from 'watchdog' groups such as the Gay London Policing Group (GALOP), it still is.

[9] In 1984 Liberal MP William Wallace moved an amendment to the Police and Criminal Evidence Bill to amend Section 32 of the Sexual Offences Act 1956 so as to limit the power of arrest for importuning to uniformed police officers whose evidence would require the corroboration of a member of the public who had been offended by the behaviour in question. Although he received widespread support in the House, the Government resisted the change on the spurious grounds that the use of plain-clothes officers was 'essential' to prevent public nuisance and to protect children from molestation. But, as always, the Government 'deplored' the use of *agent provocateur* tactics!

[10] Law Commission Report no. 50: *Inchoate Offences* (HMSO, 1973).

those which were no longer unlawful – was contrary to public policy constituted 'a worrying threat to those who are endeavouring to assist homosexuals and members of other sexual minorities'.

The working party had produced a brave report. Within hours of its release to the press it attracted a deluge of instant comment from the 'moral guardians'. 'A thoughtless and callous document, blind and bigoted, showing an immense lack of compassion for young people' (Mrs Whitehouse); 'totally evil', 'sexual anarchy', 'unpardonably and morally frivolous' (the Responsible Society); 'A Lolita's charter from the permissive Pied Pipers of our time, piping away and taking children and young people to destruction' (Dr Rhodes Boyson MP); 'We're sick of listening to do-gooders who want to help the criminal instead of the victim' (the chairman of the Police Federation).

The report was 'a perfect recipe for child-rape and child-fornication' and 'further encouragement to lust and licence', according to the Bishop of Leicester (chairman of the Church of England's Board for Social Responsibility). 'Like most of what these so-called reform societies bring out these days', said a Lincoln vicar, 'I would consign the whole of this report to my dustbin'. 'When they have completed their programme of legalising moral filth, it is hoped they are ready to answer for the chaos they are causing', wrote a nonconformist minister to the *Eastern Daily Press*.

The newspapers went to town. 'KILL THIS CASANOVA CHARTER', urged the *News of the World*; 'the plan is a charter for pimps, prostitutes, proselytising homosexuals and perverts. It is SICK, SICK, SICK.' And Boofy Arran most unhelpfully chose to slam the report in his *Evening News* column as 'totally amazing': 'it is the sheer impracticality of these liberal-minded folk that I find so surprising'. 'The public tends to be hypnotised into silence by any self-appointed "expert" who stands up to testify, as though to a revealed and absolute truth, that even the most unspeakable beastliness is therapeutically "good" for somebody', lamented Ronald Butt in *The Times*. All these critics studiously ignored the basis of the SLRS' argument, which was that the law as it stood did far more harm than good.

The working party's report was, however, courteously welcomed by the Criminal Law Revision Committee and its Policy Advisory

Committee,[11] who responded in their working paper on the age of consent[12] to what they described as the SLRS's 'challenge' by asking themselves how best young girls could be protected. Their conclusion was that 'the criminal law had an important role to play'; and they settled unanimously for retaining the existing age of consent of sixteen for girls. For homosexual behaviour they recommended lowering the age of consent (or, as they preferred to term it, the minimum age) to eighteen, commenting that the Wolfenden Committee had reported at a time of great prejudice against homosexuals and ignorance against homosexuality – ignorance and prejudice which the PAC thought (too optimistically) was now diminishing. It was increasingly being realised, they said, that many homosexuals experienced intense difficulty in coming to terms with their sexual orientation and could best be assisted by a compassionate legal framework; the law had a part to play in bringing about acceptance of homosexuals by not discriminating unnecessarily against homosexuality; but it could not go too far too fast. A minority of the PAC,[13] however, urged that the homosexual minimum age should be sixteen: the law ought not to discriminate between the sexes unless there were very strong reasons for doing so, and by sixteen the individual should be free to make his or her own decisions on these matters.

One encouraging feature of the PAC's working paper was their acceptance and endorsement of the 'Wolfenden principle' that in the sphere of sexuality, the law's function should be primarily protective rather than punitive. This was a most welcome declaration – although contemporary practice was (and still is) in many respects far out of line with the principle. Pointing this out in our response to the working paper, the SLRS questioned the basis for the PAC's apparent assumptions that there was some unspecified psychological (as distinct from moral, emotional or physical) harm caused to young people by their indulgence in what the PAC described as 'premature' sexual

[11] I was gratified to be told subsequently by one of its members that the CLRC treated the SLRS's submissions as among the most important of the many they received, and that they always gave our arguments very careful consideration in their deliberations. Our aim was indeed to act as a 'pacemaker', and we laid down a benchmark for ultimate sexual law reform which still constitutes a highly relevant agenda.

[12] Policy Advisory Committee on Sexual Offences: *Working Paper on the Age of Consent in relation to Sexual Offences* (HMSO, 1979).

[13] Five out of the eight women members, but none of the seven men.

activity; and that it was desirable wherever possible to encourage 'natural' heterosexual development and to discourage 'deviant' homosexual propensities. These propositions, we said, were far from being self-evident. We also challenged their stance of 'benevolent paternalism', and reiterated our objection to the concept of 'ages of consent' as a legal fiction. The criminal law, we said, should not only be certain; it should also be truthful:

> it is not conducive to respect for the law to falsify the actualities
> of the situation – especially where sexual behaviour of a private,
> personal and intimate kind is concerned.

So we reiterated our original recommendations, emphasising that we did not wish the age of consent laws to be removed or reduced without alternative protective machinery being introduced to make constructive help, instead of destructive punishment, available to teenagers whose sexual behaviour was putting them at risk. We did not regard it as the proper function of the law to act as a 'moral signpost' in place of adequate pastoral help; in fact, the stress and misery it caused was out of all proportion to its actual effectiveness. Far from 'protecting' adolescents involved in homosexual behaviour, the existence of criminal penalties placed them at much greater social and moral risk. As Professor Herbert Hart had pointed out, laws to enforce sexual morality created 'misery of a quite special degree' through the attempted suppression of sexual impulses which affected the balance of the individual's emotional life, happiness and personality.[14] But in their final report on the age of consent[15] the PAC stuck to their original proposals, countering our views with the conclusion, drawn from the bulk of the evidence they had received, that 'it would be wholly unacceptable to public opinion' to allow adult males to have sexual intercourse with young girls, who would thereby be deprived of 'protection necessary for their well-being'. The PAC justified their majority preference for a higher minimum age for homosexual behaviour than the heterosexual age of consent by the assertions that 'because a great many people still considered homosexuality degrading and objectionable' it imposed great psychological strain; and that their high level of promiscuity was a 'further source of unhappiness' to many homo-

[14] *Law, Liberty and Morality* (Oxford University Press, 1963), p. 22.
[15] HMSO, Cmnd. 8216, April 1981.

sexual men – strange reasons, surely, for exacerbating their plight by harrying them with the criminal law! The PAC also said their (unspecified) experience was that 'between the ages of sixteen and eighteen girls are on the whole more mature than boys in their approach to sexual relationships'. As the Joint Council for Gay Teen-agers had pointed out in their response to the working paper, the PAC were alert to the imagined dangers which homosexuality posed to heterosexual young men, but seemed oblivious to the weight of pressure exerted by heterosexual society and its institutions upon homosexuals of both sexes.

> Gay people are not going to go away [the JCGT wrily pointed out]; they will only prosper or suffer according to the way society – including the law – regards them. The situation is analogous to the way the law influences race relations or sex equality.

The heterosexual age of consent had also come under assault from a different quarter. In a report, *Pregnant at School*, issued in September 1979 by a joint working party of the National Council of One Parent Families and the Community Development Trust, the age of consent law was condemned as on balance a hindrance to good welfare prac-tice, and its abolition was accordingly proposed. While the age of consent was only one aspect of the CLRC's review, it attracted the bulk of attention and was the focus of a fierce battle between those who saw it as an effective protection and those who experienced it as destructive of human happiness. As Secretary of the SLRS I was the recipient of voluminous correspondence on this issue. One of our out-of-London supporters did a great deal of single-handed lobbying and wrote several papers and articles. Among them was an amusing fable about a school where the children had been taught to worship the 'Cow of Consent' which, on closer inspection, turned out to be a heavily whitewashed and distinctly bogus animal. The children restored it to its original colour, and set it free to graze at will, where-upon they became happily self-governing and dispensed with artificial discipline – to the horror of the school governors, who promptly rewhitewashed and tethered the cow and made the children miserable again. I sent a copy of this story to Dame Margaret Miles, the former London headmistress who had chaired the *Pregnant at School* working party, and whom I knew well in her role as much-loved president of the British Association for Counselling. She replied, inimitably, by postcard: 'Thank you so much for the Cow! It seems marginally over involved, but the message certainly comes through.'

In their working party on sexual offences,[16] the CLRC discerned 'an important difference between the law governing sexual behaviour and other parts of the criminal law', arising from the fact that there was not the same degree of consensus about what sexual behaviour the law should rightfully cover as there was in relation to most other crimes.[17] They accordingly asked for the views of the public before making decisions about some of these contentious issues. While they broadly adopted the 'Wolfenden' approach,

> few would dispute the need for the law to protect the vulnerable, but how far such protection should extend and the most suitable way to provide it are matters over which differing opinions are held.

While moral condemnation alone could not be regarded as sufficient ground for making consensual adult behaviour a criminal offence, 'nor do we consider . . . that the mere fact that sexual conduct is consensual should always be decisive against its criminality'.

Though this was understandable with reference to some aspects of incest, the phrase 'mere fact' in relation to the presence or absence of consent struck me as suggestively indicative of the CLRC's instinctive paternalism, despite their lip service to the 'Wolfenden' philosophy. In our response to their working paper the SLRS urged that 'there should be a general presumption that mutual consent should be a sufficient answer to criminal charges of a sexual nature', and that any departures from this presumption should be exceptional and require ample justification in terms of public policy. The need to secure acceptance of this principle was underlined in December 1990, when several men who had indulged in mutually desired consenting sado-

---

[16] HMSO, October 1980.

[17] This was borne out by some of their own views, which struck some of their readers as quite quaint. For example, 'Most of us think that acts such as oral sex are extremely serious (perhaps more likely to disturb a young girl meeting them for the first time than ordinary sexual intercourse)'. The notion that meeting ordinary sexual intercourse for the first time is 'disturbing' for young girls, as distinct from arousing, seems extremely odd; as is the statement 'it is for society to decide what should be the age at which sexual familiarities are allowed with its young' – as if this is always something which is done *to* young people, and not sought *by* them.

masochistic genital torture resulting in minor injuries (some of them self-inflicted) were sentenced to terms of imprisonment for indecent assault.[18] Surely it is high time to incorporate into the law the positive right to sexual freedom advocated by Professor Tony Honoré in his book *Sex Law*, in which he urges recognition of the right of bodily integrity – the proposition that each of us may use our body as we please, provided we do not touch another without their consent:

> It is my right to express myself and my personality in a certain intimate way which involves the use of my body but reaches beyond it. . . . It embraces the right to love, to be loved and to express love or, in some cases, just friendship. For this reason, and because sex can be physically so intense, many people value it more highly than, say, religion, though freedom of worship, unlike sexual freedom, has long been listed as a basic human right. . . .
>
> The principles which should guide legislators and lawyers who want to give effect to a right of sexual freedom are . . .
>
> > (a) The right to sexual freedom consists in the right to use our bodies as we choose and to touch others with their consent, together with accessory rights designed to ensure reasonable sexual opportunities.
> >
> > (b) Sexual freedom may be exercised by those who have reached maturity. The age of maturity is also the age of full responsibility (eighteen).[19]

On the age of consent the CLRC provisionally endorsed the proposals of their Policy Advisory Committee, saying that the minimum age for homosexual relations should be 'no higher than' eighteen, and that the current age of majority was a most important factor in determining this. They rejected the notion of a lower general minimum age combined with special protection against abuse of authority as unlikely to work satisfactorily – though why, when such provisions operate in various European countries and in Canada, was not convincingly explained. While recommending that consensual heterosexual buggery

---

[18] *The Independent*, 22 December 1990. In February 1992 the Court of Appeal upheld the convictions, while reducing the sentences. (*Independent*, 20 February 1992.)

[19] Tony Honoré, *Sex Law* (Duckworth, 1978), pp. 172–174. This plea echoes, down 275 years, the pathetic puzzlement of the man trapped by the police in 1726 and accused of intent to commit sodomy: 'I think there is no Crime in making what Use I please of my own Body.' (Cited in Richard Davenport-Hines, op. cit., p. 65.)

should cease to be a crime when the woman involved had attained a minimum age of sixteen or eighteen, they proposed to retain nonconsensual buggery as a separate offence with a maximum penalty of life imprisonment. They suggested rationalising the different maximum penalties for indecent assault[20] to a single maximum prison term of five years, but rejected one member's idea[21] that there should be two degrees of indecent assault – ordinary and aggravated – carrying maxima of two and five years respectively, on the ground that 'the majority of us are not convinced that any form of aggravated offence could be created which would satisfactorily identify those indecent assaults which should be punished with special severity'. And, retrogressively in my view, they rejected the same member's plea to get rid of descriptive moralisms such as 'indecent assault' and 'gross indecency'; indeed, they wanted to extend the scope of the latter.

Turning to sexual acts committed in public (or not 'in private'), the CLRC advanced the welcome proposition that the law with respect to these should be the same for heterosexual and homosexual behaviour. Their view of the 'Dilhorne' definition of homosexual privacy was that it was designed 'in an attempt to reduce the risks of corruption, especially of young adults'. Many of those who had submitted evidence had been critical of this provision, and the PAC had said that in their opinion it was discriminatory and an excessive interference with privacy. They had been told that clubs for homosexuals were generally well conducted:

> indecencies in the presence of others do not take place on their
> premises, and while no doubt people may visit them in search
> of partners they cater for people who have already adopted a
> homosexual way of life.

However, the PAC had felt unable to forecast what might happen to standards in these clubs if the 'Dilhorne' rule were to be repealed without any replacement so that homosexual acts in the presence of others became allowable. They considered that the right to privacy did not require that conduct in clubs should be unregulated by law,

---

[20] Two years for an indecent assault against a girl aged thirteen or over; five years where the girl is under thirteen; and ten years where the offence is against a man.

[21] The dissentient was Professor Glanville Williams, an eminent Cambridge academic lawyer whose views were more libertarian than those of most of his colleagues.

and recommended accordingly that the law should continue to prohibit homosexual acts in the presence of others in clubs, as well as acts
in public 'in the ordinary sense of these words'.

The CLRC accordingly proposed that a new law, for both homosexuals and heterosexuals, should cover sexual intercourse and other
sexual conduct 'which might be expected to cause serious offence to
members of the public observing it' in accordance with the 'prevailing
standards in the community', taking place in circumstances where the
defendants knew that it was 'likely to be seen' by others or were
reckless as to this. An alternative would be to introduce such a law
covering heterosexual behaviour, while retaining the 'Dilhorne' rule
for homosexual behaviour with an exception for acts occurring in the
home or 'on a domestic and private occasion'.

As another possible way of covering the 'club' situation, the CLRC
suggested a provision making it an offence for

> anyone to engage (whether alone or with another person) in acts
> of gross indecency in the presence of others when in a building
> constituting premises of common resort

(which for this purpose would include private property requiring
club membership for entry). This trend of thinking revealed their
continuing obsession with group consensual acts which the committee obviously found it distasteful to contemplate, even when performed in circumstances which could not obtrude upon the public
at large. They seemed unable to escape from the lawyer's traditional
moralism, and their espousal of the 'Wolfenden' distinction between
sin and crime was at this point less than half-hearted. They themselves recognised this, but denied any inconsistency with the feeble
argument that

> the sorts of places that we have in mind are likely, we believe, to
> constitute a source of outrage to neighbours and a public scandal.

Another course, they tentatively suggested, would be to provide that
the actual causing of offence to others was irrelevant if they were
'likely' to witness the behaviour in question. The CLRC had gone
round in circles and ended up almost back with Lord Dilhorne! Some
of them, at any rate, seemed to be in the unhappy situation, mocked

at by Lady Wootton in the Arran Bill debates,[22] of constructing a law to deal with visions which tormented them of what might be going on elsewhere, unable to recognise this was their own private misfortune and no reason for imposing their personal standards of taste and morality on a minority of their fellow citizens.

In our response to this rather disappointing document, the SLRS reiterated that our approach to the law concerning sexual behaviour was 'minimalist':

> We believe that the shouldering of personal responsibility by individuals for their sexual behaviour is the essential prerequisite for a healthy social morality. As Lord Hugh Cecil so aptly put it . . . , 'Virtue is attained in proportion as liberty is attained: for virtue does not consist in doing right, but in choosing to do right.'

In our view proof of the necessity for every legal curb on people's freely made sexual choices lay four-square upon the legislator. We also questioned the practical utility of paternalistic laws in this sphere, pointing out that the resentment they aroused damaged respect for law in general. We urged the CLRC to seize the opportunity, in finalising their review, to sort out the 'untidy and confusing mess' the law was in by getting rid, so far as possible, of 'victimless crimes'. There was no valid place in a modern, rational and humane system of law for criminal penalties which merely expressed moral revulsion at sexual activities which did not infringe upon the rights and freedoms of third parties, or for punishment designed to protect people from themselves: the 'consent principle' should be paramount. The hypothetical 'harm' of any form of freely chosen behaviour had to be weighed against the tangible harm done by the law in its interference with the lives of individuals. While it was necessary to protect the immature from exploitation, the law must not add to the damage by inappropriate intervention. The criminal law, we said, should properly be concerned with protecting people from sexual behaviour they did not want to engage in – not with prohibiting or preventing that which they willing sought. In particular, we disagreed with the CLRC's apparent assumption that homosexuality required the deterrence of the criminal law during adolescence to prevent its adoption as an adult lifestyle. It was fundamentally mistaken, we urged, to criminalise the

---

[22] *House of Lords Official Report*, 13 July 1967, col. 1317. See p. 125 above.

homosexual behaviour of adolescent boys at a stage in their sexual development when doing so was likely to blow up what for some were only transient inclinations into something far more significant and problematic. It should not be the function of the law to protect people *from themselves* – least of all in the peculiarly personal sphere of sexual relationships.

On the vexed question of 'public' offences we hoped the CLRC would come round to viewing the matter, as we ourselves did, as essentially one of *nuisance*, depending on whether actual offence had been caused to identifiable persons who gave evidence to that effect. There should be a limited but strict liability not to cause such an offence. On the 'club' issue, we maintained that

> what goes on in unobtrusive circumstances between people, all of whom are consenting, and who do not themselves find the behaviour offensive, should not come within the purview of the law. . . . We think it is time to disentangle the enforcement of sexual morality from the promotion of public policy.

The new offence proposed by the CLRC was, in our view, too wide:

> To interfere with or snoop upon the activities of consenting people in circumstances of effective privacy simply because neighbours or the public at large experience feelings of outrage or are scandalised by what they imagine *might* be taking place within constitutes in our view a dangerous and unwarrantable precedent for the extension of police supervision and control over many activities of a non-sexual nature which might be held to scandalise the neighbours (e.g. a freethinkers' meeting at a private house next door to a church).

Alas, our attempts to cajole the CLRC to take a more robustly libertarian stance, or even to follow through to its logical conclusion the 'Wolfenden' principle which they had nominally endorsed, cut no ice with them. They were faced, they said in their final report,[23] with persisting fundamental disagreements as to the proper function of the law; and, while adopting the Wolfenden Committee's approach as a guideline, they had to balance against this the view of many commentators that the State, through the criminal law, should bear some responsibility for maintaining moral standards in society and that the

[23] HMSO, Cmnd. 9213, April 1984.

258

relaxation of existing laws may appear to condone conduct which many find objectionable.

> On the other hand [they conceded], it may not be necessary for the State to proscribe particular sexual practices merely because a great many people regard them with revulsion.

This was indeed tightrope walking with a vengeance. By and large the CLRC also adhered to the other proposals of their working paper. After a lengthy discussion of the pros and cons they remained unconvinced as to the practicability of introducing two categories of indecent assaults ('ordinary' and 'aggravated'), and revised their proposed maximum penalty for this offence upwards to ten years. They recommended that consensual heterosexual buggery should no longer be an offence if the woman was aged over sixteen, and that if she was under that age but over thirteen the man (but not the girl) should still be punished, even when the girl had consented, with up to five years' imprisonment, and with a maximum of life imprisonment if she was under thirteen. They recommended extending to men over eighteen accused of homosexual buggery with another man aged under eighteen the defence already available in the case of unlawful sexual intercourse with a girl that he genuinely believed she was over eighteen. Yet they wished to retain the existing maximum sentence of two years' imprisonment in the case of two consenting men each of whom was under eighteen.

With regard to the 'fictional' element in charges of indecent assault in situations where there was in fact consent, they proposed that such situations should be dealt with as a new category of heterosexual gross indecency towards girls of under sixteen – i.e. by simply changing the designation of what was still a victimless crime, instead of abolishing it outright. After discussing various alternatives they elected to retain the designation 'gross indecency', in preference to explicit descriptions of proscribed acts. They proposed that incest between brother and sister should cease to be criminal when both parties were aged over twenty-one, and that daughters, granddaughters and sons should not be punished if they were aged under twenty-one. They confirmed their working paper proposal to replace the present laws relating to public indecency with a new offence, triable either summarily or by jury, with a maximum penalty of twelve months' imprisonment, 'designed to penalise sexual conduct, homosexual or heterosexual, between two or more persons, which would be likely to cause serious offence if seen by members of the public'. While one of their members did not think this provision should apply to situations where all those taking part or present had attended specifically for the purpose of sexual activity, the majority considered it 'inimical to the public interest to allow to flourish clubs where numbers of people can participate in, or watch, sexual acts'.[24] They proposed retaining bestiality as a crime, with a maximum penalty of six months' imprisonment (it was currently a life sentence), and of five years for procuring it.

This series of proposals could not be described as radical, and fell short in many respects of the SLRS' guiding principles. But they did at least mark some progress in official discussion of the social situation and characteristics of homosexual men, who were no longer described in the various PAC and CLRC working papers and reports as if they were all sad, pathetic people and/or an especially nasty species of criminal. Rather, the tone had shifted some way beyond that of the Wolfenden Report, and it seemed that our evidence and that of the numerous gay and civil liberties organisations had paid off to the extent that the CLRC recognised the existence of homosexual people as not being necessarily antisocial, even if it still regarded their activities as reprehensibly distasteful and placed far too much emphasis upon protecting them from themselves and too little upon protecting them from the ignorance, prejudice and sometimes vicious hostility of others.

Even these cautious proposals for modest change met with a loud chorus of outraged disapproval. As the 1970s and 1980s wore on it was increasingly difficult to engage in rational civilised debate on sexual topics. On the Second Reading of the Whitehouse-inspired Protection of Children Bill in February 1978, for instance, Eldon Griffiths MP, who was parliamentary adviser to the Police Federation, referred to the SLRS working party's report as illustrating 'the moral decline of our society'. So I wrote to challenge his apparent belief that our proposals 'formed part of some malign conspiracy to undermine

---

[24] This still struck the SLRS as being much too wide and hypothetical. We adhered to our view that the correct test should be whether the behaviour in question had *in fact* offended anybody. But on this issue 'morals police' remained firmly entrenched in the minds of the CLRC.

the morals of the nation and to debauch children'; and asked him to acknowledge that, while he might disagree with them, they were not discreditable to those who had prepared the report. I sent him a copy of Bishop Robinson's lecture *The Place of Law in the Field of Sex*, and he ultimately had the good grace to reply that, having read it, he agreed that it merited the most careful consideration, adding 'certainly his arguments lead me to accept that however much I disagree with them, your proposals are in no way discreditable'. But not all his parliamentary colleagues were prepared to admit the integrity of those of us who took a different view to theirs on these contentious issues. Indeed, the frequent imputations of sinister motive debased the standards of public debate.

By the time the CLRC's final report was published in 1984 there was less likelihood of a favourable government response than there would have been if Roy Jenkins had still been in office as Home Secretary. Apart from the Conservatives' traditional disinclination to tackle such emotive areas of reform, Mrs Thatcher's second term of office saw much more deferential attention being paid by her ministers and MPs to the views of those who were highly critical of most of us dealing with the problems and needs of young people at the 'coal face' of counselling and youth work. It was the start of a more doctrinaire approach by government which, coupled with growing stringency of financial resources, left social workers increasingly disgruntled by the end of the decade. This was not a climate in which to look for early liberalisation of the sex laws, even along the timidly hidebound lines formulated by the CLRC.

So there has as yet been no further action on a general programme of sexual law reform, save for incorporation of the CLRC's recommendations into the Law Commission's Draft Criminal Code for England and Wales, published in 1989.[25] While drafting these sections in accordance with the CLRC's recommendations[26] the Law Commission, in their accompanying commentary, criticised some remaining anomalies in the law and expressed some viewpoints differing

[25] HMSO: *Law Com. No. 177*: A Criminal Code for England and Wales, vols. 1 & 2, Part II, Chapter II.
[26] And in accordance with their own policy of incorporating without amendment recommendations for law reform made by the CLRC and other official bodies into the draft code. This, the Law Commission pointed out, did not imply their own assent to, or dissent from, such proposals. (*Law Com. No. 177*, Vol. I, Report, para. 3.34.)

from those of the CLRC. They would have preferred to provide a definition of 'gross indecency', which the CLRC had decided against doing; they would have preferred not to discriminate between the ages at which men and women might lawfully consent to buggery; they criticised the situation whereby a man aged over eighteen would not be guilty of an offence committed with a youth of under eighteen if the man believed the youth to be over that age, although this defence would not be available to a youth aged under eighteen who wrongly believed that his consenting partner was older; some of them wished to abolish the offence of bestiality; some of them questioned why it should remain an offence for a third person to procure a lawful homosexual act between two men when prostitution was not involved.

The Law Commission were in fact prepared to go further in several respects than the Criminal Law Revision Committee. But while enactment of their Draft Criminal Code would constitute an improvement in several respects on the existing state of affairs, it would still be a long way behind the 'minimalist' goal of the Sexual Law Reform Society. Although the small print of law reform, and properly drafted statutes, are always important, the general acceptance within the community of attitudes towards sexuality in all its aspects that are very different from the prevailing ones is the essential prelude to sound and satisfactory law reform. What is required for a healthier, happier twenty-first century is nothing less than a sexual revolution.

XXI

Towards Sexual Sanity

'In abandoning toleration one loses other values as
well - self-respect and natural dignity, a regard for
truth and a dislike of cruelty. The worst thing about
intolerance would seem to be the harm it does to
the intolerant.'

R. J. Cruikshank
'Roaring Century'

There is still a long way to go before gay rights are recognised by
most people as a basic human freedom. Yet the claims of homosexual
people to be socially accepted, and to live our mutually consenting
lives as we choose, are undeniable. At the end of the twentieth century
we should no longer have to beg, plead, or even argue for our fundamental rights and dignities as citizens and human beings.

How, during the coming decade, can progress be made towards
the sexually sane – or, at least, sexually saner – society which I envisaged in the 1960s for people of all sexual orientations? There has been
some improvement during the past twenty-five years, but not as much
as I looked forward to in the victory glow of 1967. For the 1967 Act,
with all its shortcomings, *was* a victory, to which I am proud to have
contributed. If I had not done what I did reform might have come at
a different time, and could have been marginally better or worse; but
I do not believe that any other new law on homosexuality passed in
the 1960s or early 1970s would have differed radically in its approach
and its limitations from the Arran/Abse Bill, even before the onset of
the 'backlash' which defeated Lord Arran in 1977. The tone of the
Wolfenden Report, and the political constraints of the time, ruled out
acceptance by Parliament of the proposition that homosexuality has a
valid alternative lifestyle, let alone one which merited evenhanded
treatment, legally or socially, with heterosexuality.

The pressure groups campaigning for social reform in the 1950s and 1960s – typified by the National Campaign for the Abolition of Capital Punishment, the Abortion Law Reform Association, and the Homosexual Law Reform Society – were professionally efficient and strategically effective. They achieved their objectives of swaying public and parliamentary opinion through hard, sustained and sophisticated lobbying carried out over a period of years on shoestring budgets. They could not have done so without the devoted work of a few poorly paid, and many more unpaid, supporters who were willing to sacrifice leisure time and peace of mind for their chosen causes.

When the reforms for which they had fought at last reached the Statute Book, many of these workers were exhausted as well as elated. Some (notably the stalwart spirits behind the Abortion Law Reform Association) had perforce to carry on for years fighting a rearguard action no less strenuous than their original campaign so as to prevent the parliamentary emasculation of their victory. While this was not necessary in the case of homosexual law reform, the Albany Trust had insufficient resources to push ahead with its programme of widespread sex education and public enlightenment.

I myself saw the 1967 Act as a foundation to be built upon. During the years of campaigning it had been borne in on me that the basic problem was widespread ignorance about sexuality generally, and not only ingrained public hatred of homosexual people. Though there were a few stridently homophobic voices in public life and the media, they were not then as numerous or as provocative as they became during the later 1970s and the 1980s in counterpoint to the emergent campaign for gay rights.

With the 1967 Act on the Statute Book public education towards a better understanding of all aspects of human sexuality became the highest priority for the Albany Trust, and was an attainable goal. So far as further law reform was concerned it seemed a tactical mistake to single out homosexual issues, when the whole tattered array of sexual laws cried out for reform; gay rights were likely to be most easily accepted as part of a wider package deal of sexual rights generally. For both these tasks we needed the help of a broader grouping than the gay activists. For this reason the Albany Trust never was, and never became, a 'homophile' organisation, incurring considerable resentment from some gay groups (because we were not) and misrepresentation by some opponents (who wrongly insisted that we were).

'Outreach' to the wider public had always been a major priority of the HLRS' ten-year campaign. My diary for the mid-1960s records a steady flow of meetings with a wide range of political, religious and professional groups all over the country. It is a pity that too little effort since has gone into extending such work. Making direct contact of a persuasively conversational (rather than a provocatively confrontational) kind with a broad cross-section of the general public is essential if the case for full social acceptance of homosexual people and their overdue integration into the mainstream community is to be made effectively. And until that case is made, and other positive steps are taken to diminish the pernicious influence of homophobic individuals and organisations, and of media misinformation, the prospects for saner sexual attitudes, better public health provision and improved legislation will remain dim.

The eruption of AIDS has made the need for sex education even more urgent. Sadly, progress remains bogged down by the pressures deployed by the 'moral majority' brigade. Official timidity, unscientific attitudes and homophobic bias have condemned generations of teenagers (heterosexual as well as homosexual) to grow up in fundamental ignorance of their own and others' natures, and without any supportive behavioural yardsticks. Recently the punitive prophets of gloom and doom have seized upon the AIDS crisis to advocate more repression, less sexual frankness, even recriminalisation of homosexuality and repeal of the 1967 Act.

Why has the 1980s backlash occurred? I think there are several reasons. After the 1967 Act was passed, problems were harder to tackle, because more diffuse and less clearly focused, than the single-issue campaign for a 'Wolfenden' Bill. The Albany Trust was almost swamped by counselling needs, because in the widespread absence of other suitable agencies to deal with those seeking our help we were unable to limit ourselves to the purely referring role we wished for. Requests for our participation in educational and training activities multiplied, while at the same time our post-reform income dwindled. The Sexual Law Reform Society's proposals to the Criminal Law Revision Committee could not be adequately publicised or followed through by the Society because of lack of funds and staff.

The gay rights movement which grew up after 1967 was itself split between the conventionally functioning Campaign for Homosexual Equality and the Gay Liberation Front, which presented a radical challenge not only to heterosexual susceptibilities but also to socially conservative homosexuals. Everyone has the right to 'do their own thing', and it is often healthy for a topic to be tackled simultaneously from several different perspectives. A diversity which is too exuberant does, however, weaken effort and blunt impact.

Unfortunately, a good deal of the copious energy, time and money generously poured into gay rights over the past two decades has, in my view, been largely wasted. The failure of the post-reform homophile movement, and of the 1980s gay rights campaigners, to get their act really together and to devise and implement a sound, broadly based strategy has been disappointing and self-defeating. It is a great pity that so much of the good will contributed over the years by very many gay people has been squandered in unnecessary divisiveness and mutual suspicions.

The likely success of campaigning tactics in achieving desired changes must be one of the main yardsticks for adopting them: personal pleasure or excitement, or a craving to release pent-up energy, is merely self-indulgent if it does not win us battles and new allies. Street theatre, however spectacular, is no substitute for the prosaic, colourless daily grind of political persuasion which in the end depends upon knowledge, competence, integrity and good repute.

Self-discipline, though sometimes tedious and frustrating, is necessary in personal, social and political life. I had to exercise it a great deal (and sometimes very much against the grain in my dealings with Leo Abse and other politicians) during the law reform campaign. But I believe the outcome proved that Paris *was* worth a mass; and that to dress, behave and speak in ways calculated to win the sympathetic attention of those whom you wish to influence is simply common sense.

Now (as then) there needs to be carefully planned, precisely targeted, long-term political action designed to persuade the heterosexual man and woman in the street that if their MPs enact further homosexual or – preferably – general sexual law reform they are not barmy or foolhardy, but are actually doing the sensible thing for everyone. To win our future battles gay people need non-gay allies who recognise this, and are willing to speak out. For gay rights are human rights. Homosexual equality is not a bizarre, immoral or shocking notion but a necessary component of a civilised, decent, democratic society. It is the interests of society *as a whole* which count; and it is in those interests that personal, social and legal equality are called for. There could be no more false impression than that principled demands for justice, equality and fair treatment in society are a form of special pleading for an unmerited degree of toleration for a mode of sexuality which goes against the grain of what is best for the rest of society. It is this fallacy, of course, which the implacable homophobes wish to foster and to reinforce; any action which appears to validate it plays straight into their hands.

I can appreciate and sympathise with the sense of self-respect which led Ray Gosling to declaim to a 1975 gay rally in Trafalgar Square: 'Last time it was done by an elite, who did it by stealth. . . . This time it has to be done by us, brothers and sisters;' and also with the desires of present-day campaigners to 'take centre stage' and 'have our own show'.[1] But 'this time' has not materialised yet; and I confess to some scepticism as to whether 'our own show' can achieve our objective unaided. In any case, because our cause is a just one, we should not have to 'go it alone'.

A massive brake on the progress of gay rights has been the effect of the 'closet', whose morality is so hotly debated. Sexual hypocrisy is not practised only by those who are gay or bisexual. As Freud said:

> People in general are not candid over sexual matters. They do not show their sexuality freely, but to conceal it they wear a heavy overcoat woven of a tissue of lies, as though the weather were bad in the world of sexuality. Nor are they mistaken. It is a fact that sun and wind are not favourable to sexual activity in this civilised world of ours; none of us can reveal his erotism freely to others.[2]

If this is true of people in general, how much more true it is of the wholly and partially gay? Of course the closet is a distorting mirror; it befogs public perceptions of who homosexual people are, how many of them there are, and where they are; and it warps the representation

---

[1] Ray Gosling, 23 November 1975 (*Gay News* 84); Peter Ashman, *Gay Times*, July 1990.

[2] Sigmund Freud, *The Complete Psychological Works*, trans. and ed. James Strachey, The Institute of Psycho-Analysis and Hogarth Press, 1957.

of gay people in the community by a self-denying process. The late Gilbert Harding is supposed to have said that if everyone who was homosexual or bisexual turned an appropriate shade of blue overnight, there would be so many 'blues', ranging from pale lilac to deep purple, to be seen on the streets the next morning that the true extent of homosexuality would be revealed and society's perceptions of it drastically transformed. As it is, what the general public sees is the merest tip of the gay and bisexual iceberg; and so they get a very misleading impression of how many people actually are attracted to their own sex, and also of what varied kinds of people they are, personally, socially and politically.

When does personal prudence slide over into group betrayal? 'Solidarity' is the watchword of the radicals, with their taunting call to their hidden brothers and sisters to 'come out, come out, wherever you are'. 'What is there to hide?' they ask, a trifle disingenuously. The pertinent question, surely, is: 'What is there to lose?' – and the answer to this must be different for each individual.

The notion that the 'reluctant debutantes' who are unwillingly flushed out by their militant brethren will constitute any sort of an asset to the fight for gay rights seems to me naïve, for are they not far more likely to constitute a resentful fifth column? The numerous gay politicians, judges, lawyers, policemen, doctors, teachers, businessmen, engineers, who remain invisible and shrink even further into their shells when confronted with militant gays marching down Whitehall with banners, need persistent friendly encouragement, not taunts and hostility, if they are to be persuaded to make a constructive contribution to the emancipation of their own kind. I hope many more of them will do so in the near future, by coming out voluntarily – preferably in an organised way and in impressive numbers. If they were 'out', many of them would be in positions of influence in the gay movement where their knowledge, experience and contacts would be significantly engaged on behalf of us all. The most effective way to demolish the closet (like the Berlin Wall) is to attack the ignorant and bigoted people whose crass attitudes have constructed it rather than the timid souls cowering inside.

Had the gay movement been much more out, cohesive and effective it would still have had to contend, during the 1980s, with the negative political climate of Thatcherism. It is a striking paradox that so many market 'free choicers' jib at free choices in those intimate personal matters of lifestyle, cultural tastes and sexual behaviour where effective freedom matters most to the individual. It is also curious that a lot of people who abhor any controls over economic life are eager to secure legal backing for the moral codes which they consider should regulate sexual behaviour. The damage which such people do to individuals and to society is real and lasting. Let us hope that their influence is now on the wane.

Even without them, we would not be living in an emotionally healthy society. There is a great deal wrong with our traditional systems and institutions, with our ways of doing things, and with our personal, social and sexual patterns of thinking and relating. The morbid mix of 'sex 'n' violence' (as inseparable in the media as fish 'n' chips), of traditional male macho postures of toughness which spasmodically erupt into mindless ramboism, of the spread of domestic violence and child abuse – all testify to the loveless emotional desert which far too many people inhabit. If there is to be any real prospect of a sexually saner British society in the twenty-first century, there has got to be a seismic shift in thinking. Sexual ignorance and misery should no longer be regarded as 'respectable', and still less as 'virtuous'. They are certainly neither necessary nor inevitable. It is high time we were more civilised.

What is required? First and foremost, abandonment of the artificial, outdated and often hypocritical tenets of conventional morality based on codes and rules (whether regarded as divinely inspired or not), and a communal shift to a reality-based ethic hinging on *motivation*. There needs to be general recognition that sexual relationships and activities cannot be meaningfully categorised as 'good' or 'bad', 'right' or 'wrong', 'moral' or 'immoral', according to whether they are homosexual or heterosexual, within or outside marriage, or depending upon which orifices are utilised. What matters is whether such actions are initiated and performed with a loving and caring intent, compassionately as well as passionately, and with the wellbeing of the other as well as of oneself in mind.

Benign intent does not always avoid unfortunate outcomes; 'the road to hell is paved with good intentions', and there must always be an ethical duty of care (even when there is not a specific legal one).

But without such consciously benevolent intent no sexual relationship or activity, however conventionally legal or 'moral', can qualify as being 'good'. Where such intent exists, and is mutual, the consenting relationships and actions of the parties are essentially their own personal and private affair and should not come within the scrutiny of society or the purview of the law. Unhappily there are a great many sexual relationships and activities which are *not* well-meaning: it must be the aim of society, acting through education, through the weight of public opinion and (in the case of physical assault and the violation of personal rights) through the law, to reduce the number of these and to minimise their harm.

The problem of sexual violence, which to judge from the media is far more prevalent now than it was a decade ago, is part and parcel of the wider question of violence in society. Discerning the causes of this upsurge, and suggesting how to curb it, are beyond the scope of this book. I do, however, strongly believe that a less condemnatory and punitive public rhetoric around sexual issues would diminish the guilt induced in a great many sexually inadequate and unhappy people, who would then be less likely to resort to sexual assaults and child abuse.

Where the law is concerned I hope that a radical restructuring, broadly along the lines forecast by the Sexual Law Reform Society's proposals, will not be long delayed. The sexual rights of every citizen preferably should be enshrined in any Bill of Rights which is enacted for Britain. The entire body of law relating to sexual offences should then be recast in accordance with such a Bill of Rights. The time has long passed when sexual acts which have been committed with mutual consent in circumstances which have not offended members of the public, and which do not breach provisions intended to protect children and those in situations of dependency, ought to have been removed from the calendar of crimes. It is ludicrous in this day and age for the police and prosecuting authorities to misuse their scarce resources and public funds in hunting down and prosecuting those who infringe the daft 'Dilhorne' definition of 'in private', or who misbehave in public lavatories or open spaces without upsetting any accidental spectators. The correct test should be actual *nuisance*, not an abstract notion of 'indecency'.

In 1899 Havelock Ellis wrote:

It may safely be said that in no other field of human activity is so vast an amount of strenuous didactic morality founded on so slender a basis of facts. In most other departments of life we at least make a pretence of learning before we presume to teach; in the field of sex we content ourselves with the smallest and vaguest minimum of information, often ostentatiously second-hand, usually unreliable.[3]

This is still true almost one hundred years later. Although English people (as E. M. Forster remarked) dislike having to think about homosexuality – or any other aspect of sex – they nowadays chatter about it unceasingly in an uninformed way. Homosexuality, which when I was a youth was scarcely ever mentioned except in shocked whispers, has become the staple fare of the tabloids on the family breakfast-table; though whether the presumably avid readers really know any more about it than they used to when it was taboo is a moot question.

Because of AIDS it has now become a matter of life and death to have completely frank and honest public dialogue, especially with the young, about the physical aspects of sexual behaviour both heterosexual and homosexual.

There is still confusion about what to say. Having spent so much of my life attempting to educate the public about the real nature of homosexuality and the problems arising out of pervasive ignorance, I put forward the following basic points which should be incorporated into sex education programmes:

⁎Homosexuality is a natural variation of temperament and sexual impulse. It is a state of being: a mode of experiencing oneself. It is not a disease, a disability or an impairment; and it is compatible with the highest physical, creative, moral, spiritual, and social development. Homosexual people constitute a typical cross-section of humanity, not differing significantly (save in their sexual orientation) from their fellow men and women. Homosexual people down the ages have been amongst those of outstanding achievement in all walks of life. Their manifold contributions to human creativity, science and culture deserve acknowledgment.

[3]   Preface to first edition of *Studies in the Psychology of Sex* (1899).

271

*Despite persistent myths to the contrary, homosexuality is not acquired through seduction or corruption in youth. Rather, the common experience of homosexual men is that they battle painfully throughout their adolescence and youth against their strengthening attraction to others of their own sex, often making vain endeavours to conform to the heterosexual pattern that is presented to them as the only 'natural' and 'healthy' one. Many women do not realise that they are lesbian until a time in their lives when they have become wives and mothers. The trauma of these demoralising experiences is exacerbated by the lack in our educational system of adequate reliable information about homosexuality, and by the invisibility of respected adults capable of providing the young with worthy examples of responsible homosexual lifestyles and relationships. Such information, and such role models, should be as freely accessible to adolescents as are equivalent heterosexual images.

*People of a homosexual or bisexual disposition are no less worthy as citizens, and no less deserving of respect and consideration from others, than anyone else. There is no cause for the law to take special cognisance of their sexuality, their sexual lifestyles, or their mutually consenting relationships, which are entirely private and personal matters and should be so regarded and treated by others. However, they should not be expected to hide these aspects of their lives and personalities any more than heterosexuals have to do.

*Homosexuality and homosexual behaviour are separate and distinct matters. Not all homosexual people behave homosexually, and not all those who behave homosexually possess a primarily homosexual temperament. The arbitrary classification of people on the basis of assumptions about their sexuality reinforces the false belief that society consists of two distinct and easily identifiable groups – those who are heterosexual and those who are homosexual. In reality there is and always has been a considerable overlap between these groups, and various degrees of bisexuality are widespread.

*There is no such person as a 'typical homosexual', and the vulgar stereotypes are false. The open, self-declared gay person does

272

not have a monopoly on homosexual feelings or behaviour. Those who identify themselves as gay, lesbian or homosexual are themselves a minority (and quite a small one) of those who actually are homosexual or bisexual. Accusations of 'hypocrisy' because of concealment are hypocritical in circumstances where openness can be dangerous. The entire community should work together to foster a social climate in which all homosexual and bisexual people feel free to be open about their sexual preferences.

✳Homosexual people are currently the objects of more ignorance, prejudice, unnecessary fears and irrational hostility than any other minority group of comparable size. Homophobia (the irrational fear and hatred of homosexuals which serves as a pretext for abusing and mistreating them) is a social evil akin to anti-semitism, racism, slavery and religious bigotry, harmful both to the victimised individuals and to the society which it infects. It is a scandal that far too many homosexual men, women, and especially the young who are in the process of growing up to discover their sexual identity, still have to live a lie; still endure discrimination, loneliness and despair; still fear to give and receive love and affection from like-minded human beings; and are still sometimes driven to suicide and other forms of severe self-damage by the attitudes of others.

✳The issue of prejudice must be candidly addressed by everyone of goodwill. Discrimination against anybody because of his or her sexual orientation must become as unacceptable in our society as are other forms of sexual, racial and religious discrimination. The validity and value of people's freely chosen personal and sexual relationships, whether heterosexual or homosexual, must be affirmed, respected and socially acknowledged. While minority opinions and tastes should not be imposed upon others, neither should minorities (racial, religious or sexual) be forced to conform to majority standards so long as their behaviour does not damage others or infringe upon legitimate rights and freedoms.

✳Homosexual people are entitled to be themselves, and to value their own sexual identity: indeed, there is a moral obligation

273

upon them to do so in the face of unjust prejudice and discrimination. Those who are homosexual are in duty bound to resist and refute the ignorance, contempt, ridicule, derision, scorn, spite, denigration, belittlement and outright hatred which they commonly experience as a barrage of assaults upon their self-esteem and personal integrity.

*The right of homosexual and bisexual people to communicate and associate freely with one another, and to publish their views on issues affecting themselves, must be safeguarded. A society which does not guarantee such rights to minorities is itself unfree.

I grew up through my 'teens knowing that the prevailing laws and social attitudes were hideously unjust and harmful to thousands of people besides myself. I lived through my twenties experiencing in myself the 'misery of a quite special degree' which Professor Herbert Hart has attributed to the legally enforced suppression of sexual impulses. My thirties were absorbed by the ten-year campaign which began with the publication of the Wolfenden Report and culminated with the passage into law of the 1967 Sexual Offences Act. My forties were taken up with endeavouring to build upon that triumph, and to advance beyond it towards the sexually saner society which would be at once better educated, more relaxed and more responsible in its attitudes towards sexuality. My fifties were increasingly preoccupied with the 'war situation' precipitated by AIDS.

Now I am in my sixties, I am not overoptimistic that greater sexual sanity will be widespread by AD2000, but nor am I unduly pessimistic for the twenty-first century. Being a historian by training and inclination I know that, while human shortsightedness and folly are persistent, human hope and achievement are born anew in each generation.

Sexuality will always be of the greatest interest to the young as they discover its potentially ecstatic joys and sometimes lacerating miseries. But sexuality is by no means the exclusive preserve of the young; and 'ageism' is as stultifying and impoverishing as any other form of prejudicial '-ism'. The sexuality of the mature, as well as that of the youthful, calls for recognition and fulfilment.

In this book I have recorded some of the events in which I have been involved, especially the twenty years of my life which were closely associated with the Homosexual Law Reform Society and the Albany Trust. Some of these happenings are already public knowledge; others have not previously been recounted. All will, I hope, be of interest to my readers and lead them to a clearer understanding not only of what I did, but of why and how I did it. I see my life's work as a quest for justice. In the face of injustice and cruelty I say with Martin Luther:

'Here I stand. I can do no other'.

APPENDICES

———

BIBLIOGRAPHY

———

INDEX

APPENDIX 1

My letter to *The Sunday Times*, 2 April 1954

Your admirable and forthright leading article emboldens me to offer deeply felt thanks for the ray of hope which your sane approach to the grievous problems of homosexuality offers to the abnormal. Recent months have seen a public ventilation of the subject which would have been unthinkable even a year ago. This is all to the good; for although one cannot but be dismayed at some of the deep-rooted prejudices and misconceptions which have been expressed, it does at last seem possible that a sustained and purposeful campaign by the many authoritative voices (not the least of which, Sir, is yours) who believe that the present state of the law is not only unjust but is productive of some distinctly harmful social consequences, may result in legislation within a measurable time.

I write this letter, not to make once again any of the valid objections to the present state of the law which have been cogently canvassed in your recent pamphlet, in that of the Church of England Moral Welfare Council, and elsewhere, but to ask you to assist in educating public opinion to look above and beyond the immediate legal issues to the deeper problems posed by the fact of homosexuality.

As you rightly say, it is a Social Problem; it is also an individual problem, and there is perhaps no such person as 'the typical homosexual'. Newspaper accounts and the proceedings of the criminal courts must together give many ordinary people the idea that all male homosexuals are by definition habitually promiscuous, addicted to constant vice and liable to indecently assault any other male, given the slightest opportunity. Yet there must be very many like myself – perhaps even a majority – who, without ever having been approached by another, have known themselves to be irrevocably 'queer' from early adolescence; have for one reason or another – idealism, inhibitions or timidity – denied themselves any physical relationships; and who reach the later twenties or thirties with the energy-consuming stresses, imposed by their unsatisfied emotional needs and the constant mental dilemma of their general situation, heightened every year. Even if not technically criminals, like our practising brothers, we are oppressed perhaps even more keenly than they by our consciousness of the injustice of the law against the private acts of consenting adult inverts.

But there would be little improvement, even though the law were altered, if we were only transferred from the lawyer's frying pan into the psychiatrist's fire. The present lamentable tendency of 'criminologists' to attribute crimes of whatever variety to mental illness is leading both law and psychology sadly astray. If certain forms of behaviour are antisocial they must be prevented by the law; and though the mental abnormality of the offender may be an explanation of his behaviour, it is not an excuse. The homosexual wishes the law to redefine more justly what are in fact antisocial activities on his part; he should not rush to surrender all personal responsibility for his character by accepting the hypothesis that he is mentally ill. Abnormal, yes, and in a small minority; subject to certain inherent disadvantages which call for understanding rather than for pity from his normal fellow men and women; neurotic only insofar as that understanding is lacking.

We shall not get any nearer to such necessary understanding by holding that, even if all those of homosexual temperament should not be in prison, they should all be on psychoanalysts' couches twice a week. In the first case (as a recent letter in *The Economist* showed) there would not be nearly enough prisons; in the second, there would not be nearly enough couches. And the differing opinions of the medical profession on homosexuality, on its origins and on its 'cure' are extremely disconcerting to those who might seek for guidance if they felt convinced that it existed. In fact, they get the collective impression that most so-called 'mental experts' are no better at running other people's lives than the average person is at running his own. And I would earnestly question whether the growing modern psychological fashion of postulating a hypothetical norm as 'healthy' and all divergencies from it as unhealthy, with the consequent repression of individuality and accentuation of the nonconformist's 'neuroticism', is wise or in the end likely to lead to a mentally healthier community. (I myself think it may be largely responsible for much of the mental illness we see around us in this age when mental health is so much emphasised.)

There is a third alternative, which offers far more hope to the homosexual, and, I believe, to Society. It is for us all to work for the integration of the homosexual individual into society, rather than for his degradation or transformation. For, like the poor, some homosexuality will always be with us. Even granting for the sake of argument – though I am far from convinced – that the whole cause of this phenomenon lies in the parental relationships of the earliest years, it will be long before we breed a race of potential parents enlightened enough to be a hundred percent successful in giving every child the right start necessary for a normal life. We have only to look at the depressing evidence of probation officers and other social workers to realise this. In these spheres of social education lies, perhaps, one of the most important preventives, but it is not a work which will be accomplished in one generation.

A most deplorable aspect of homosexuality, from any point of view, is the promiscuity which characterises the behaviour of so many homosexuals and justifies the strictures of viciousness which are commonly brought against them. The most urgent aim of those who are enlightened enough to seek to integrate the invert into society must be to heighten his sense of moral responsibility and self-respect, which can only be done by creating a moral climate throughout society as a whole such that the mere fact of his inversion will no longer cause him to be regarded as a pariah. It is perhaps asking a great deal to seek recognition of the fact that the nature of his love is no more 'unnatural' to the invert than normal heterosexual attraction is to the heterosexual person – but I believe that nothing less than some degree of social acceptance of this fact, with a concomitant encouragement of the ideal of constancy and disapprobation of promiscuity can effect an amelioration of the homosexual problem.

One recognises, of course, that no homosexual relationships can ever be 'moral' in the sense that marriage is the only truly moral sexual relationship; but by frowning less heavily upon an invert's attempt to attain a permanent connection based upon affection than upon promiscuous behaviour akin to prostitution, society would be pointing the way to a solution of the invert's personal problems, and thus helping to lessen his incidence as a social problem. It is not really surprising that those who, when they discover that they have the misfortune to be abnormal discover also that the very thought of love on their part is tainted with criminality, are likely to throw moral restraint aside more readily than do the general run of people – or that this trait is liable to spread beyond the sexual sphere of character. By denying the invert any claim to morality or respectability, society thus conferred upon him the gift of moral irresponsibility. Development of moral stature, of any kind of responsibility, can only take place in conditions of freedom; our own political history since 1688 provides abundant illustration of this truth. By acknowledging that a man who remains a homosexual can aspire to and attain a certain moral integrity without demanding of him an involuntary sacerdotal celibacy, Society would take the essential step towards solving some of these anxious problems, and could enforce far more effectively the protection of youth.

There is one final aspect of the homosexual's present dilemma to which I would call attention. A widespread demand for enquiry seems likely to lead to the appointment of a Royal Commission to investigate the whole subject and enlighten public opinion. Yet it seems the paradoxical fact that, under their present stigma, many of those most deeply concerned, as inverts, are unlikely to feel able to contribute their views and experience, which are surely essential to a satisfactory outcome of such a Commission's deliberations. Further, if an official body of enquiry were to consist entirely of the so-called 'experts' whose external knowledge of inversion is derived from court proceedings, criminal statistics, the confessions of the psychologist's consulting room, or prison visiting, it may well mislead rather than clarify. Your article rightly says, Sir, that we are riddled with hypocrisy in this matter, as many known inverts occupy eminent places. I would urge that the strongest possible pressure be brought to bear to ensure that, on this occasion at least, hypocrisy is cast aside and one or two of these people, of known honesty and probity, be appointed to any Royal Commission that is set up. If that were done I do not believe that they would inevitably issue minority reports.

It is regrettable that I am unable to offer any proofs of my own integrity other than the views which I have inadequately expressed. I cannot expect you to publish a long and unsigned letter, but I trust that you will make any use of it which you think proper in your efforts to shed light on the homosexual problem and to promote social health.

Yours faithfully,

HOMOSEXUAL

*(1992 footnote: While I no longer hold all the views expressed in the letter, it stands the test of time well.)

APPENDIX 2

Albany Trust Social Needs Survey (1970)

This unstructured sample, obtained through (a) organisations (e.g. Albany Trust, Minorities Research Group), (b) magazines (e.g. *Jeremy*), (c) external contacts in pubs, clubs etc. in all parts of the country, was the largest sample of homosexuals questioned in Britain up to that time. It did not claim to be representative of the homosexual population as a whole; securing a truly random sample would not have been feasible. But although the sample had its own biases – educational status, a degree of socialisation, and a preponderance of Londoners – it was freer of some other biases – e.g. psychiatric patients – than previous samples.

Of the 2672 respondents, 2082 said they were male and 588 female. Two ignored the question. 1310 men and 304 women regarded themselves as being wholly homosexual, and 607 men and 211 women as predominantly so. 1736 of the men and 497 of the women said they were well-adjusted to their homosexuality. Only 25 per cent of the men and 18 per cent of the women had been in any sort of trouble (self-defined) because of their orientation. Approximately half of both the men and the women in the sample had sought advice and help (mostly from psychiatrists and doctors) over their homosexuality, and two-thirds of those who did so had found this helpful.

1203 men and 421 women were aged between twenty-one and forty. There were 770 male and 134 female respondents aged over fifty, and 107 men and 33 women under eighteen. There was a significantly larger percentage of older men than women. Predictably, 88 per cent of the sample were single; 248 men and 121 women were married, divorced or separated.

The educational level of the sample was above the national average: 56 per cent of the sample had attended university or a college of higher education. Over half lived in a big city – 44 per cent in London.

A current homosexual love relationship was being enjoyed by 58 per cent of the women and 42 per cent of the men, while 76 per cent of the women and 40 per cent of the men had a regular sexual partner. As many as 80 per cent of the women and 67 per cent of the men had at some time had an affair lasting more than six months at some time in their lives: all figures contradicting the myth of homosexuals as rootlessly promiscuous.

There was a closer correspondence for the men than for the women between the age at which they first realised they had homosexual desires and the age of their first homosexual experience. The critical point when most of the men had grappled with such feelings was very young – under thirteen for 640, and between thirteen and fifteen for another 708. Half of the women, on the other hand, realised their feelings for their own sex between the ages of thirteen and eighteen. First experiences were as follows:

	Men	Women
Under 10	216	22
10 – 12	318	36
13 – 15	680	79
16 – 18	348	127
19 – 21	175	102
Over 21	303	206

Loneliness was a problem to 851 men and 216 women, but the majority of both sexes did not regard themselves as lonely people. But nearly two-thirds of both sexes moved in a world where hardly anyone else knew them to be homosexual. Only 315 men and 84 women were 'out of the closet' to most of their social friends, and 233 men and 58 women to their employers. However, only 329 men and 100 women thought that they would lose their jobs if their employers found out about their homosexuality – 928 men and 224 women did not believe this would happen.

APPENDIX 3

I

Extracts from Mrs Mary Whitehouse's speech to Christian Lunch and Dinner Clubs, 24 November 1976

The calculated attack against religious education in schools on the one hand and on the other the move to establish wholly amoral sex education in schools and youth movements throughout the land, leaves our children totally exposed to the exploitation of the sexual anarchists and the internationally financed sex exploitation industry.

That the government either condones or is indifferent to these pressures upon the young is a matter of political fact. Moral teaching is frowned upon, the Christian ethic is discarded by atheistic trend-setters in education. Children and young people are left to flounder in a philosophical no-man's-land, at the mercy of the 'Gay' liberators and the advocates of the contraceptive society.

*   *   *   *

One constantly has to ask oneself – does the right hand of the government know what the left hand is doing? And I MEAN the left hand. One wonders if the Chancellor of the Exchequer, concerned as he is about public expenditure, is aware that a government grant is made to the Albany Trust, the homosexual lobby front runner. This Trust, which is partially subsidised by public money, now has its own youth officers to counsel what it describes as 'the gay teenager'.

Some of these youth counsellors – who work through the schools and the youth clubs – are otherwise engaged in giving what is euphemistically termed 'psychosexual advice' through the columns of various pornographic magazines. Furthermore, the support given by this organisation to paedophile groups means that we are all subsidising and supporting, at least indirectly, a cause which seeks to normalise sexual attraction and activity between adult males and little girls.

The Albany Trust's reply to Mrs Whitehouse

The Trustees have considered the terms of the address which you gave, in your capacity as Honorary Secretary of the National Viewers' and Listeners' Association, to a meeting of Christian Lunch and Dinner Clubs at the Central Hall, Westminster, on 24 November 1976.

It is evident that you have been materially misinformed about the Albany Trust and its activities. As a result you have, it is to be hoped inadvertently, misled the audience who heard your address on 24 November and all those very many more who have read or heard reports of what you said.

To enumerate the inaccuracies in your speech:

Firstly, you stated erroneously that the Albany Trust is 'the homosexual lobby front runner'. The Trust is in fact a registered charity whose objects are to promote psychological health through research, education and appropriate social action. While in its early years the Trust concentrated upon the provision of counselling and other assistance for homosexuals in need of it, since at least 1970 our work has lain in the broader field of psychological health and education, with especial concern for members of sexual minorities. We do not have close links with any specifically homosexual organisation. We receive public funds from the Voluntary Services Unit of the Home Office and from the Department of Education and Science, in addition to private subscriptions and donations.

Secondly, not one of us is conscious of any influence emanating from 'left' elements in the government or elsewhere – as distinct from the middle or the right – to gain or to maintain government support for the Trust; and we consider that your remark: 'And I *mean* the left hand' carries implications which are wholly unwarranted, so far as we are aware. In fact, we have throughout our existence received both moral and material support from members of all the three main political parties.

Thirdly, you said that the Trust 'now has its own youth officers to counsel what it describes as "the gay teenager".' In fact, the Trust employs one Youth Officer, funded by the Department of Education and Science and supervised by a steering group which includes a representative of that Department. His functions are to create a greater awareness of the situation and needs of members of sexual minorities in sex education and youth work training programmes generally. It is no part of his task to counsel teenagers – nor indeed to work directly with them to any great extent. He is primarily concerned with adult education programmes.

Fourthly, you claimed that 'some of these youth counsellors – who work through schools and through youth clubs – are otherwise engaged in giving what is euphemistically termed "psychosexual advice" through the columns of various pornographic magazines.' The Trust employs or uses no 'youth counsellors'; neither its Field Officer nor its Youth Officer 'work through the schools' nor 'through youth clubs'; nor are either of them or anyone else employed or engaged by the Trust to give 'psychosexual advice' through the columns of any magazines – pornographic or other.

Fifthly, you alleged that 'the support given by this organisation' (meaning the Trust) 'to paedophile groups' meant that (presumably as tax-payers) 'we are all subsidising and supporting, at least indirectly, a cause which seeks to normalise sexual attraction and activity between adult males and little girls'. The Albany Trust does not 'give support' (financial or otherwise) to 'paedophile groups'; nor does it promote or encourage any person or group in seeking to 'normalise' – whatever that may mean – sexual attraction and activity between adult males and little girls: or, for that matter, sexual attraction and activity between adult males or adult females and little boys.

Your address, so far as it concerned the Albany Trust, is most seriously inaccurate and damaging, as well as being personally false and libellous of each of the Trustees individually and as a body.

We accordingly feel bound, for the protection and furtherance of our Charitable objects, to call upon you to withdraw publicly each of the false statements I have listed above, and to join with us in seeking to obtain as wide a circulation for your retraction as you achieved for the original publication of your remarks.

Please let me hear from you in very early response to this letter with your confirmation that you will co-operate, as a matter of urgency, to put the record straight.

17 December 1976

BIBLIOGRAPHY

When I first sought reading material on homosexuality, books which referred to it were rare and those entirely devoted to it almost non-existent. So in 1953 I was extremely surprised to discover, in a small London bookshop, a copy of D. W. Cory's *The Homosexual Outlook* – a trail-blazing work which, although written from an American standpoint, transformed my own perceptions. (I did not then know that Gordon Westwood had published *Society and the Homosexual* in Britain the previous year.) Nowadays, whole library shelves are filled with works (good, bad and indifferent) on the subject. The following bibliography is not intended to be comprehensive, nor is it an exhaustive record of my own forty years' reading: I have included in it only those books I have found informative (whether reliably or provocatively), and useful.

*Denotes contribution(s) by Antony Grey.

1. GENERAL SURVEYS

Albany Trust *Winter Talks 1962–63*
Loraine, J. A. (ed.) *Understanding Homosexuality* (MTP, 1974)
Magee, Bryan *One in Twenty* (Secker & Warburg, 1966)
Rees & Usill (eds) *They Stand Apart. A Critical Survey of the Problem of Homosexuality* (Heinemann, 1955)
Walker, Kenneth *Sexual Behaviour, Creative and Destructive* (William Kimber, 1966)
Weltge (ed.) *The Same Sex: an appraisal of homosexuality* (Pilgrim Press, 1969)
West, D. J. *Homosexuality* (Duckworth: 1st edn. 1955, 3rd edn. 1968; Penguin Books: 2nd edn. 1960)
—— *Homosexuality Re-Examined* (Duckworth, 1977)
Westwood, Gordon *Society and the Homosexual* (Gollancz, 1952)

2. HISTORICAL

Brandt, Allan M. *No Magic Bullet: A Social History of Venereal Disease in the United States since 1980* (Oxford University Press, 1987)

Costello, John *Love Sex & War: Changing Values 1939–45* (Collins, 1985)

Davenport-Hines, Richard *Sex, Death and Punishment* (Collins, 1990)

De Becker, Raymond *The Other Face of Love* (Spearman, 1967)

Frost, Brian (ed.) **The Tactics of Pressure* (Galliard, 1975)

Heger, Heinz *The Men With the Pink Triangle* (GMP Publishers, 1986)

Hyde, H. Montgomery (ed.) *Trials of Oscar Wilde* Foreword by Sir Travers Humphreys (Hodge, 1948)

—— *The Cleveland Street Scandal* (W. H. Allen, 1976)

—— *The Other Love* (Heinemann, 1970)

Jeffrey-Poulter, Stephen *Peers, Queers, and Commons: The Struggle for Gay Law Reform* (Routledge, 1991)

Newburn, Tim *Permission and Regulation: Law and Morals in Postwar Britain* (Routledge, 1991)

Plant, Richard *The Pink Triangle* (Mainstream Publishing, 1987)

Simpson, Chester and Leitch *The Cleveland Street Affair* (Little, Brown, 1976)

Weeks, Jeffrey *Coming Out: Homosexual Politics in Britain* (Quartet, 1977, 1990)

—— *Sex, Politics and Society* (Longman, 1981)

3. ETHICAL, LEGAL

Abse, Leo *The Sexual Offences Act* (*British Journal of Criminology*, January 1968)

Bennion, Francis *The Sex Code: Morals for Moderns* (Weidenfeld & Nicolson, 1991)

Benson, R. O. D. *In Defense of Homosexuality: A rational evaluation of social prejudice* (Julian Press, New York, 1965)

Berlin, Sir Isaiah *Four Essays on Liberty* (Oxford University Press, 1969)

Blom-Cooper, Louis & Drewry, Gavin (eds.) *Law and Morality: A Reader* (Duckworth, 1976)

Cohen, Steve & seven others *The Law and Sexuality. How to cope with the law if you're not 100% conventionally heterosexual* (Grass Roots Press, 1978)

Crane, Paul *Gays and the Law* (Pluto Press, 1982)

Criminal Law Revision Committee (CLRC) Policy Advisory Committee *Working Paper on the Age of Consent in relation to Sexual Offences* (HMSO, 1979)

—— *Working Paper on Sexual Offences* (HMSO, 1980)

—— Policy Advisory Committee *Report on the Age of Consent in relation to Sexual Offences* Cmnd. 8216 (HMSO, 1981)

—— *Working Paper on Offences relating to Prostitution and allied Offences* (HMSO, 1982)

—— *Fifteenth Report: Sexual Offences* Cmnd. 9213 (HMSO, 1984)

—— *Seventeenth Report: Prostitution: Off-street activities* Cmnd. 9688 (HMSO, 1985)

Cross, Rupert *Unmaking Criminal Laws* (University of Melbourne Law Review, vol. 3 no. 4, Nov. 1962)

Devlin, Patrick *The Enforcement of Morals* (Oxford University Press, 1965)

Edwards, Quentin *What is Unlawful? Afterthoughts on the Wolfenden Report* (Church Information Office, 1959)

Grey, Antony *The Citizen in the Street* (Albany Trust, 1969)

—— (with D. J. West) 'Homosexuals: New Law but No New Deal' (*New Society*, 27 March 1969)

—— 'Civilizing Our Sex Laws' (*Journal of the Society of Public Teachers of Law*, 1975)

—— 'Sexual Law Reform Society Working Party Report' (*Criminal Law Review*, June 1975)

Hart, Herbert *Law, Liberty and Morality* (Oxford University Press, 1963)

HLRS *Homosexuals and the Law* (1958)

Home Office: *Report of the Committee on Homosexual Offences and Prostitution* (Cmnd. 247, HMSO, 1957)

——Working Party on Vagrancy and Street Offences *Working Paper; Report* (HMSO, 1974; 1976)

Honoré, Tony *Sex Law* (Duckworth, 1978)

Howard League Working Party Report *Unlawful Sex* (Waterlow, 1985)

Law Commission: Report no 50 *Inchoate Offences* (HMSO, 1973)

—— *A Criminal Code for England and Wales* (1989)

Mill, J. S. *On Liberty* (1859)

Mitchell, Basil *Law, Morality and Religion in a Secular Society* (Oxford University Press, 1967)

Bibliography

National Council of One Parent Families and Community Development Trust *Pregnant at School* (1979)

Report of the Committee on Homosexual Offences and Prostitution (Wolfenden Report) Cmnd. 247 (HMSO, 1957)

Richards, Peter G. *Parliament and Conscience* (Allen & Unwin, 1970)

Robinson, Rt. Rev. John A. T. *The Place of Law in the Field of Sex* The Beckly Lecture for 1972. (Sexual Law Reform Society, 1972)

Scruton, Roger *Sexual Desire* (Weidenfeld & Nicolson, 1986)

Smith, John C. **The Reform of the Law of Sexual Offences* (with comments by Antony Grey) (University of Leeds, Centre for Social Work and Applied Social Studies, Occasional Paper no. 6, 1981)

St John-Stevas, Norman *Law and Morals* (Burns & Oates, 1964)

Stephen, J. F. *Liberty, Equality, Fraternity* (1873)

Sturgess, Bob *No Offence. The Case for Homosexual Equality at Law* (CHE/SMG/USFI, 1975)

Sunday Times 'A Social Problem', 1 November 1953 (reprinted in pamphlet form with subsequent correspondence.)

———— 'Law and Hypocrisy', 28 March 1954

Szasz Thomas The works of American psychiatrist Thomas Szasz are essential reading for anyone interested in a libertarian critique of the ethical basis, assumptions and practices of orthodox psychiatry and psychotherapy. Beginning with *The Myth of Mental Illness* (Secker & Warburg, 1962), Szasz wrote a series of books, the main relevant ones for our topic being *Law, Liberty and Psychiatry* (Macmillan, New York, 1963); *The Manufacture of Madness* (Paladin, 1973); *Ideology and Insanity* (Calder & Boyars, 1973); *Sex: Facts, Frauds and Follies* (Blackwell, 1980); *Thomas Szasz: primary values and major contentions* (ed. Vatz & Weinberg, Prometheus Books, 1983).

West, D. J. (ed.) **Sex Offenders in the Criminal Justice System* (Papers presented to the 12th Cropwood Round-Table Conference, December 1979. Institute of Criminology, Cambridge, 1980)

Wilson, John *Logic and Sexual Morality* (Pelican, 1965)

4. PSYCHOLOGICAL, SOCIOLOGICAL

Bene, Eva 'On the Genesis of Male Homosexuality: An Attempt at Clarifying the Role of the Parents'; 'On the Genesis of Female Homosexuality' (both in *British Journal of Psychiatry*, September 1965)

Benjamin, Harry *The Transsexual Phenomenon* (Julian Press, New York, 1966)

Chesser, Eustace *Live and Let Live* (Heinemann, 1958)

——— *Odd Man Out* (Gollancz, 1959)

Churchill, Wainwright *Homosexual Behavior Among Males: A Cross-Cultural and Cross-Species Investigation* (Hawthorn Books, New York, 1967)

Cook, Mark & McHenry, Robert *Sexual Attraction* (Pergamon, 1978)

Crompton, Louis *Homosexuality and the Sickness Theory* (Albany Trust, 1969)

Dannecker, Martin *Theories of Homosexuality* (Gay Men's Press, 1981)

Eglinton, J. Z. *Greek Love* (Neville Spearman, 1971)

Ellis, Havelock *Psychology of Sex* (Random House, New York, 1936)

——— *Sexual Inversion* (Random House, New York, 1936)

Freud, Sigmund *The Complete Psychological Works*, vol. II (Hogarth Press, 1957)

Gagnon, John H. & Simon, William *Sexual Conduct: The Social Sources of Human Sexuality* (Aldine, Chicago, 1973)

George, Bill 'Young homosexuals and the corruption theory' (*Social Work Today*, 16 November 1976)

Hart, John & Richardson, Diane (eds) *The Theory and Practice of Homosexuality* (Routledge, 1981)

Hauser, Richard *The Homosexual Society* (The Bodley Head, 1962)

Hocquenghem, Guy *Homosexual Desire* (Allison & Busby, 1978)

Kraemer, W., Gordon, R., Williams, M., and Lambert, K. *The Forbidden Love. The Normal and Abnormal love of Children* (Sheldon Press, 1976)

Maddox, Brenda *The Marrying Kind. Homosexuality and Marriage* (Granada, 1982)

O'Carroll, Tom *Paedophilia: The Radical Case* (Peter Owen, 1980)

Perrott, Roy 'A club for homosexuals' (*The Observer*, 13 January 1963)

Plummer, Kenneth *Social Stigma. An interactionist account* (Routledge, 1975)

——— (ed.) *The Making of the Modern Homosexual* (Hutchinson, 1981)

Psychiatry and the Homosexual. A brief analysis of oppression (Gay Liberation pamphlet no. 1, 1978)

Ross, Michael W. *The Married Homosexual Man* (Routledge, 1983)

Rossman, Parker *Sexual Experience Between Men and Boys* (Temple Smith, 1979)

Schofield, Michael *Sociological Aspects of Homosexuality* (Longmans, Green, 1965)

Bibliography

Singer, June *Androgyny. Towards a New Theory of Sexuality* (Routledge & Kegan Paul, 1977)

Speijer Report (1969)

Ullerstam, Lars *The Erotic Minorities* (Calder & Boyars, 1967)

Weeks, Jeffrey *Sexuality and its Discontents* (Routledge, 1985)

Weinberg, George *Society and the Healthy Homosexual* (Colin Smythe, 1972)

Westwood, Gordon (M. Schofield) *A Minority: Male Homosexuals in Great Britain* (Longmans, Green, 1960)

Wolff, Charlotte *Bisexuality: A Study* (Quartet, 1977, 1979)

―――― *Love Between Women* (Duckworth, 1971)

5. HOMOSEXUAL/GAY POLITICS

Altman, Dennis *Homosexual Oppression and Liberation* (Angus & Robertson, 1971)

Bosche, Susanne *Jenny Lives with Eric and Martin* (Gay Men's Press, 1983)

Cory, Donald Webster (Edward Sagarin) *The Homosexual Outlook* (Peter Nevill, 1953)

Galloway, Bruce (ed.) *Prejudice and Pride* (Routledge, 1983)

Gay Left Collective *Homosexuality: Power and Politics* (Allison & Busby, 1980)

Gide, André *Corydon* (Secker & Warburg, 1952)

Greater London Council *Changing the World: A London Charter for Gay and Lesbian Rights* (1985)

Hanscombe, G. E. & Lumsden, A. *Title Fight: The Battle for Gay News* (Brilliance Books, 1983)

Hodges, Andrew & Hutter, David *With Downcast Gays* (Pomegranate Press, 1974)

The Joke's Over (Gay Prints/Rat Studies, 1973)

Lauritsen, John & Thorstad, David *The Early Homosexual Rights Movement* (Times Change Press (USA), 1974)

Norris, Stephanie & Read, Emma *Out in the Open* (Pan, 1985)

'Plummer, Douglas' *Queer People* (W. H. Allen, 1963)

Seabrook, Jeremy *A Lasting Relationship* (Allen Lane, 1976)

Shepherd, Simon & Wallis, Mick (eds) *Coming On Strong* (Unwin Hyman, 1989)

Stafford, J. Martin *Gay Lib/Homosexual Equality: A Reactionary Appraisal or a Realistic One?* (1973)

―――― *Homosexuality and Education* (Stafford, 1988)

Teal, Donn *The Gay Militants* (Stein and Day, New York, 1971)

Thompson, Mark (ed.) *Gay Spirit: Myth and Meaning* (St Martin's Press (USA), 1987)

Towards a Charter of Homosexual Rights (Campaign for Reason, 1978)

Tsang, Daniel (ed.) *The Age Taboo* (Gay Men's Press, 1981)

Walter, Aubrey (ed.) *Come Together: the Years of Gay Liberation* (Gay Men's Press, 1980)

Capital Gay

Gay News

Gay Scotland

Gay Times

Lunch

Pink Paper

6. RELIGION

Bailey, Derrick Sherwin *Homosexuality and the Western Christian Tradition* (Longmans, Green, 1955)

—— *Sexual Offenders and Social Punishment* (Evidence submitted to the Wolfenden Committee on behalf of the Church of England Moral Welfare Council, 1956)

Barnett, Leonard *Homosexuality: Time to Tell the Truth* (Gollancz, 1975)

Beck, A. & Hunt, R. (eds) *Speaking Love's Name. Homosexuality – Some Catholic and Socialist Reflections* (Jubilee Group, 1988)

Blamires, David *Homosexuality from the Inside* (Society of Friends, 1973)

Boswell, John *Christianity, Social Tolerance, and Homosexuality* (University of Chicago Press, 1980)

Coleman, Peter *Christian Attitudes to Homosexuality* (SPCK, 1980)

Heron, Alastair (ed.) *Towards a Quaker View of Sex* (Friends' Home Service Committee, 1963)

James, Eric *Homosexuality and a Pastoral Church* (Christian Action, 1988)

Kuhn, Donald *The Church and the Homosexual* A Consultation Report. (Glide Urban Center, San Francisco, 1964)

Macourt, Malcolm (ed.) *Towards a Theology of Gay Liberation* (Student Christian Movement, 1975)

Oberholtzer, W. D. (ed.) *Is Gay Good?* (Westminster Press (USA), 1971)

Pittenger, Norman *Time for Consent* (SCM Press, 1967, 1970)

Wood, Robert W. *Christ and The Homosexual* (Vantage Press, 1960)

Bibliography

7. SEX EDUCATION, COUNSELLING

Babuscio, Jack *We Speak for Ourselves* (SPCK, 1976, 1988)

Cousins, Jane *Make it Happy: What Sex is all About* (Virago, 1978); (revised edition) *Make it Happy, Make it Safe* (Penguin Books, 1988)

Dallas, Dorothy M. *Sex Education in School and Society* (National Foundation for Education Research, 1972)

Hansen, S. and Jensen, J. *The Little Red Schoolbook* (Stage 1, 1971)

Hart, John *So You Think You're Attracted to the Same Sex?* (Penguin, 1984)

Hill, Maurice & Lloyd-Jones, Michael *Sex Education: The Erroneous Zone* (National Secular Society, 1970)

Lee, Carol *The Ostrich Position* (Unwin, 1986)

Morrison, Eleanor S. & Price, Mila Underhill *Values in Sexuality* (Hart, New York, 1974)

Pomeroy, Wardell B. *Boys and Sex* (Pelican, 1970)

Righton, Peter *Counselling Homosexuals* (Bedford Square Press, 1973)

Whitehouse, Mary *Whatever Happened to Sex?* (Wayland, 1977)

Woodman, Natalie J. and Lenna, Harry R. *Counseling with Gay Men and Women* (Jossey-Bass (USA), 1980)

Yates, Alayne *Sex Without Shame. Encouraging the child's healthy sexual development* (Temple Smith, 1979)

8. CENSORSHIP

King & Nugent (eds) *Respectable Rebels: Middle Class Campaigns in Britain in the 1970s* (Hodder & Stoughton, 1979)

Sutherland, John *Offensive Literature* (Junction Books, 1982)

Yaffe & Nelson (eds) **The Influence of Pornography on Behaviour* (Academic Press, 1982)

9. BIOGRAPHICAL, MEMOIRS

Abse, Leo *Private Member* (Macdonald, 1973)

Alexander, Peter F. *William Plomer. A Biography* (Oxford University Press, 1989)

Annan, Noel (Lord) *Our Age* (Weidenfeld & Nicolson, 1990)

Brabazon of Tara, 1st Lord *The Brabazon Story* (Heinemann, 1956)

Butler, Lord *The Art of the Possible* (Hamish Hamilton, 1971)

Cant & Hemmings (eds) *Radical Records: Thirty Years of Lesbian and Gay History* (Routledge, 1988)

Crisp, Quentin *The Naked Civil Servant* (Cape, 1968)

Croft-Cooke, Rupert *The Verdict of You All* (Secker & Warburg, 1955)

Crossman, Richard *The Diaries of a Cabinet Minister* Volume Two (Hamilton/Cape, 1976)

Daley, Harry *This Small Cloud* (Weidenfeld & Nicolson, 1986)

De-La-Noy, Michael *A Day in the Life of God* (Citadel Press, 1971)

————(ed.) *The Journals of Denton Welch* (Allison & Busby, 1984)

Draper, Alfred *Smoke Without Fire. The Swabey Case* (Arlington Books, 1974)

Furbank, P. N. *E. M. Forster: A Life* (Secker & Warburg, 1979)

Harvey, Ian *To Fall Like Lucifer* (Sidgwick & Jackson, 1971)

Jenkins, Roy (Lord Jenkins of Hillhead) *A Life at the Centre* (Macmillan, 1991)

Parker, Peter *Ackerley* (Constable, 1989)

Porter & Weeks (eds) *Between the Acts: lives of homosexual men 1885–1967* (Routledge, 1991)

Rolph, C. H. *Living Twice* (Gollancz, 1974)

'Rowley, Anthony' *Another Kind of Loving* (Axle Publications, 1963)

Tatchell, Peter *The Battle for Bermondsey* (Heretic Books, 1983)

Wilde, Oscar *De Profundis*, in *The Letters of Oscar Wilde* (ed. Rupert Hart-Davis, Hart-Davis, 1962)

Wildeblood, Peter *Against the Law* (Weidenfeld & Nicolson, 1955)

———— *A Way of Life* (Weidenfeld & Nicolson, 1956)

Wolfenden, Lord *Turning Points* (The Bodley Head, 1976)

Wolff, Charlotte *On the Way to Myself* (Methuen, 1969)

———— *Hindsight* (Quartet, 1980)

———— *Magnus Hirschfeld* (Quartet, 1986)

10. FICTION

Forster, E. M. *Maurice* (Penguin, 1972)

Renault, Mary *The Charioteer* (Longmans, Green, 1953)

Selby, Hubert (Jr) *Last Exit to Brooklyn* (Calder & Boyars, 1966)

INDEX

* = footnote